AF321530

Paula
Modersohn-Becker

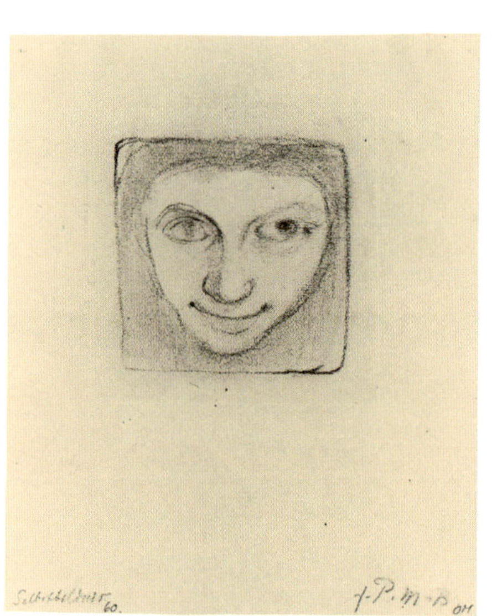
Selbstbildnis
60.
J. P. M.-D. 011

Uwe M. Schneede

Paula Modersohn-Becker

A Life in Art

With 120 illustrations

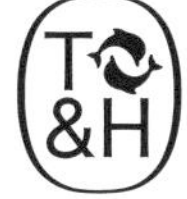

Translated from the German by Lorna Dale

First published in the United Kingdom in 2022 by
Thames & Hudson Ltd, 181a High Holborn,
London WC1V 7QX

First published in the United States of America in 2022
by Thames & Hudson Inc., 500 Fifth Avenue, New York,
New York 10110

Original edition © 2021 Verlag C.H.Beck oHG, Munich
This edition © 2022 Thames & Hudson Ltd, London

British Library Cataloguing-in-Publication Data
A catalogue record for this book is available from the
British Library

Library of Congress Control Number 2022932307

ISBN   978-0-500-02562-8

Printed and bound in China by RR Donnelley

Contents

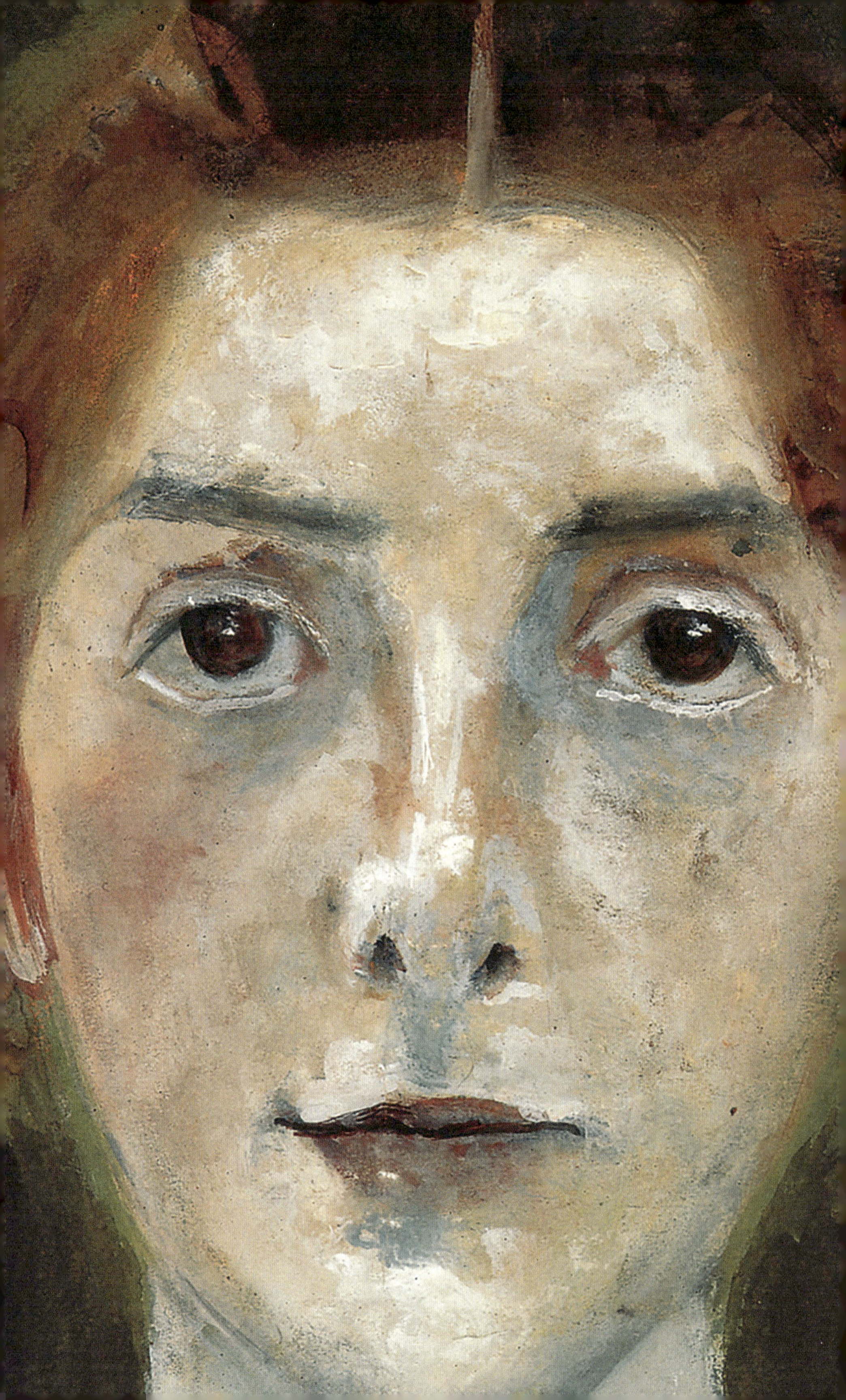

Preface

We now know the German painter Paula Modersohn-Becker as one of the great pioneers of modernism. When she died in 1907, at the age of 31, she had made her artistic mark on the short epoch between the old and the new. Art was stagnating at that time, at least in Germany. It was only after her death that avant-garde movements like Die Brücke and Der Blaue Reiter started the wider revival.

Paris, at that time the world capital of art, was the turning point for Paula Modersohn-Becker. She visited the city several times and soon became interested in contemporary French painting. In 1906 she moved to Paris from the Worpswede artists' colony in northern Germany, planning to live there permanently and escape the narrow provincial environment in which her fellow painters had taken very little notice of her work. Young German artists usually stayed in Paris for only a short period to find inspiration, but she was fiercely independent and, with rare courage for a female artist, she followed her own

Detail of ill. 1

path. People were not ready for her art at the time and most found it hard to accept.

This monograph looks in greater detail at the way Paris influenced Modersohn-Becker's work. In Germany, she could not find the stimulus she so longed for. She enjoyed the peaceful working environment in Worpswede, and her motifs and the depth of her colours were inspired by its harsh landscape. But both concept and imagery drew on the wide range of cultures with which she came into contact in Paris's museums and exhibitions, as well as at the studios of well-known fellow artists. The work that resulted was independent and distinctive. During her final stay in Paris, in 1906–7, she created her most important works, which were produced in parallel to Picasso's groundbreaking new forms. She was a female artist who tenaciously forged a career in the modern art world, in her words 'happy as a modern person and a child of my time'.

The Paris self-portraits were a high point. She portrayed a different version of herself, a figure whose hieratic bearing gave her the look of both a ruler from ancient times and an embodiment of independent art. In the last two years of her life, Modersohn-Becker depicted scenes in which the figures she paints and the natural attributes they hold are part of a strange-looking ritual. This imagery was a response to the stylistic specializations associated with avant-garde movements that sought to restore classical artistic standards to modern art. Nowadays, Paula Modersohn-Becker is seen as a unique artist who created a new iconography and made a pioneering contribution to modern art in the period immediately before the emergence of the German avant-gardes.

Many of my ideas came from authors – Simone Ewald, Karin Schick, Frank Schmidt and especially Rainer Stamm – whose recent research and new insights have given us a more detailed picture of Modersohn-Becker's work. I am grateful to the administrator of her estate, Wolfgang Werner, for his invaluable advice, support and suggestions. I have previously drawn on his wide knowledge for the exhibition of the artist's drawings at the Kunstverein in Hamburg in 1976 and the 2017 exhibition of her work at Bucerius Kunst Forum, also in Hamburg. Thanks as well to Alexandra Schumacher for her meticulous and dedicated work on the manuscript and production of this book. And special thanks to my wife for her contribution, which was, as always, thoughtful and stimulating.

1896–99: Sheltered Beginnings in an Artistic Backwater

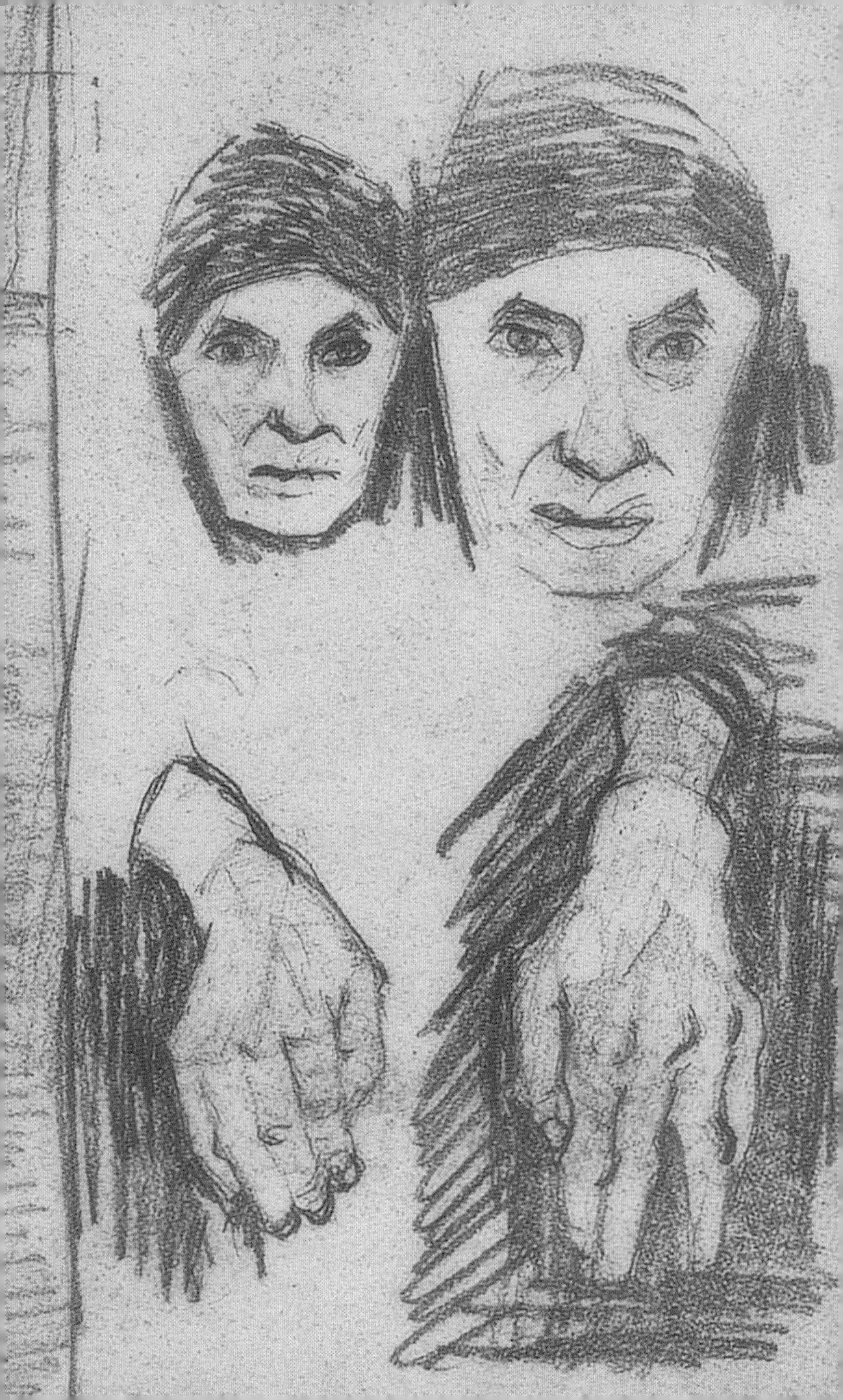

'A passion that excludes everything else'

When, in the late 19th century, a young woman like Paula
Becker from a solidly middle-class family decided not simply to
develop the dilettante taste for drawing and painting so admired
by society but to dedicate herself completely to art, that called
for exceptional determination and self-assurance. Women were
usually prevented from becoming serious professional artists
and the state did not yet offer them training. As usual at that
time with women who had ambitions to be independent, when
Paula Becker was considering that step she was accused of
behaving selfishly when she should have been thinking of the
interests of her family. She constantly had to justify herself to
the world and especially to her family. She responded to the
doubts of those around her with courage and self-confidence.
In July 1897, for instance, she wrote: 'You just have to accept
my egoism. I can't help it – it is part of me like my long nose.'
Her decision to remove herself from her middle-class environment, to embrace the world of art, further complicated her

Detail of ill. 6

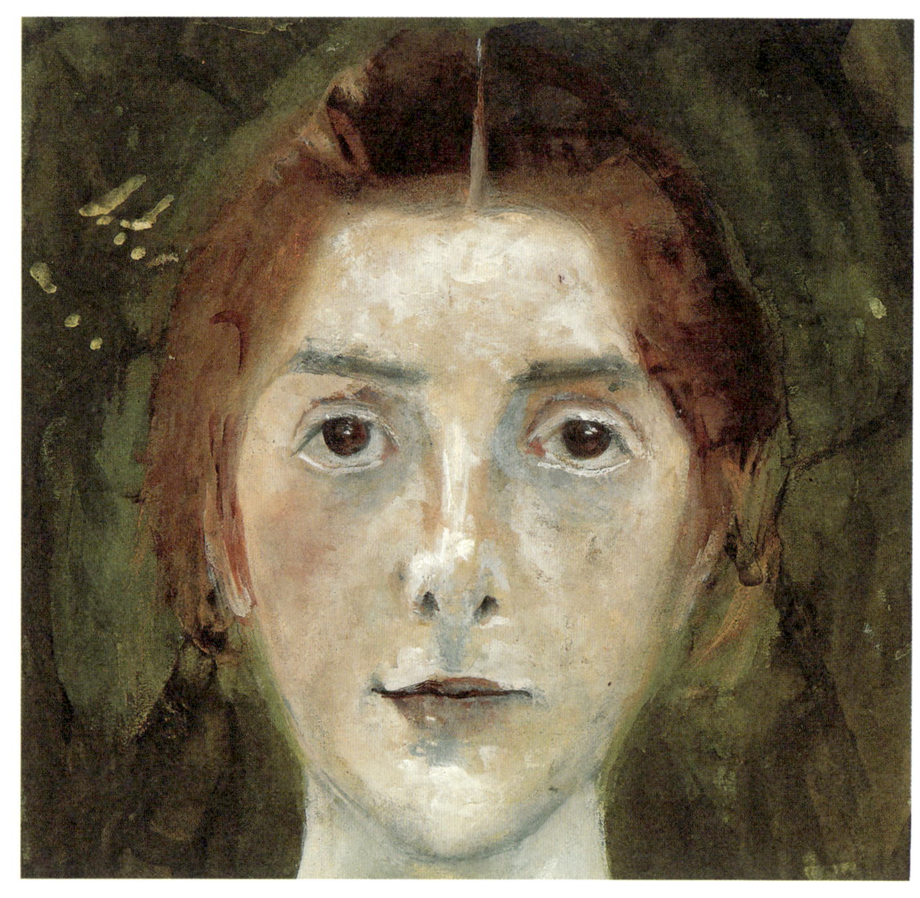

1 *Self-Portrait, c.* 1897

                    CHAPTER I

relationship with her immediate circle. Becker quickly realized the implications: 'I think if you want to achieve anything, you have to be totally dedicated.' She wrote this in February 1897. At the end of October, when she was 21, she added firmly: 'I am working with a passion that excludes everything else.' She had decided to defy bourgeois convention and dedicate herself exclusively to art.

Minna Hermine Paula Becker was born in Dresden in 1876, a generation after Max Liebermann and a few years before Ernst Ludwig Kirchner and Max Beckmann. She was the third of seven children; her siblings were Kurt, Bianca Emilie (known as Milly), Günter, Hans (who died when he was two), Herma and Henry. She became close to Milly, who married a businessman, and Herma, who obtained a doctorate and became a high-school teacher (see p. 212). None of them had any connection with the art world. Her father, Carl Woldemar Becker, a building and maintenance inspector on the Berlin–Dresden railway, was the son of a prominent academic in Odessa. Her mother, Mathilde, was a von Bültzingslöwen, an aristocratic and military family originating in Thuringia, whose father had been commanding officer of the city of Lübeck. When Paula was 12, the family moved to Bremen, where her father worked as a building surveyor for Prussian railways. They were interested in literature and art. Paula and her mother often went to events held by the local artists' association on the Domsheide square, and her father regularly attended viewings of artworks in the prints and drawings section of the art gallery.

During a seven-month stay with an aunt in England when she was 16, Paula took drawing classes at St John's Wood Art School in London. Her family then persuaded her to go to a teacher training college in Bremen, where she also had private drawing lessons. In 1896, at the age of 20, Paula was able to fulfil her original ambition, beginning an 18-month course in painting and drawing at the Association of Female Artists and Art Patrons in Berlin, which was based at 38 (now 98) Potsdamer Strasse. She was thrilled to be able to 'devote myself totally to drawing!' she wrote in February 1897.[1] During this period she lived with her uncle, Wulf von Bültzingslöwen, in Berlin-Schlachtensee. At the Association's painting school, she received a thorough training and was particularly inspired by one of the teachers on the course, the Swedish painter Jeanna Bauck. But 'I still put too much on the paper that is not essential' and 'my heads are still too wooden and stiff', she wrote in April 1896. As an aspiring artist who started out in a different field before turning to her real passion – painting – Becker was in good company: Vincent van Gogh was originally an art dealer and preacher, Paul Gauguin had been a stockbroker, Paul Cézanne a lawyer, and Henri Matisse had worked as a paralegal after studying law.

If they wanted to avoid being labelled amateurs, aspiring female artists needed academic training, but until 1919 the German state academies still largely denied them that opportunity. They therefore had to resort to private art schools at which academic teachers earned extra money or worked unpaid. This was a way for prospective female artists to create a social and artistic grounding for their own work. At the Berlin institution there were classes on drawing from plaster casts and live models (nudes and portraits), on landscape painting and art history. 'I spend my two free mornings, on Friday and Sunday, at the museum,' Paula wrote in a letter in April 1896. 'I know quite a lot about the German artists and Holbein now, but Rembrandt is still the greatest.' In the print room, where she 'really felt like an interloper in the Holy of Holies', she looked at works on paper by such artists as Botticelli and Michelangelo ('The legs that man draws!').

The Joy of Exhibitions

Berlin was still emerging as a city of art. The city's art scene was dominated by Anton von Werner, a history painter who enjoyed the patronage of the Kaiser, and thus was politically opposed to anything modern. In 1893, Alfred Lichtwark commented: 'In Berlin a brutal variant of academic art dominates, its colours more mundane than reality and its people more ordinary than nature.'[2] However, artists resisted. Led by Max Liebermann and Walter Leistikow, Berlin artists joined together in the so-called Association of the XI – known as the 'Elfer', the Eleven – to exhibit their work independently. The first exhibition was held in 1892 in private premises, at the Eduard Schulte art gallery on Unter den Linden. The last was at the same gallery six years later. Paula Becker's teacher Jacob Alberts was a member and she was there. The Eleven paved the way for the Berlin Secession, founded in 1898.

As well as the Eduard Schulte gallery, modern Berlin galleries at the time included the Fritz Gurlitt gallery and the art dealers Keller & Reiner. Becker also visited them. She may have seen a Munch exhibition at Keller & Reiner in 1898. She went to 'a very interesting lithographic exhibition with wonderful etchings and colour prints from all over the world' at the Museum of Decorative Arts, one of her first encounters with contemporary international graphic art – from Edouard Manet and Pierre Puvis de Chavannes to Félix Vallotton and Edvard Munch.

Despite these occasional glimpses of contemporary art, the budding artist was mainly interested in the old masters, not just in the Berlin National Gallery and the print room, but also on her frequent travels. She stopped off in Munich during a summer holiday to visit the Pinakothek and the Schack-Galerie. In 1897 she went to the International Art Exhibition and the Gemäldegalerie in Dresden. In Vienna she visited the Kunsthistorisches Museum and the Liechtenstein Gallery, mentioning works by Leonardo, Titian, Rubens, Dürer, Cranach and Holbein ('I was absolutely captivated by the old Germans'). She stopped in Zurich and Geneva while she was travelling in Switzerland and then in Munich and Nuremberg ('to really get a feel for Dürer'), in Leipzig and then Dresden for the German Art Exhibition, in which the Worpswede artists also exhibited. After her marriage in 1901, she and Otto Modersohn travelled via Berlin and Dresden to Prague ('the ghetto and the Jewish cemetery were enormously interesting'). Finally, they went to Munich and Dachau to see Hans von Marées's works in the Schleissheim Palace. In 1904 they went on a 'short art trip' to Kassel and Braunschweig just to see Rembrandt's paintings. 'I am learning to understand these giants more and more, and I hope it is doing me good.'

Her aim in visiting exhibitions, travelling mainly to see the old masters, was partly to look at the great achievements in art history – in other words (and this would include her initial experiences in Paris in 1900), to learn how the old masters worked and see their paintings first-hand rather than simply studying them in books. But travel could also help her focus on assessing and harnessing her own creativity.

The encounter that obviously made the most lasting impression took place in the summer of 1901 at the Schleissheim Palace in Bavaria. The important Marées works donated by Konrad Fiedler, a friend of the artist, had been on show there since 1892. They are now in the Neue Pinakothek in Munich (see ill. 88). Paula Modersohn-Becker wrote afterwards that she and her husband were 'deeply impressed by this extraordinary person'. In June 1906, in a letter to a painter friend, Emmi Walther, who

CHAPTER I

had recommended the visit, she went on to give this interesting explanation: 'He has managed to remain in his world all through his life.' That was 'all that I wish for myself and my husband'. She goes on to thank Walther 'for expanding our vision and our emotional range'. Her enthusiasm for the colours in Marées's work and the ideas it gave her for creating her own world through painting, and being and remaining in that world, are discussed in Chapter 6. The encounter with Marées would have a decisive influence on her later work.

The Worpswede 'wonderland'

Still in the Berlin period, in the summer of 1897, Paula Becker stayed for several weeks in Worpswede, north-east of Bremen on the Teufelsmoor, while on holiday. Having met painters who lived there, Hans am Ende, Fritz Mackensen, Otto Modersohn, Fritz Overbeck and Heinrich Vogeler, and come to love the area ('a wonderland, a land of the gods'), in September 1898 she decided to take a risk and move to Worpswede, leaving her bourgeois world behind.

In the late 19th century, like-minded people gathered in artists' colonies such as Worpswede, Ahrenshoop (on the Baltic Sea) and Dachau (in Bavaria) to live and work communally. They avoided cities and despised the academies; they sought a simple life that was as natural as possible, and needed their art to be close to nature, often working outdoors in a manner modelled on the *plein air* painting of the French Barbizon School. In Worpswede, Paula Becker came to love 'the misty landscape, green meadows and brightly coloured rape fields', 'the shining canals reflecting the blue sky, with the black turf barges', and finally, as she wrote at the beginning of September 1898, 'the brown heath, dotted with cheerful sparkling birch trees, a strange mixture of melancholy and lightheartedness'. Above all, the communal life in the countryside offered her a safe environment in which she could work freely, since deliberately formed avant-garde groups of artists like Die Brücke and Der Blaue Reiter that had specific artistic programmes did not yet exist.

The Worpswede painters were relatively successful, especially when they exhibited in the annual international exhibition at the Glaspalast ('Glass Palace') in Munich in 1895, so Becker was joining an already functioning artists' community. She was taught by Mackensen, but she never became an equal partner to her fellow artists. 'My work goes on very quietly,' she said in November 1901, by which she meant that none of the other artists paid any attention to what she was doing. The only exception was Otto Modersohn, who wrote in March 1902, 'No one ever asks about her work', and in June that year he commented that no one in the artists' colony knew her, 'no one appreciates her'.[3] Rainer Maria Rilke, who lived in Worpswede for a time, reported that she certainly did not show her work willingly.

Becker felt particularly drawn to the budding sculptor Clara Westhoff and to Otto Modersohn. When she was first able to exhibit a few works to the public in 1899 in the Kunsthalle Bremen with Clara Westhoff and the Worpswede painter Marie Bock, the painter and writer Arthur Fitger wrote a devastatingly scathing review in the local paper.[4] She withdrew her work from the Kunsthalle the very same day.

CHAPTER I

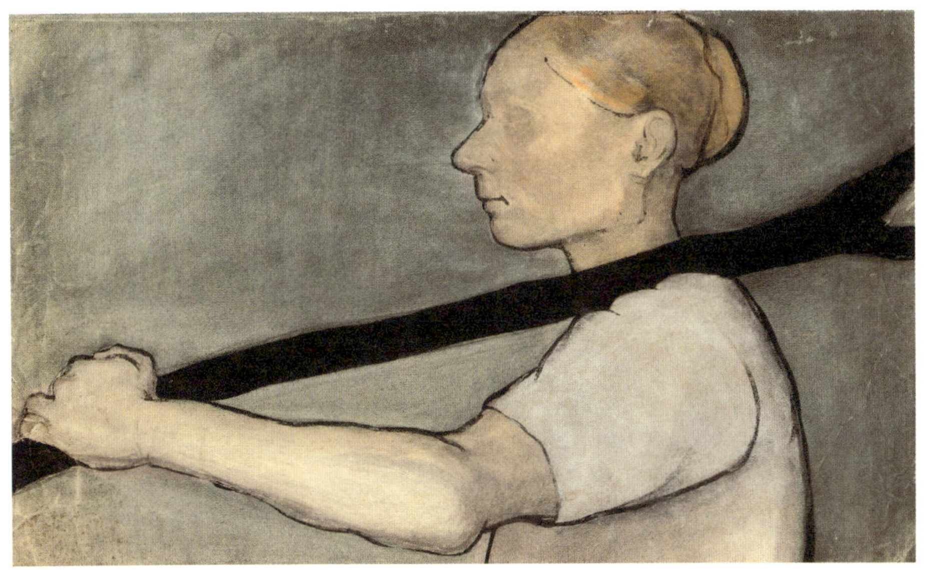

2   *Peasant Woman Carrying a Forked Branch*, 1898–99

Early Works

Paula Becker's early works were mainly drawings: nudes and heads at the Berlin Association of Female Artists; depictions of residents of the local poorhouse under Mackensen's guidance in Worpswede. However, one group of sketches from the Worpswede period in 1898 and 1899 is in a completely different category. These sketches are not polished life drawings but free compositions, ideas for paintings or etchings.

In one, a particular motif – a front view of an old woman on a chair – is repeated as an outline drawing four times on a sheet with only slight variations (ill. 4). In another, the woman is shown on a sheet from different angles: from the left, then the right, then frontally (ill. 3). On another sheet, there are several views of the sitter in silhouette against a background of trees (ill. 5). Details are merely hinted at, combinations of figure and background explored for their visual compactness and workability. These experiments were also carried out with purely natural motifs: a marsh canal from different perspectives with one or more boats, various reflections of turf barges in the water.

Even at this early stage, it is clear how systematically the artist worked on her compositions. Her drawings focus mainly on the position and stance of the figure – in other words, the basic form – and then incidentally on the details: a hand may be drawn fully or simply hinted at; a face may be given individual features, roughly indicated or totally obliterated; trees may support the figure in the composition or form part of the natural environment. Elements of the sketches could all be kept in reserve for similar future paintings.

The sketches provide a rare insight into Becker's artistic process. The process starts with reduction to a simple basic form

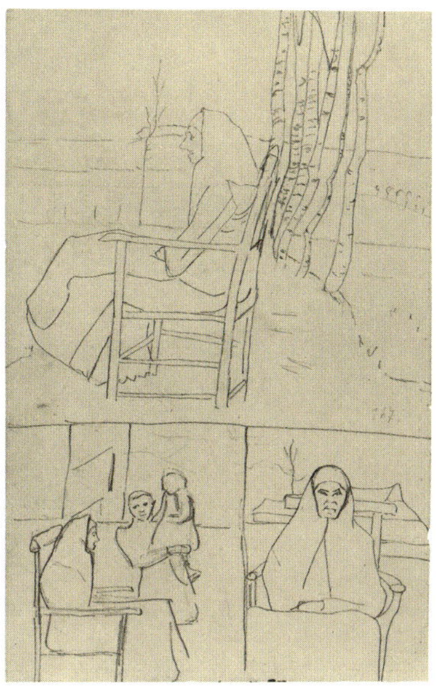

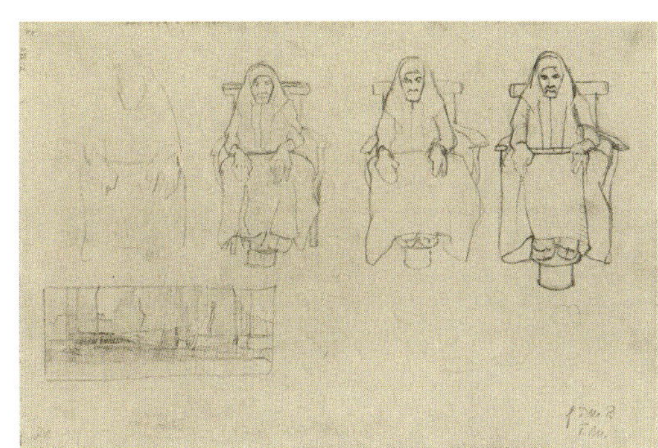

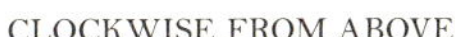

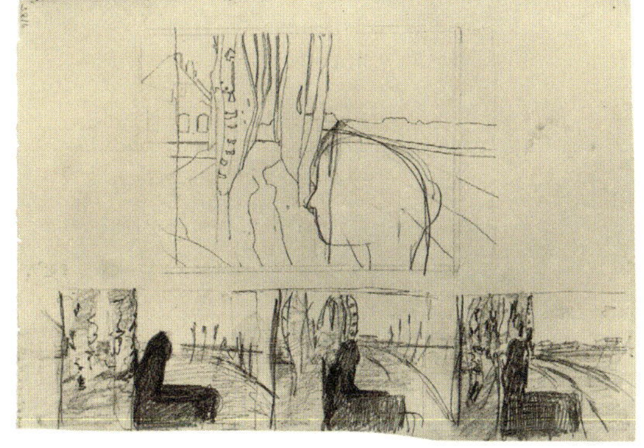

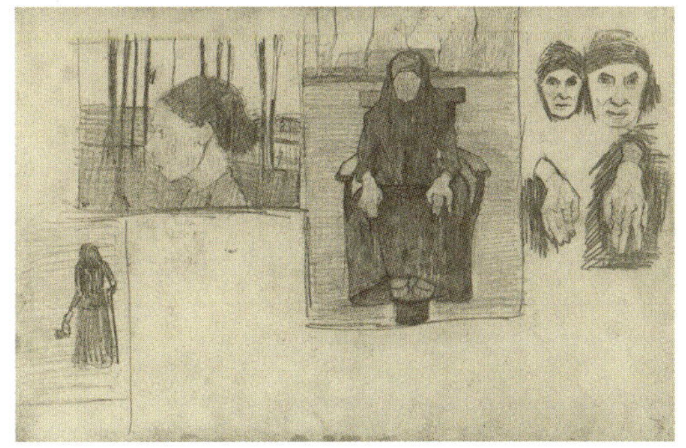

CLOCKWISE FROM ABOVE

3 Three studies in pencil for the etching *Seated Old Woman*, 1898–99

4 Sketches in pencil for the etching *Seated Old Woman*, 1899

5 Compositional studies in pencil: *Head in Front of Landscape / Three Sketches of Woman Seated in a Landscape*, 1898–99

6 Preparatory drawings in pencil for the etchings *Portrait of a Peasant Woman* and *Seated Old Woman*, 1898–99

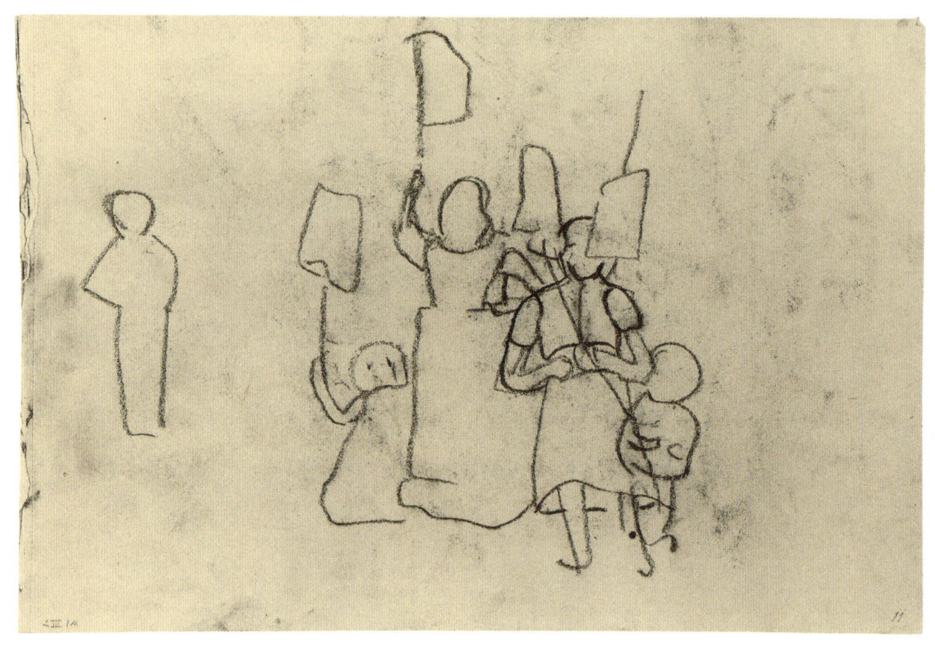

7 Study in charcoal, *Children with Lanterns, c.* 1901

                    CHAPTER I

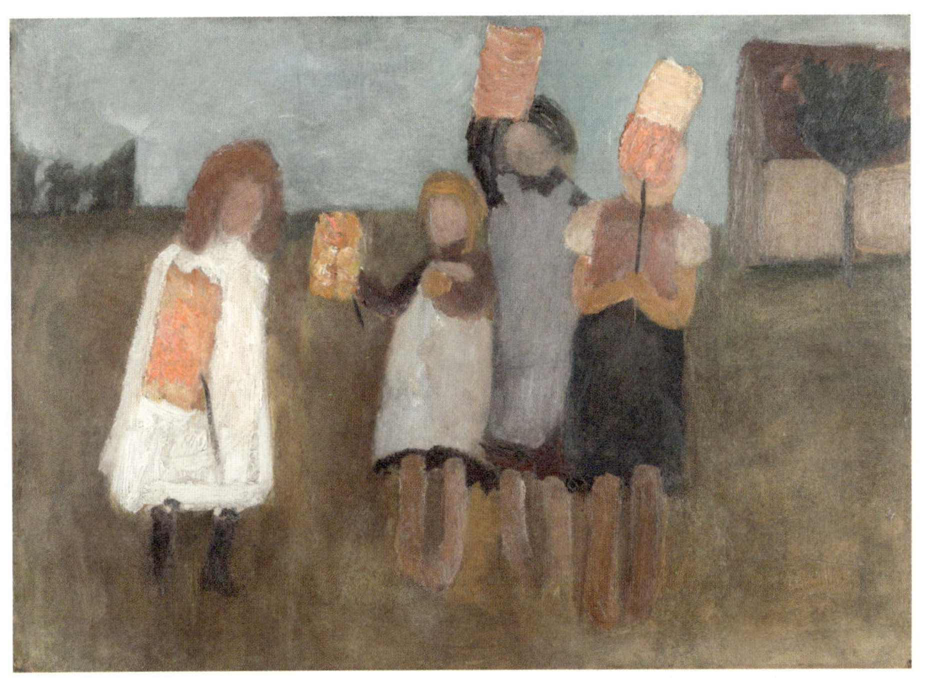

8   *Children with Lanterns in Front of House, c.* 1901

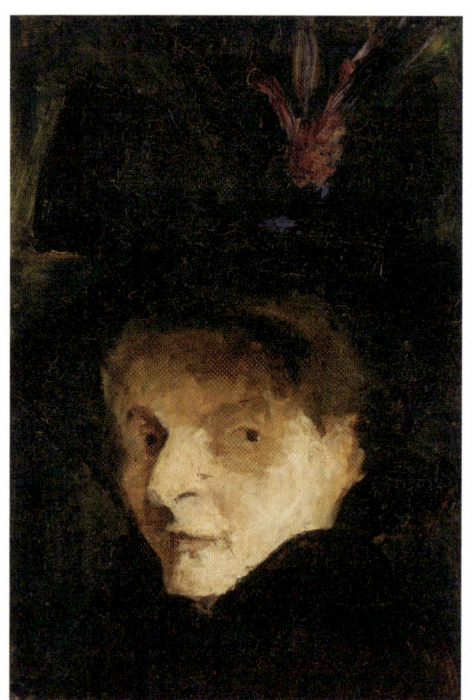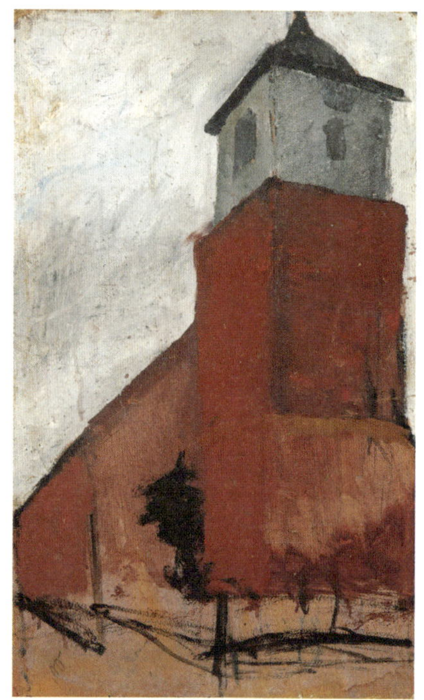

ABOVE LEFT

9 *Lady with a Feather Hat*, 1897–98

ABOVE RIGHT

10 *Church in Worpswede*, 1900

  CHAPTER I

with minimal, only essential details. This provides the structure, the framework of the picture. The artist then works on this initial analysis of what she sees and builds on it, enhancing it graphically. Finally, the painting is completed with whatever media she deems appropriate for it – brush and paint, for example, or etching with a needle and acid.

This transition from sketch to painting can be clearly seen in *Children with Lanterns* (*c.* 1901, ill. 7). The sketch shows a group of figures, with a child standing to one side. The drawing is a mere outline; it simplifies, keeps the forms transparent and, in particular, shows the places where they intersect, merging large and small. In the painting *Children with Lanterns in Front of House* of the same year (ill. 8), there are fewer children in the group. The details of the faceless figures are primarily painted in greyish-brown tones, while the child who stands apart is shown in contrasting white. The scene is brightened by the coloured lanterns. Whereas in the sketch the principal feature is the semi-abstract composition with no background indicated, in the painting the transition from the natural background to the figures is defined by colour. The figures seem almost to blend with the background, with the naturalness of the scene reflected in the earthy tones.

Composition and form are carefully planned; nothing is left to chance. However, the studies and preparatory works are in black and white, and show only form and structure. The colour that will ultimately define the picture introduces the element of freedom, spontaneity and thus vividness. The sketches reveal why it would be a mistake to consider Modersohn-Becker a fore-runner of the Expressionists. Her work is essentially characterized by systematic planning, although perhaps not in such an obvious way as in these sketches – more as a fundamental principle.

Becker did her first oil studies in 1897–98, mostly in small format on cardboard: women's heads, self-portraits, the church at Worpswede, landscape elements. Stylistically they vary in composition, but it is possible to identify basic features that recur in other works. *Lady with a Feather Hat* (1897–98, ill. 9), from the Berlin period, is a quick sketch. The face stands out from the dark as a patch of light with few details. Even the eyes are only sketched in. The figure has characteristic features: a large nose, a pointed chin, a sharp gaze. These early colour works are unlike any of the dominant trends of that period in Germany: the late Impressionism of Liebermann, the popular naturalistic scenes of Wilhelm Leibl or Arnold Böcklin's symbolism. They are entirely her own.

Therefore, while *Portrait of a Woman with Poppies* (c. 1898, ill. 12), for instance, has a Jugendstil-inspired composition and reflects an intention to create a deliberately constructed image, *Interior (Studio in Bremen)* (1897, ill. 11) is ahead of its time in that the paint is applied with a freedom suggesting the possibilities of true abstraction. *Church in Worpswede* (1900, ill. 10) is completely different, consisting of simple, compact cubes whose relationships are made clear with roughly executed black lines, which provide a marked contrast with the red and the unfinished nature of the coloured form.

Various styles of painting are already evident in the modern approach, the construction process, the spontaneous application of paint, the cubic forms and the *non finito* execution of the works. The characteristic that connects these experiments in colour and form is 'subjective sensation'. In 1902, Paula Becker elaborated on her ideas in her journal, saying, 'I believe that when painting a picture, you should not think about nature at all', at least not as 'the concept of the painting'. First of all, it was necessary to decide on the basic idea of the picture. If that then conveyed a natural impression, the major element was 'subjective sensation'. Once the form and colour of that 'subjective

CHAPTER I

sensation' had been defined using her own style and media, the reference to reality would naturally follow: 'Then I have to bring in from nature the features that make my picture look natural.' In this way, a paradox could be introduced into this new form of art: the naturalistic effect of a personal concept, 'so that a layman would think I had painted my picture from nature'. Consequently, the pictorial means became independent, autonomous. As she wrote in her journal, she had truly felt how suddenly 'everything in the picture can change its localized colour', by means of 'the same principle that gives all muted tones a uniform relationship'.

This was a breakaway from 'localized colour', a breakaway from the natural colours of materials and objects in favour of colours that were subjective and at the same time specific to the painting. But the colours needed to follow certain rules and possess a 'uniform relationship'. In other words, there must be a new, naturalistic coherence of pictorial media that are themselves independent. This process of shifts of tone to achieve artistic autonomy was fully developed in Modersohn-Becker's studies for the seated portraits of 'Dreebeen' (ills 23, 24) in 1902–4 (and, therefore, after her first trip to Paris). But it was already becoming clear how precisely and specifically Modersohn-Becker could express her views on her own work. This freedom in explaining aesthetic processes is rare among her contemporaries.

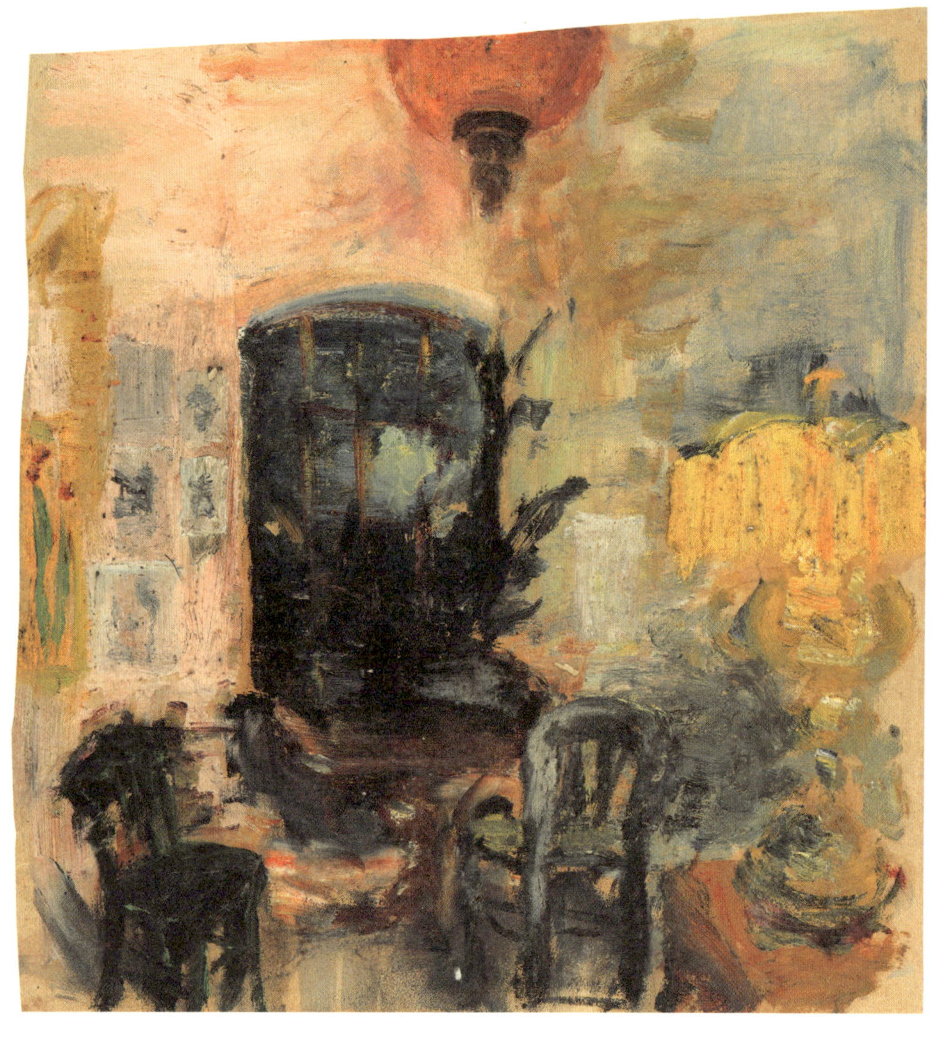

ABOVE

11 *Interior (Studio in Bremen)*, 1897

OPPOSITE

12 *Portrait of a Woman with Poppies, c.* 1898

   CHAPTER I

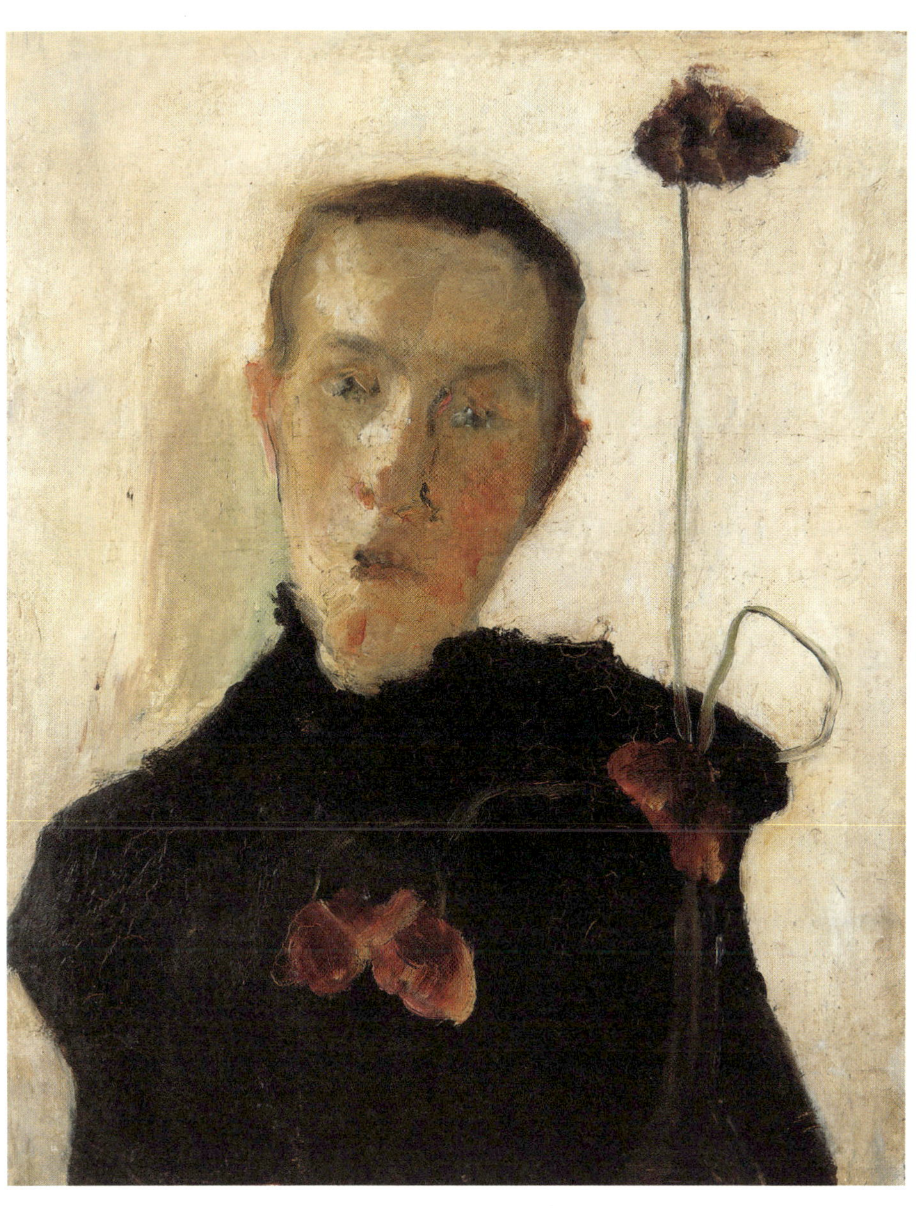

Withdrawal from Worpswede

Paula Becker enjoyed the isolation from the world in Worpswede because it allowed her to concentrate on her art. Perhaps she also felt secure among fellow artists, so different from the unenlightened bourgeoisie who, in the German Romantic tradition, she liked to call 'philistines'. On Sundays they met at Heinrich Vogeler's house, Barkenhoff (see p. 218): Otto Modersohn and Paula Becker, Heinrich Vogeler and his future wife Martha Schröder, Clara Westhoff and Marie Bock, and occasionally Paula's sisters Herma and Milly Becker. Rilke was also a frequent visitor. On Thursdays they played skittles.

However, the village community, attitudes to art and the world, and the lack of stimulus soon became too restrictive for Paula Becker. She seems to have accepted that people were not interested in her art. Artistically, at any rate, she distanced herself openly and decisively from the Worpswede artists. She thought Vogeler's work touching and charming; you could only 'shake your head over it'. In December 1900, she described his art as 'shoddy'. Mackensen's ideas were 'not big enough, too generic'. Overbeck was 'like an unproductive worker bee'. She felt his work lacked 'inner urgency'. The only person she found worthwhile was Modersohn. She wrote in February 1899, 'I think I shall move on from here. The number of people I can bear to talk to about anything meaningful to me is getting smaller all the time.' She had no personal freedom or hopes for the future. The community in Worpswede (and probably other figures such as Max Liebermann) was not 'forward-thinking enough; artistically they are living in the past'. So she withdrew into herself, already turning away from the 19th century in favour of modernity. Single-mindedly she stood up with confidence to all those who, as she said at the beginning of July 1902, 'treated my art pityingly and tactfully like an amusing little eccentricity'.

In September 1898, having escaped her bourgeois surroundings and moved to Worpswede, she was already thinking seriously of broadening her horizons. On her first day in Worpswede, she wrote: 'Paris is glowing, shining in the distance.' Paris was her 'most secret, heartfelt desire'. It was as if the northern German village was just a temporary place to stay, a stepping stone to eventual freedom. She was initially thinking of staying in Paris for six months. The world capital of art was a way into modernity, uncertainty, novelty, the longed-for future. She arrived there on New Year's Day 1900. Not long before, she had written to her sister Milly that she could see her goals as an artist 'are moving further and further from yours, you will be less and less in favour of them'. But she had to pursue them: 'I cannot go back.' She needed to keep moving forward, 'in my mind, in my flesh and in the way I feel I must'. The rest of her short life would be defined by this resolute inner strength.

Paris 1900: A Symbolic Journey into a New Century

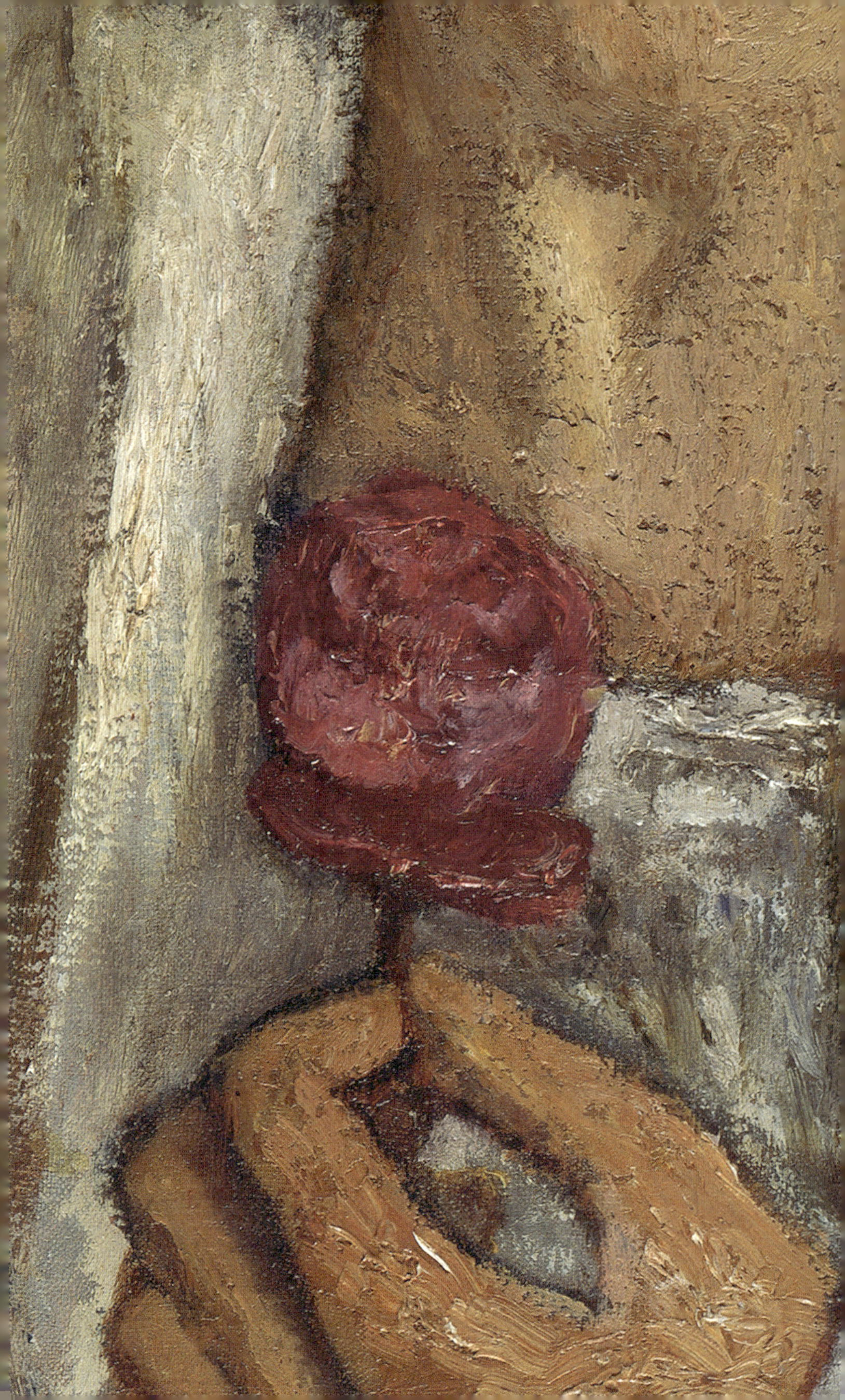

Exploration

What awaited Paula Becker in Paris was a new year, a new century and a new dawn. On New Year's Eve 1899, she boarded a train in Bremen in northern Germany. After a 17-hour journey in the ladies' compartment, she arrived at the Gare du Nord in Paris on New Year's Day. It must have taken an unusually strong will for this 23-year-old, privately educated painter from the provinces to risk travelling on her own – at a time when women would normally have been accompanied by companions – in pursuit of art. This was a symbolic journey as much as a physical one. It did not take long for Becker's hopes to be realized. Although she found the big city 'horrifying' at first, she was soon writing in her journal: 'I feel a new world being born in me.'

At the time, it was common for aspiring artists to spend a few weeks or months in Paris to enjoy the unique attractions of the Louvre and the academies, the sensational, sometimes scandalous works of their contemporaries, the innovative art dealers and the non-state-controlled exhibitions showing thousands of

Detail of ill. 14

contemporary works of all kinds and levels. The flow of German artists into Paris around 1900 was essentially an act of resistance to the state academies and academic art. Paris offered a freedom they did not have at home. This was especially true for women, who were not usually permitted to study art. German artists Käthe Kollwitz, Ida Gerhardi, Julie Wolfthorn, Clara Westhoff and Maria Slavona spent time in Paris because the teaching in the private academies was more professional than in artists' studios in places like Munich or Berlin. Paula Becker, too, was particularly attracted by the possibilities of academic study that were not available to her at home.

Becker's friend from Worpswede, Clara Westhoff (see p. 213), who was a year younger than her, was already in Paris and awaiting her arrival. She was studying sculpture at the private Académie Julian, which Emil Nolde also attended at the time. Their schedule in those early days was astonishing and appears to have been typical. Becker's symbolic journey to Paris was followed by a symbolic art tour of the city. On 2 January, the two friends went to the Louvre in the morning and were captivated by the old masters, including Fra Angelico, Titian, Botticelli and Holbein. In the afternoon they went to the Palais du Luxembourg. In 1818, part of the Palais du Luxembourg had been designated as a museum of painting and sculpture by living artists, with older works being transferred to the Louvre, although this does not mean that the Palais du Luxembourg was a modern art museum: by far the largest space was occupied by French Salon painters and academicians. The – at the time controversial – bequest by the painter Gustave Caillebotte, which included extraordinary works by Cézanne, Manet, Degas and the Impressionists, was simply packed into an end room measuring about 9 × 6 metres. These works must have appealed especially to the two young artists (and still stand out in the Musée d'Orsay today). They visited the medieval treasures in the Musée de

Cluny and the nearby Gallo-Roman thermal baths on the same day. But Paula Becker said a few days later, 'For me the Louvre is most important … that seems to me the only thing in Paris without a catch.'

On 3 January, Becker went to an art history lecture at the Sorbonne. She began a course at the Académie Colarossi (see p. 214) soon after that. In 1904, Max Beckmann had advised his friend Caesar Kunwald to go to the Colarossi rather than the Julian, commenting that with the women there you could work more easily and peacefully.[5] At the end of her second month in Paris, Becker reported that in the morning they did life drawing:

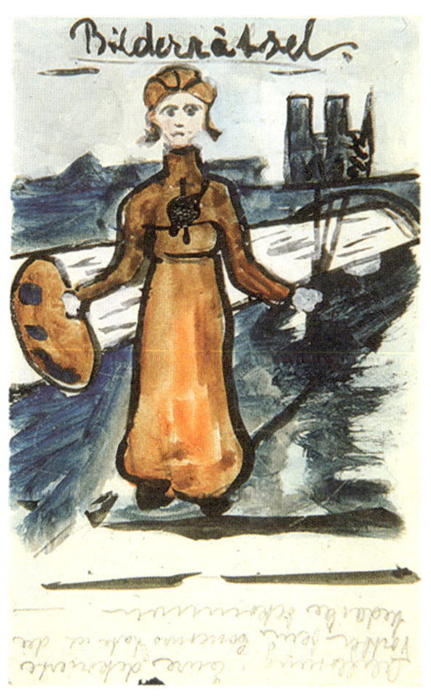

13 *Picture Puzzle*, postcard to the artist's mother,
Paris, 1 March 1900: 'Your decorated daughter – I have
been awarded a medal in the *concours*.'

'Among the "little women" in the morning, you see a lot of uncombed hair and unpolished boots, a few clever students and not much talent. They work more like a herd of cattle, with no idea what it is all about.' In the afternoon they had a brief spell of life drawing; otherwise, they were free to work in their small living room, the 'doll studio', at 9 Rue Campagne-Première, not far from the Académie Colarossi at 10 Rue de la Grande Chaumière in Montparnasse. Later, they sometimes had more life drawing: 'At 7 in the evening with the "little men", it is even funnier. There are some comical figures there!' None of them really looked sensible like the men at home; these budding artists had to wear 'velvet suits, long hair, shirtsleeves, hand towels as neckties', the way foreign newcomers imagined Parisian bohemians dressed. On Wednesdays and Sundays, female students could go to anatomy classes at the state-run Ecole des Beaux-Arts on Rue Bonaparte. In Germany, this was considered improper for women: as Becker noted, 'That is something that is not available to us girls anywhere else but here.' Finally, at the beginning of March, she could announce to her parents in a picture puzzle (ill. 13) that she had been awarded a medal in the Colarossi *concours*.

A Whole World of Art

Becker visited Charles Cottet, a painter much admired at the time, in his studio. In her spare time, she looked around modern art dealers. She mentions Jean-Baptiste-Camille Corot, Jean-François Millet, Charles-François Daubigny, Gustave Courbet,

14 *Half-Length Portrait of the Sculptor Clara Rilke-Westhoff,* 1905

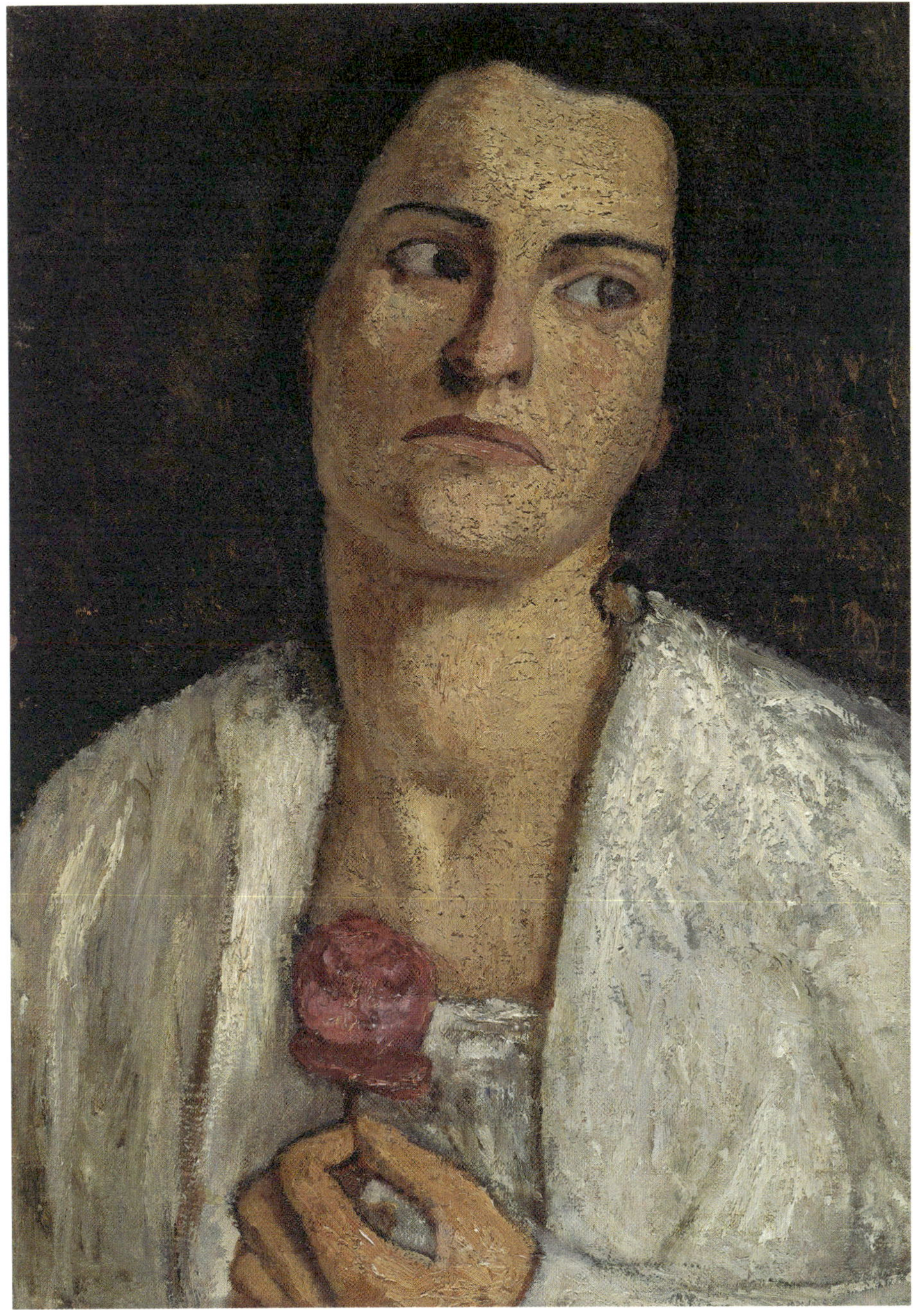

Pierre Puvis de Chavannes, Edgar Degas; she talks critically of Claude Monet and admiringly of Auguste Rodin. She saw 'much that is charming and bad and banal', while continuing to seek out 'treasures'.

According to Wilhelm Uhde, an art dealer who settled in Paris in 1904, 'it was easy at that time to have an overall view of what was happening in the art world in Paris.' It was possible to visit every modern art gallery within the space of two hours.[6] The most interesting avant-garde galleries – Bernheim-Jeune, Durand-Ruel and later also Clovis Sagot – were on Rue Laffitte, the 'art shops street'. It was there, in search of 'treasures', that Paula Becker discovered Ambroise Vollard. Vollard had championed Cézanne and was to cause a sensation soon afterwards with the first exhibitions by the 20-year-old Pablo Picasso and the 35-year-old Henri Matisse, in 1901 and 1904 respectively. Rue Laffitte was the centre of the modern art market in Paris and, as Vollard said in his memoirs, a place of pilgrimage for all young painters. Matisse, Picasso, André Derain, Maurice de Vlaminck and many others passed through there.[7]

Clara Westhoff described how her friend had asked her to go and see Vollard, with the promise of showing her something special; Paula Becker had been struck by the works being shown there. 'They were pictures by Cézanne that we were seeing for the first time. We didn't even know his name.'[8] For the German artists, this was an extraordinary discovery. In November 1900, the art dealer Paul Cassirer was to show Cézanne's work in Germany for the first time. This must have been a revelation for Becker and, as it turned out, a momentous experience, an unexpected encounter with radical modern art.

At that point, however, she was yet to see the 1900 Exposition Universelle, which opened in mid-April of that year and would have had a major impact on any young artist looking for inspiration outside their own country. Becker would have seen the

CHAPTER 2

many pavilions showcasing cultures from around the world, but she was mainly interested in the art exhibitions. She was not particularly bothered about Art Nouveau, which had been causing such a stir in art circles; she was more interested in painting. In the specially built Grand Palais, 28 countries displayed their most recent art, and the exhibition in the Petit Palais opposite, also built for the occasion, showcased the most important 19th-century French artists, including Ingres, Delacroix, Courbet, Manet, Gauguin and Cézanne. The whole art world was on show in the two buildings: great classicists and realists, regional genre and Salon paintings, new landscape paintings and pioneers of modern art. Becker went there several times. She wrote to Worpswede at the beginning of May 1900 that every nation was 'wonderfully represented'; 'this time has simply been a landmark in my life in Paris'.

Becker seems to have gained important insights at the Paris Exposition, especially in comparing international and German art. In the German exhibition in the Grand Palais, she discovered 240 works by some 150 artists. A few works by Adolph von Menzel, Wilhelm Leibl, Max Liebermann and Max Slevogt were on display, but somewhat marginal in an overwhelmingly traditional scene. The organizer, Alfred Lichtwark, director of the Hamburger Kunsthalle, was not entirely happy with the choice himself, believing that it gave an inadequate impression of 19th-century German art (which, in his view, had still not been properly explored).[9] In fact, most of the selected artists had been forgotten. At any rate, they did not include Caspar David Friedrich or the Romantics, whose work Lichtwark would go on to highlight in 1906 at the centenary exhibition of German art in Berlin.

Nonetheless, Becker found all this 'enormously instructive'. In her letters she again expressed enthusiasm for Charles Cottet's impressive dark-toned Breton paintings of ordinary

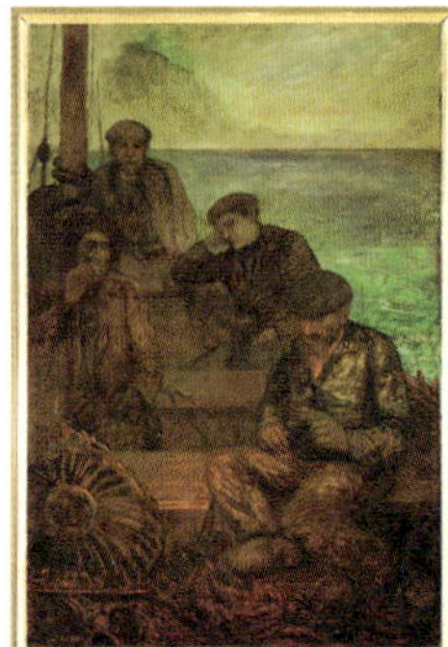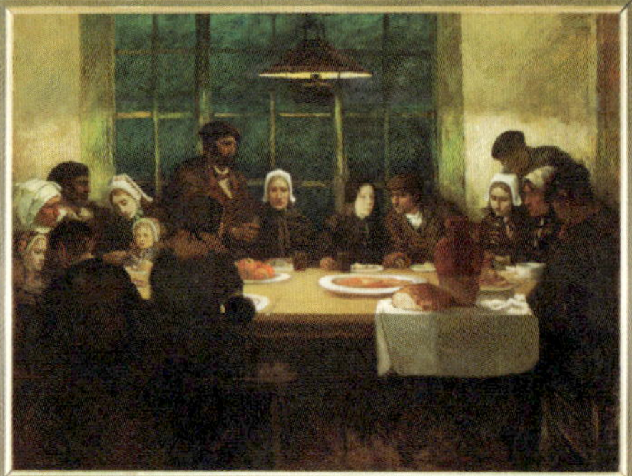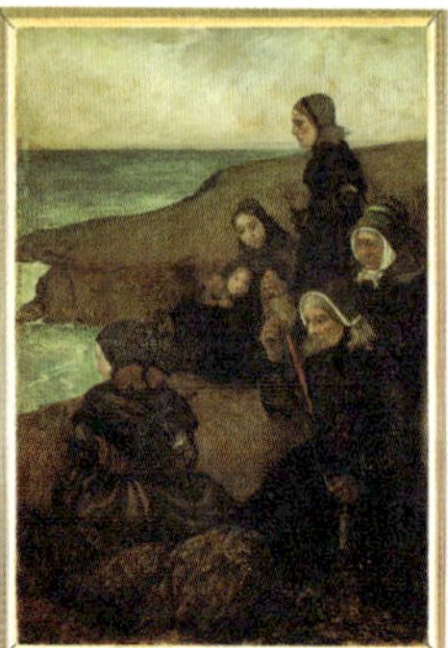

15 Charles Cottet, *Au pays de la mer*, triptych, 1898

people (ill. 15). She probably talked about them in letters to
Worpswede because they were similar to German nature painting and were therefore, in a sense, a link between Paris and
Worpswede. She mentioned very few names, presumably
because the newer artists were not understood in Germany. But
she did find a special artistic quality in members of the Bande
Noire group, such as Cottet and Lucien Simon, and in Jean-
Pierre Laurens, describing 'a deep colourful brilliance at dusk,
coloured light within shadow, light without sun', just as she
tried to achieve. In May 1900, she turned firmly away from
French Impressionism with its focus on light and returned in
her typically systematic way to her origins, 'deep, rich colour',
which she found in Worpswede rather than Paris.

Her visits to the Paris Exposition prompted her to think about
'construction', which she said was 'one of the catchwords', presumably among fellow artists. Writing about her studies in Paris, the
painter and art historian Henriette Mendelsohn said that at the
Académie Colarossi, Gustave Courtois, who taught Becker, 'criticized practically everything': *'Ce n'est pas bien construit'*, *'Ce n'est pas
mal en couleur, mais cela manque de construction'*.[10] Becker wrote that

CHAPTER 2

understanding the need for construction in a picture was, she believed, something she had learned in Paris. She did not explain exactly what she meant by that, but we can assume that she was talking about her theory that, instead of being a mere representation of nature, a painting should have a specific concept, which would give it autonomy. We'll come back to this point in her later works and, in particular, the idea of 'light without sun'.

Outdated German Art

Paula Becker only produced three paintings during her time in Paris: *Portrait of a Young Woman with Red Hat*, *View from the Studio Window* and the programmatic *Self-Portrait in Front of Window with View of Parisian Houses* (ill. 16). She took a daring approach with the latter, showing herself against the light and deliberately in shadow, barely recognizable and seen from a low angle, with distorted perspective. She was not aiming for an objective likeness. With these first steps, in fact, Becker could begin cautiously to experiment with turning a subordinate representation into an autonomous picture. That was her system.

Instead of writing in detail about particular artists or works of art in her Paris letters, Becker began to set out some general ideas that she had learned from experience. In a letter of early May 1900, she wrote that the French led the field. She felt 'that for a long time we in Germany have not broken free enough, not kept up to date with what is happening' and, above all, 'still cling too much to the past'. Liebermann, Mackensen and 'their crowd' were 'still too conventional. All our German art.' And a few days later: 'the couple of French greats are totally unconventional'. In comparison, 'we Germans [are] rather bourgeois and philistine'. Surrounded by

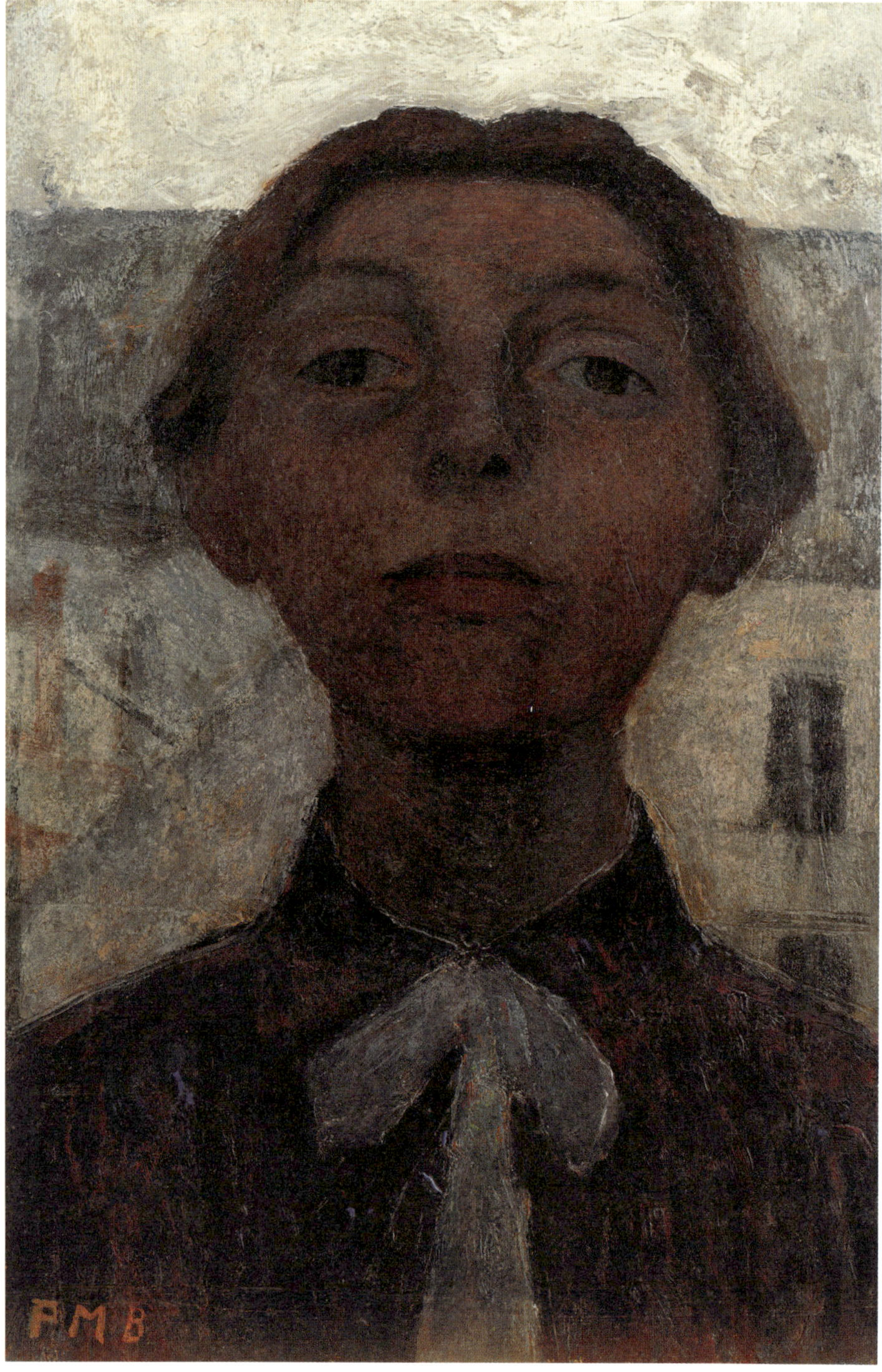

international art and influences, the 24-year-old boldly criticized the state of German art.

With a self-confidence that was already typical of her, she stated: 'I think more of people who are free, who deliberately make convention themselves.' Encouraged by the artistic freedom all around her, she urged her younger brother – who was to become a businessman – to be an idealist. He should stop being rooted in the previous generation: 'Be idealists until you are old. Idealists who embody an idea. Then you have lived.' The alternative meant becoming a 'philistine'. It is as if she is encouraging herself: the world will progress if we strive for the ideal. 'And the great swamp will dry out and become fertile soil. We are still too deep in the swamp.' In a similar vein, she added in her journal in April 1902: 'art that is rich and inventive only looks to the future'. This intellectual step into the 20th century at its very dawn anticipated the avant-gardes who would follow.

Becker's criticism of German art applied particularly to its main representatives at the time, Liebermann and Lovis Corinth, who had emerged from the late Impressionism of the previous generation. In her eyes, they stood for outdated art.

Between Two Generations

In Germany (which, at that point, was still the German Empire), the time had not yet come when modern art would start to take shape in all its diverse forms and with a passionate desire for

16 *Self-Portrait in Front of Window with View of Parisian Houses,* 1900

change. The break between the newer and the old took place at the end of the first decade of the 20th century.

Some of the key movements in this transition were taking form in Modersohn-Becker's lifetime and in the years following her death. The Brücke group of artists were founded by Ernst Ludwig Kirchner, Erich Heckel, Karl Schmidt-Rottluff and Fritz Bleyl in Dresden in 1905, and by 1909, two years after Modersohn-Becker's passing, they had developed a shared Expressionist style and a new understanding of art. Also in 1909, the Italian Futurists announced themselves with a widely circulated manifesto. Franz Marc, Wassily Kandinsky, Gabriele Münter and others held their first exhibition as Der Blaue Reiter in Munich in 1911 and published their almanac on the new concept of art under the same name in 1912. In the early years of the 20th century, however, with German art stagnating, Paris was where Modersohn-Becker had to look for role models and inspiration.

It must also be remembered that, in those days, the new art had very few real patrons. Paul Cassirer, the Berlin art dealer who had until then supported the Van Gogh generation, opened the 1907 winter season with Cézanne and Munch. It was only in the next few years that he worked specifically with younger French artists and the Germans. Heinrich Thannhauser started promoting contemporary artists in Munich in 1909. In 1912, Herwarth Walden's dynamic Sturm Gallery opened in Berlin, specializing in international avant-garde art. In 1913, Alfred Flechtheim opened his first gallery in Düsseldorf. Therefore, it was not surprising that during her second period in Paris, in 1903, Paula Modersohn-Becker noted that in Germany there were few 'strong artistic art dealers' like those to be found in Paris.

With the exception of Karl Ernst Osthaus in Hagen, Germany also had very few contemporary art collectors. The first major, internationally focused collective exhibitions establishing modern art as a new era in art history – the Sonderbund exhibition in Cologne (which included Paula Modersohn-Becker's *Old Peasant Woman* of *c.* 1905, now in the Detroit Institute of Arts), the Armory Show in New York and the First German Autumn Salon in Berlin – were held in 1912 or 1913.

In Germany, therefore, Becker could not depend on institutions being open to newcomers like her. The Secessions, with their major exhibitions in Berlin and Munich, had already become outdated organizations of the late 19th century. If groups of like-minded artists wanted to establish themselves, they first had to develop their own artistic programmes.

With the lack of internationally active supporters, dealers, collectors and patrons at the time, Becker had to make her own way. Her exposure to all sorts of art at the Paris Exposition would be the culmination of her first stay in Paris in 1900. Becker planned to return to 'isolation from the world in Worpswede' for 'a little while', although the 'heavy air' there made her 'sad'. Barely six months after her arrival in Paris, she was back in Worpswede. Later, she would write in her journal that 'there was something so happy' about her first stay in Paris: 'I had such great hopes', it gave her 'such a proud strength'. In Paris she had entered a new year, a new century: the century of modernity.

Despite her love of Paris, Becker did not find motifs for her paintings in the city or on excursions into the surrounding countryside or in the work of French artists. In almost all her art, the motifs and colours – although, it must be noted, only the motifs and colours – were rooted in Worpswede.

1901–5: The Unfamiliar in the Familiar

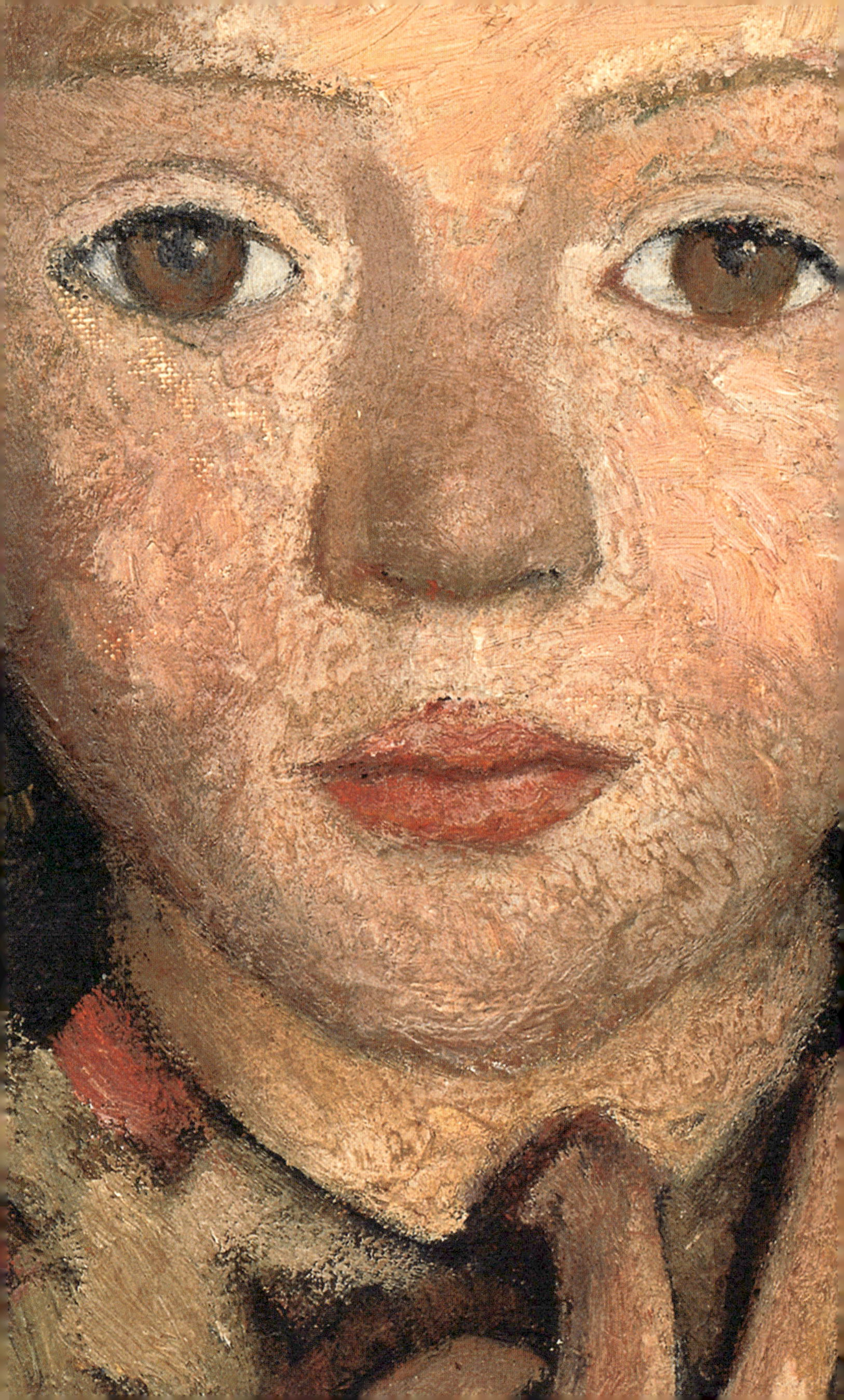

'I recognize no rules'

At the end of June 1900, Becker returned to Worpswede to start work again in seclusion. She was planning to go back to Paris in the autumn of that year, but her parents prevented her. After her engagement to fellow Worpswede artist Otto Modersohn in September 1900, they persuaded her to spend the first two months of the following year in Berlin, learning to cook in preparation for married life. She went to a cookery and housekeeping school for daughters of well-to-do families in Barbarossastrasse in Schöneberg. She often visited Rainer Maria Rilke, whom she knew from Worpswede, in the Schmargendorf area of Berlin. They had long talks about art and literature, and went to events together. However, she did not take to Berlin, describing it as 'a horrible city, hard and angular, new and pedantic'; 'here there are walls, walls and more walls, and over-ornate Renaissance flourishes wherever you look'. Moreover, she had to put up with 'too much convention' there. In short, 'I don't fit in, in a city like this.' Paris was quite a different story.

Detail of ill. 33

At the end of May 1901, at the age of 25, Becker married 36-year-old Otto Modersohn. Modersohn was a widower with a three-year-old daughter, Elsbeth (see p. 216). Describing him to her aunt in October 1900, Becker said: 'He is like a man and like a child … he has a pointed red beard and soft hands, and he is seventeen centimetres taller than me. He is a man of intense feeling. That is really what he is all about. Art and love, those are the two little pieces he plays.'

The couple were half a generation apart in age, but artistically they belonged to two different generations. On her return from Paris, Becker had taken lodgings with a farmer, Hermann Brünjes, in the Ostendorf area of Worpswede. She now used the room as a studio. It was fitted out for that purpose with a large skylight (see p. 217). She painted there every morning and every afternoon, except on Sundays ('that is one of the few Christian things I still do'). In June 1902, Otto Modersohn commented on her work: 'Remarkable how great these things are, looked at so much with the eye of a painter. There is actually no one here in W. who interests me nearly as much as Paula. She has intelligence, spirit, imagination, she has a wonderful sense of colour and form.'

Immediately after the engagement, Becker had announced that she was not prepared to give up art, stating categorically: 'Just because I am getting married, that is no reason not to become somebody.' She determinedly pursued her aim of remaining independent and becoming an important artist. She often wrote scathingly about the 'ossification process' that she observed in many people, mostly artists, including those around her. They started off with great momentum but then 'most of them came to a stop'. Artistically, they lived 'too much in the past'. In April 1900, thinking about her return to Worpswede, she had written: 'Will I then sit on the sofa too and keep my petty emotions to myself?'

 CHAPTER 3

She also wrote in her journal after reading Nietzsche's *Thus Spoke Zarathustra*, a key text for artists at the time: 'I feel happy again as a modern person and a child of my time.' In a letter to Rilke in November 1900, she insisted: 'I don't recognize any rules, not a Rilke rule, not a Becker rule, etc.' She wanted to go her own way as a modern person. This would not be easy for her. When Rilke took her with him to see Rodin, he introduced her as the wife of a painter; and when he published a book on the Worpswede artists in 1903, he did not mention Paula Modersohn-Becker. In a letter to Rilke in February 1906, she ended with the pithy, self-confident statement: 'I am Me', adding, 'and I hope to become more and more Me.'

Barely a year after getting married, Paula Modersohn-Becker was already having to admit soberly that she was completely on her own in the marriage, but at the same time she reassured herself that this solitude might be good for her art: 'Perhaps in this solemn silence it will grow wings.'

Simple Motifs

Modersohn-Becker's subjects in her village in the middle of the Teufelsmoor, with its population of 400, were not extraordinary, dramatic or mythological. She painted the subjects that were nearby: children in Worpswede, old people in the poorhouse, herself, still lifes, small landscapes of the surrounding area. She wanted to create images from the ordinary and the everyday. To do that, she was radical in her approach, stripping away the features sometimes found in the work of the Worpswede paint-ers and other nature-loving artists of the time: the local, the anecdotally decorative details, anything that recalled genre painting, or a lyrical representation of nature. Birch trees were a recurring motif that she made her own in the period 1900–2 (ills 17, 18).

These typical moorland trees with their black and white trunks crop up again and again in works by the Worpswede painters, often surrounded or framed by the characteristic features of the region: meadows and bog ditches, farmhouses and clusters of trees, ideally with their evocative golden brown autumn foliage. Modersohn-Becker's version is quite different. She does not show the particular way the small leaves shimmer in the light, or the movement of the branches in the wind. She paints bare birch trunks in bold sections and often quite narrow formats. The white bark is peeling away in places, and the exposed black parts are usually only hinted at, not fully painted. The trees are separate or grouped together, but the groups are clusters of irregular bare trunks and not the usual rows. It has been said that, before working with others in front of this subject, Modersohn-Becker would lie down on the grass and close her eyes in order to visualize a possible picture and devise a clear concept. The intention here was not Worpswede realism. She was not concerned with representation. What mattered to her was the image.

Becker had been captivated by the birches on her first visit to Worpswede in 1897, these 'delicate, slender young girls' with their 'languid, dreamy grace' as if their life had not yet begun. You had to succumb to them, they were impossible to resist. 'Some are already quite bold and masculine, with strong, straight trunks. Those are my "modern women".' And after talking about the willows ('my old men with silver beards'), she wrote that she and the trees in the marsh 'understand each other very well'.

Does this self-assured, determined focus on the trees standing out from their surroundings – isolated, fragmented, even skeletal – mean that they are symbolic? They are often irregular,

CHAPTER 3

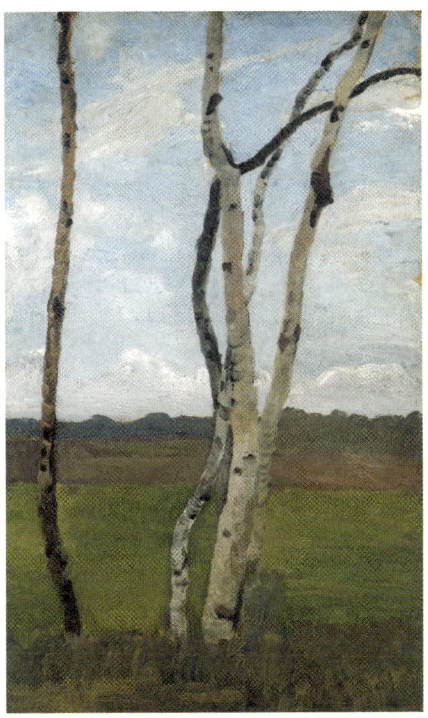

17 *Birch Trunks in a Landscape, c.* 1901

slanting into the picture, seemingly projecting from the painting towards the viewer, entangled. Although only a section of a tree or a cluster of trunks is visible, they always give the impression that they are towering upwards. The trees in the foreground have no branches, no leaves, just bare trunks; sometimes there are the beginnings of roots, like heavy boots. The motif may be simple, but the arrangements she has chosen for the trunks would seem to have an underlying meaning. They confirm the animistic view in the passage quoted from the journal: they are like people, responsive and full of movement.

In the 19th century, traditional artistic themes were replaced by observational views of nature and life. In the latter half of the century, the Impressionists abandoned formal composition and Van Gogh began to develop a new, direct symbolism centred on

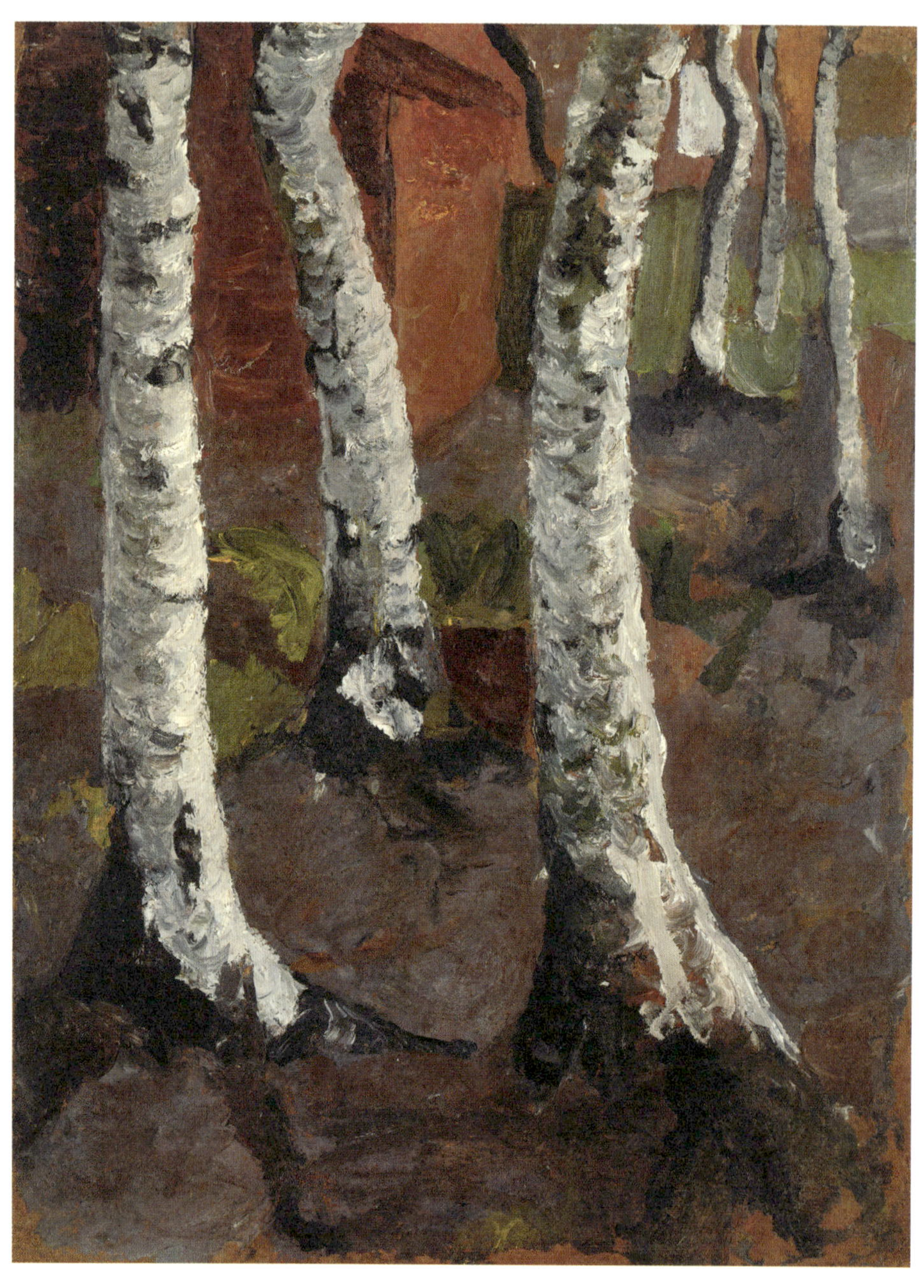

people and objects. Modersohn-Becker did the same in her early work. Just as she saw pine trees ('broad, gnarled, solid and tall, and yet with delicate fibres and nerves inside them') as 'an ideal figure for an artist', her 'subjective sensation' was that birch trees were 'as bold as men', 'modern women' and therefore symbols. In fact, they are a different kind of self-portrait. These pictures reflect – even if in a sometimes distorted form – the endurance and resistance of the nature around her, exposed without protection to the north German storms. While Modersohn-Becker's birch trees are not traditional symbols, they are a stepping stone to a new subjective iconography.

A Life Not Yet Begun

The varied pictures she painted of children during this period were part of the process. The figures, depicted individually or in specially arranged groups, are reduced to their essential forms. Often they are shown from the front; sometimes they seem distanced, viewed from a slightly low angle. Eyes, nose and mouth are merely hinted at. The children's clothes are not detailed and do not tie them to a particular period. The figures are not individualized. The artist was not interested in the children's inner life or psychology. Her focus was on their characteristic stillness, the awkward stance, their odd juxtaposition facing the viewer, holding onto a birch trunk or another person. They were a specific physical representation of nascent human beings in a totally natural, archetypal form.

18 *Birch Trunks in Front of Red House Wall, c.* 1901

These children are not individuals like those depicted by
Philipp Otto Runge. Nor are they Fritz von Uhde's playful little
things; or Edvard Munch's self-assured future members of the
bourgeoisie (ill. 19), or Pablo Picasso's sad innocents. Nor do they
show a particular social issue or make a plea for children to be
more independent. They are not in the light here; they are not
depicted as hopes for the future, as a sign of a better world. They
look isolated, self-contained, closed, shadowy beings in their own
right. In the words of Anne Buschhoff, they are 'creatures who
are part of nature and they seem to be in harmony with nature in
a way that is both mysterious and obvious'.[11] Like the birch trees,
these children look as if their life had not yet begun. They are
waiting embodiments of an uncertain future and the picture permanently suspends them in that state of uncertainty.

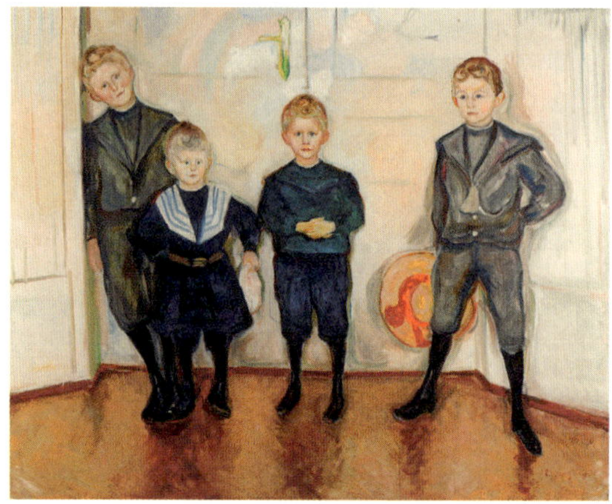

19 Edvard Munch, *The Four Sons of Dr Max Linde*, 1903

20 *Four Children in a Landscape with a Marsh Canal, c.* 1900

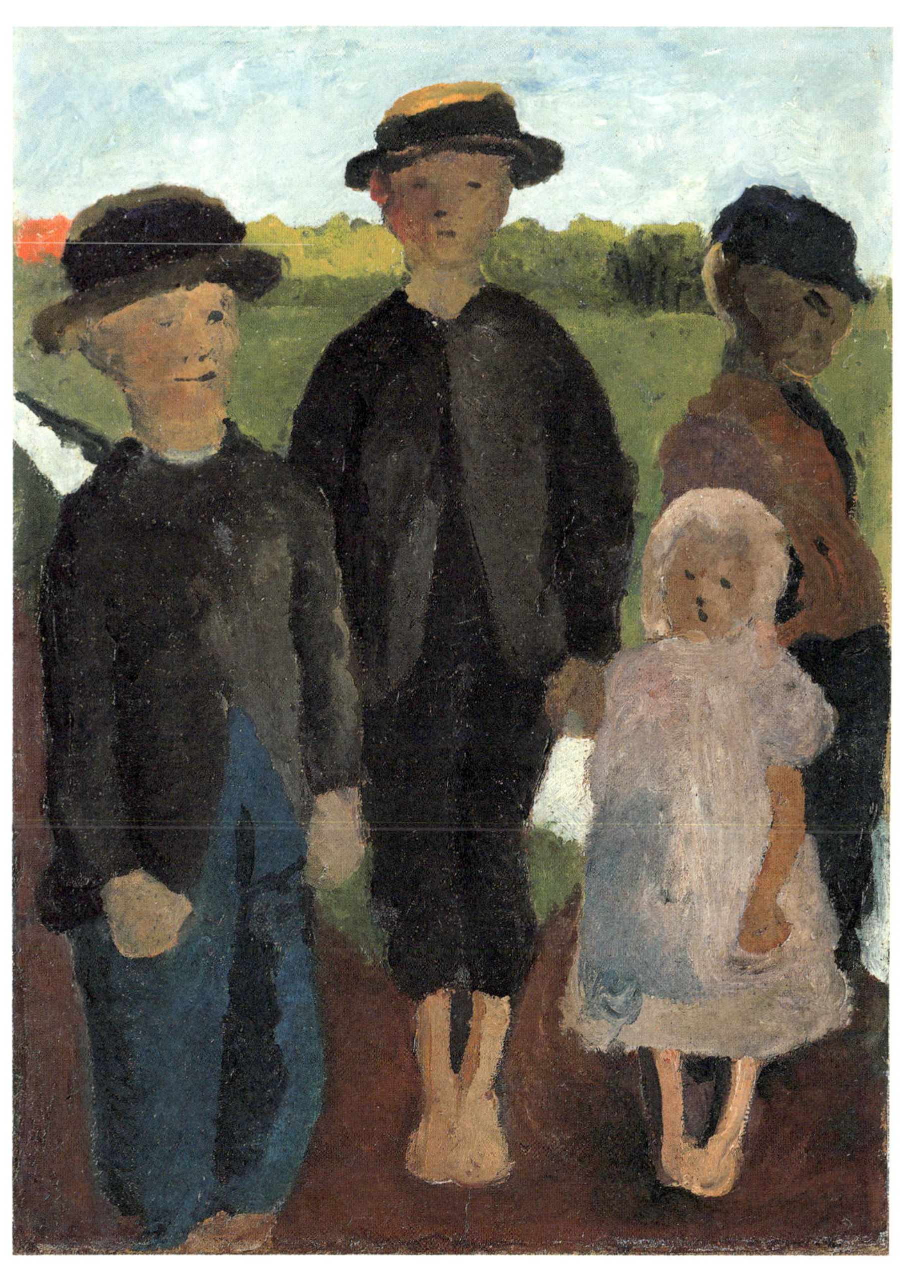

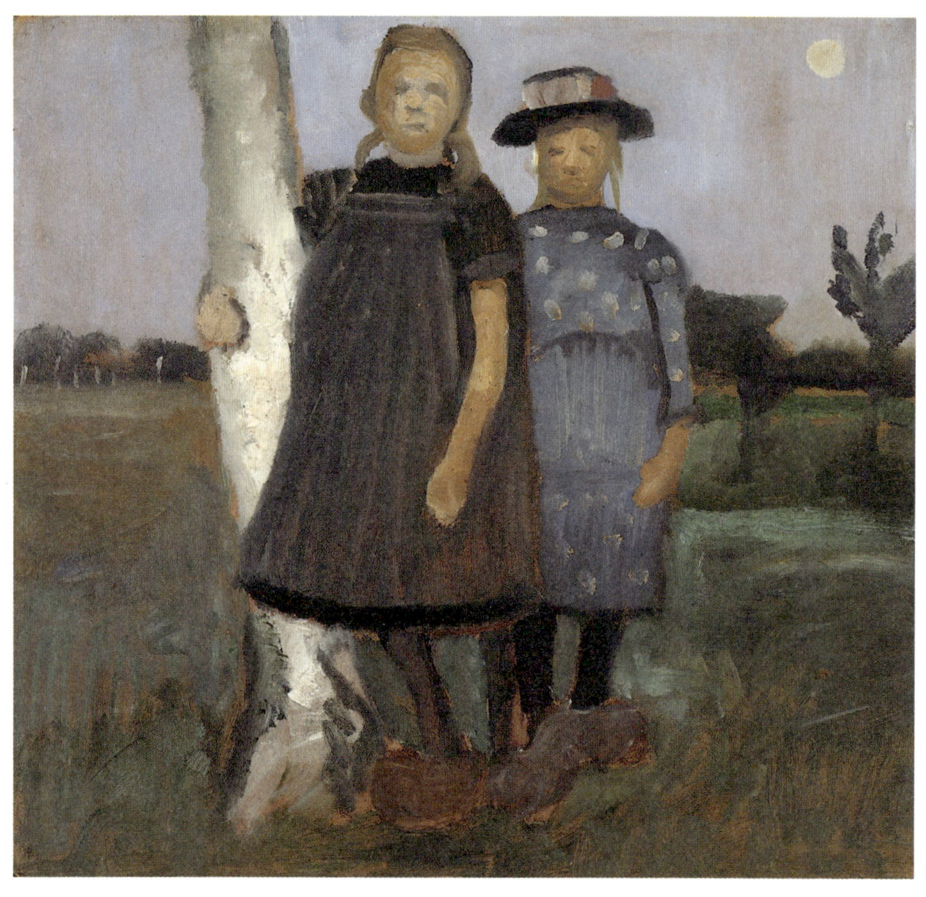

21   *Two Girls by a Birch Trunk, c.* 1902

                                    CHAPTER 3

These are children from the local area and they clearly have roots there; they are outdoors in the surrounding landscape. But their impassive immobility puts them outside everyday life. They are set apart by the powerful simplicity of the concept. This is the real point of these pictures: the unfamiliar in the familiar. The simplified forms are an essential part of that. At the time, Otto Modersohn criticized Paula because she abhorred convention and would rather make 'everything angular, ugly, odd, wooden', 'hands like spoons, noses like beaks, mouths like wounds, expressions like fools'.[12] He was right, but this was a deliberate position and not a lack of skill or mere capriciousness. She boldly brought the details together to create her own distinctive, simple style – a style that, although not true to nature, was intended to be image-specific. 'Do not for a moment', she advised her husband in a letter from Paris in February 1903, 'forget the aim, and the aim is to let your compositions develop as images', images with their own laws like those of her strange-looking, unconsciously still, shadowy beings whose life had not yet begun.

Lessons Learned in Paris, 1903

In February 1903, on her next visit to Paris, Modersohn-Becker started to 'take a critical look at Worpswede from the outside'. 'Suddenly, or in fact gradually, I had such a longing to look at old art. My dear husband let me go there.' The German art historian Rainer Stamm writes in his biography that this second trip to Paris – her first as a married woman – was intended to 'prove that an equal marriage between two artists was possible'.[13] The idea was to assert her own independence. She stayed

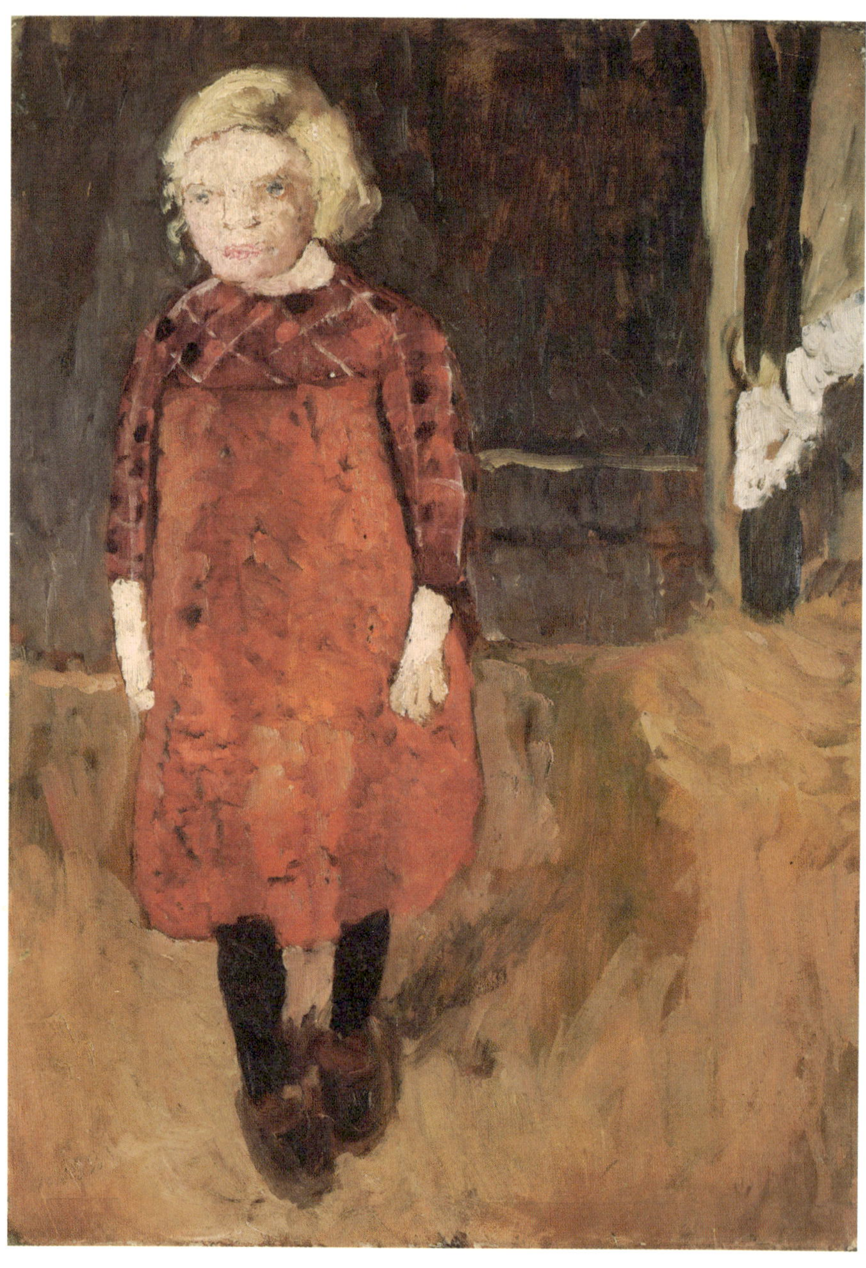

for just six weeks. Instead of going to as many art venues as possible, as she had done three years earlier, she now focused on new artistic experiences, often on the expert advice of Rilke and Clara Westhoff – now Clara Rilke-Westhoff, following her marriage in 1901.

Modersohn-Becker was particularly inspired by their visits to the Rue Laffitte, by 'the hand of the artist in art', the spontaneity and unfinished appearance of many of the new works, the small formats, the sketchiness – in short, the modernity. At the Palais du Luxembourg she found Degas's pastels 'very artistic' but also thought the colour 'capricious' – her facetious tone reflecting her stronger sense of colour. She noted with astonishment that French artists did not care whether the public understood them; the main thing was 'that it is art'. This would become a guiding principle for her.

Rilke arranged for her to see great art at Auguste Rodin's Paris studio and, the following day, at Rodin's house in Meudon. 'He is probably the greatest living artist today,' she wrote in a letter at the end of February 1903. Rodin presented her with a number of his drawings, 'these extraordinary dream forms', and it was these that made the strongest impression on her and most influenced her own drawings.

At the Hôtel Drouot auction house, she was impressed by the antique Japanese paintings from the Hayashi collection: 'The form, colour and spirit were truly remarkable.' 'Our art', on the other hand, was still too conventional, 'very inadequate' at expressing inner emotions, for instance 'expression of the nocturnal, the horrible, the charming, the feminine, the coquettish'. Her conclusion: 'concentrate on the essentials.' She meant that details should be omitted, reduced more and more, as she

22 *Girl Standing in Front of a Goat Shed*, 1902

had already done in the paintings of birch trees and children. After seeing the pictures in the auction house, she found the people she passed on the street 'much more extraordinary, much more striking, more surprising than they are ever painted'. In a letter in mid-February 1903, she wrote: 'These realizations only come to us momentarily, they are sometimes obscured by everyday life, but art must come from moments like that.' In other words, the depiction of reality in art should be striking and full of life. This would inspire other, more realistic pictures of children.

In the Louvre, Modersohn-Becker was particularly drawn to a group of classical works of art. She wrote in her journal that, until then, the art of the ancient world had felt alien to her. In particular, she had not been able to see 'any connection' between ancient and modern art. On her first visit to Paris, she had noted: 'I find the cold objectivity of ancient art oppressive. You have no sense of the personality.' It did not give her the 'subjective sensation' that was so important to her in art. Now, though, she could see the connection.

She came across mummy portraits from Fayum dating from the first and second centuries CE in the Egyptian department of the Louvre and in a publication (ill. 61). 'Great simplicity of form is wonderful.' She now realized, 'how I can learn from the heads in ancient art. They are seen as so grand and so simple! Forehead, eyes, mouth, nose, cheeks, chin and nothing else.' It sounds simple, 'and yet it is so, so much', she wrote in a letter at the end of February 1903. In the Fayum portraits, with their flat composition, the frontality of the heads, the stylized features and the animated expressions, she found vital inspiration for her future work. In particular, they gave her a real sense of 'personality'. The portraits showed her that she was on the right path to translating an impression of nature into a pictorial composition, as was her aim. She now felt that she was coming 'inwardly closer to beauty' and, above all, had 'found and thought of a great deal of form'.

Modersohn-Becker drew precise conclusions about her own work from these new artistic experiences in Paris. What she wrote afterwards sounds like a manifesto of sorts: concentrate on the essentials of the motif and leave out everything else, show what is special about the people in the picture, look for the 'great simplicity of form' and allow room for spontaneity, aim for the subjective construction of nature in the picture, and do not worry about how the work will be received. Paris brought her new insights, and she was now 'working to build on them further'.

Worpswede: Different Lives

Modersohn-Becker returned to the narrow but familiar environment of Worpswede in March 1903, after a month and a half in Paris. The models she chose to work with were not usually farmers, country folk or her fellow artists at Worpswede; they would come from the poorhouse that stood opposite the Modersohns' home. Clara Rilke-Westhoff described them as 'people who had arrived from somewhere or other and lived miserable lives'.[14] Paula's sister Herma said that the poorhouse 'offered the most convenient and available big and small models' at very little cost. They included Anna Schröder – known as 'Dreebeen', 'three-legged', so named because she had a walking stick – a woman with dwarfism who is described as having 'a disproportionately large upper body, who leant on the handle of her stick as she was talking'.[15] She was Modersohn-Becker's favourite subject for many years.

However, Modersohn-Becker did not focus on individual physical features. The solid seated figure in her sometimes impasto, sometimes fluid style merges with the natural setting. In *Study of Dreebeen Sitting in the Garden* (*c.* 1904, ill. 24), for instance, the body posture is conveyed, but the free and spontaneous application of the pictorial media to the basic composition makes the figure and background look semi-abstract – an effect that is enhanced by the uniform, earthy, natural brownish-orange range of colours. In 1902, Modersohn-Becker had written in her journal that 'all muted tones' should have 'a uniform relationship' in order to create a cohesive natural effect in the picture. The aim was to make the pictorial media that were in themselves autonomous look naturally coherent.

The artistic peculiarities of this painting become especially clear if it is compared with Otto Modersohn's *Anna 'Dreebeen' Schröder in the Garden of the Worpswede Poorhouse* (1902, ill. 25). Otto's figure is more recognizable from her clothing and her profile; the surrounding landscape is depicted, with its birch trees, hens, meadow, field and cluster of trees. The shadow in the foreground offsets the sunlit backdrop. In Paula Modersohn-Becker's painting, in contrast, Anna Schröder seems to be part of nature, to have emerged from it as a natural being. The reduction of elements and omission of detail make the scene seem timeless. There is no distinction between light and shade. What one sees is a deep colourful brilliance, the kind that Modersohn-Becker had dreamed of when she first went to Paris, 'coloured light within shadow, light without sun'. She was not trying to portray nature as it was, but to develop a method of painting that was specific and naturalistic. Like the reduction of elements to what is essential, it is a way to make the image more powerfully symbolic.

Immediately after her return from Paris, Modersohn-Becker wrote in her journal: 'I am getting close to our people here again,

I am experiencing their great biblical simplicity.' A couple of years earlier, in a letter dated September 1898, she had told her parents that in the mornings and afternoons she went to see 'Mother Schröder' in the poorhouse. She sat with 'this ancient little woman' in a big grey room and they had a very brief, simple, endlessly repeated conversation, and in between Schröder would have 'a sort of hallucination'. She talked about her youth, 'so dramatically, acting both parts in different tones of voice, that it is fascinating to listen to. You feel you want to write it down straight away.' In the same letter she added, 'I find this environment quite wonderful.'

The journals contain many entries, with occasional conversations in the local dialect, Plattdeutsch, about the characters and lives of the old women who sat for her as models, their confused interjections, and stories of curious or absurd events of the kind that Modersohn-Becker had described as 'hallucinations'. This suggests that the bourgeois Paula Modersohn-Becker, with her urban background, felt transported into a completely different world — a world of unfamiliar human experiences — while she was painting her subjects. She writes of one poorhouse resident, nearly beaten to death by her mother when she was just five years old, who has now 'wrapped herself in a web of dreams and fairy tales' and is allowed to look after the geese 'to help her recover'. Others include an educated aristocrat who worked as a gravedigger during the cholera epidemic in Hamburg, then went to sea and is now believed in the poorhouse to be a millionaire; a 'voluptuous blonde', who served four weeks in prison 'because she and her husband mistreated their illegitimate child'; a half-blind old woman who every day prays to her God not to let her go whoring or stealing. Modersohn-Becker was spellbound as she listened to them. In her first few months in Worpswede, she was full of amazement when she wrote about the poorhouse residents. Gradually, however, the

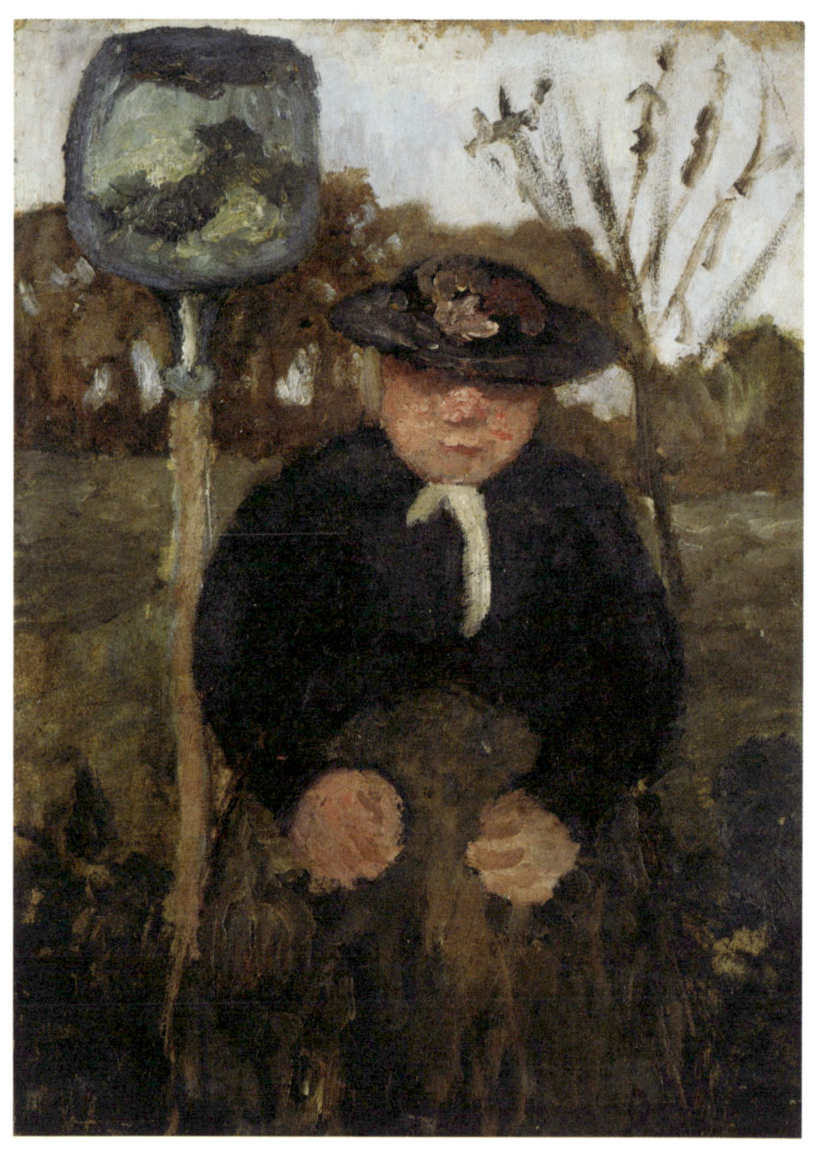

23 *Dreebeen Seated with Glass Bottle*, 1903

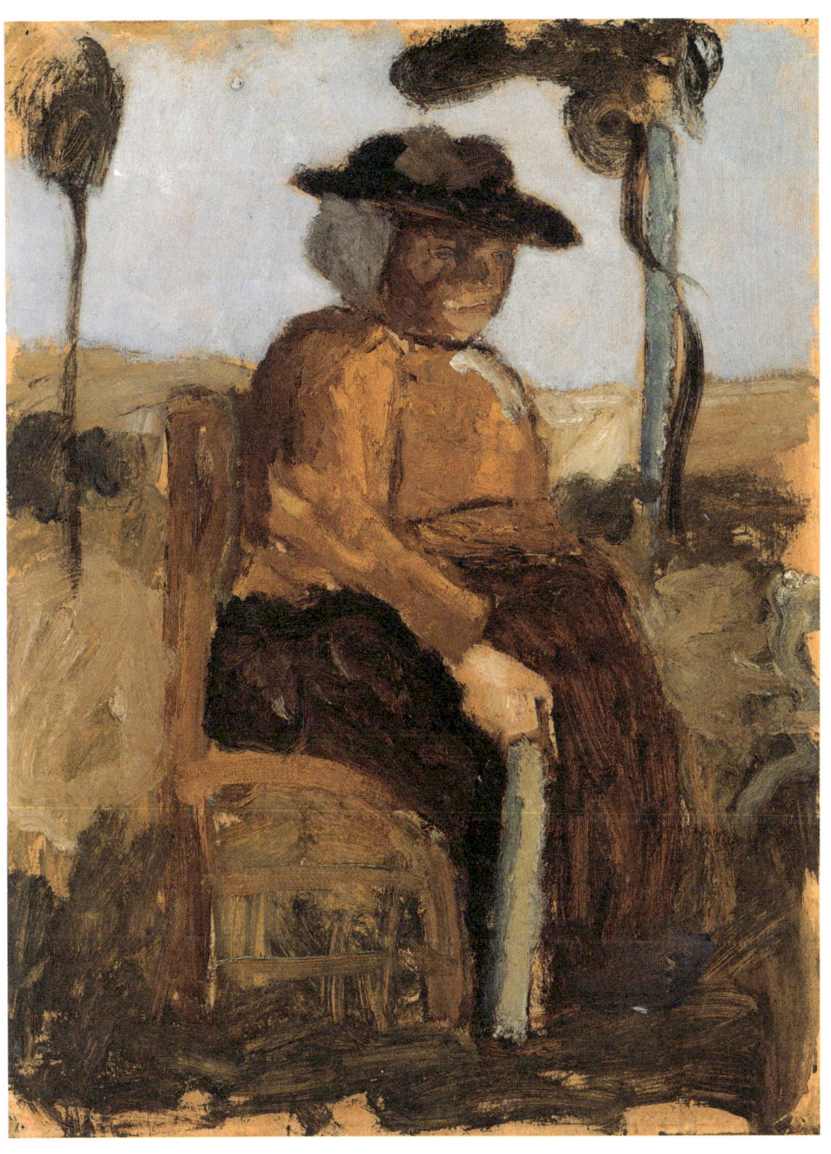

24 *Study of Dreebeen Sitting in the Garden, c.* 1904

different lives of these people became a normal part of everyday life – she and Otto liked to go and see them in the evenings to draw and paint.

Modersohn-Becker did not spend time with the residents of the poorhouse for social reasons. They had a raw honesty, genuine and unaffected, that appealed to her. That is why they loom so large in the paintings, like mythological beings. She likens a woman with her child at her breast in a smoky hut to one of the virtues. Schröder could be seen as an archetypal mother figure, like the seer Erda. Modersohn-Becker noted that Schröder had a 'sibylline voice' – another reference to mythological beings, prophetesses. This was her other world, the world of ancient stories and great biblical simplicity.

For Modersohn-Becker, perhaps Worpswede had something of that mythical strangeness that Gauguin looked for in Tahiti,

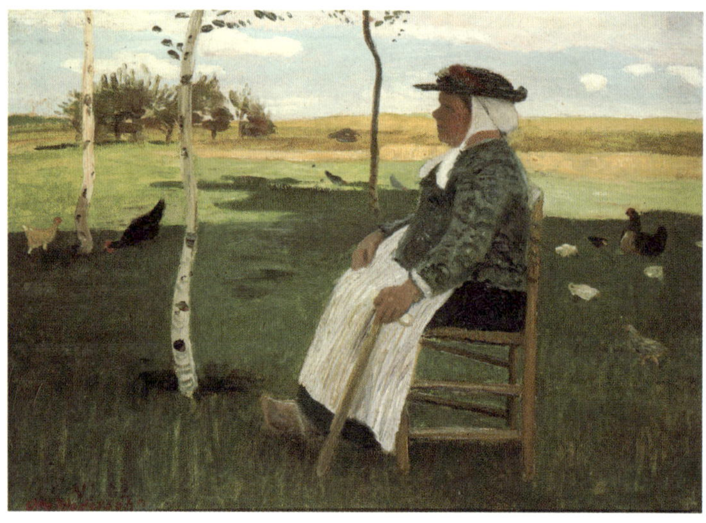

25 Otto Modersohn, *Anna 'Dreebeen' Schröder in the Garden of the Worpswede Poorhouse*, 1902

CHAPTER 3

with different people, different lives, a different language, different customs. For her, of course, it was not remote but close at hand. The birch paintings and early pictures of children had already heralded a shift from the familiar to the unfamiliar; now the unfamiliar was becoming familiar in this other world.

Back to Paris, 1905

Modersohn-Becker continued to be drawn to new experiences. Reflecting on her time in Paris, in 1905 she wrote that she once again felt a huge longing for the city. She had gone through 'a bad time with work … or in fact no work', and now she needed some 'outside stimulus'. Ultimately, Paris was *the* city for her, 'beautiful and effervescent and simmering, and you can immerse yourself in it completely'. And so, in mid-February 1905, she left again for the French capital. The trip was also an attempt to escape from everyday life at home and become independent. She met her sister Herma, nine years her junior, who was doing a language course there. After a seven-week stay, she explained to her mother that for her Paris had positively become a necessity in her life 'to complement the rather one-sided life I have [in Worpswede]'.

She found the outside stimulus in works of art old and new, which she would sketch, as she had done on previous visits to Paris. The Musée de Cluny, with its medieval treasures, and the Museum of Comparative Sculpture in the Palais du Trocadéro provided the subjects. The sketches that she produced during this period have their own place within her body of work.

At first glance, these sketches might appear to be a continuation of the exploration of art history that she had begun in

her youth, when she visited some of the great museums in
Europe to see original masterpieces in the flesh. But she was
not interested in the works from an art-historical perspective;
instead of detailed studies she made rough charcoal sketches,
focusing on the postures of the figures that caught her eye,
their positions and their relationships to each other. She was
forever seeking out the basic structure, as if collecting material
for future pictures while learning about arrangements of
figures outside her own experience. Whether it was a portrait
of a lady by Ingres (ill. 28), a Cranach Venus (ill. 27), a medieval
monument (ill. 26) or a group of Greek Tanagra figurines, she
put works by other artists through a special process of reduction. Although these were not preparatory sketches for specific
paintings, they provided essential formal practice and a foundation for future work.

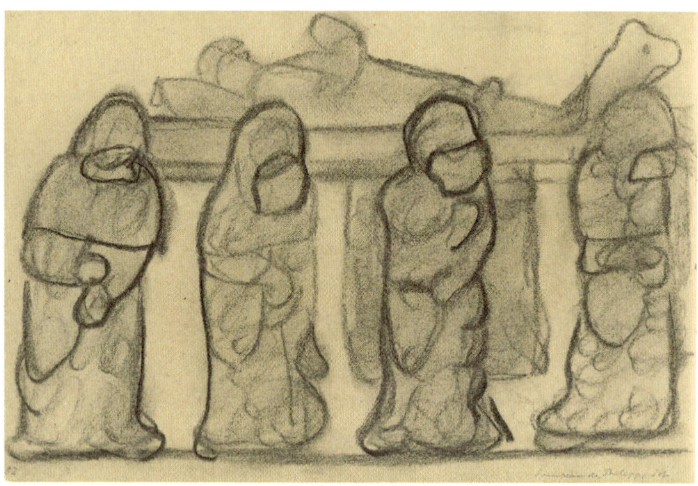

26 Sketch of the Philippe Pot monument in the Louvre, charcoal, 1903

                            CHAPTER 3

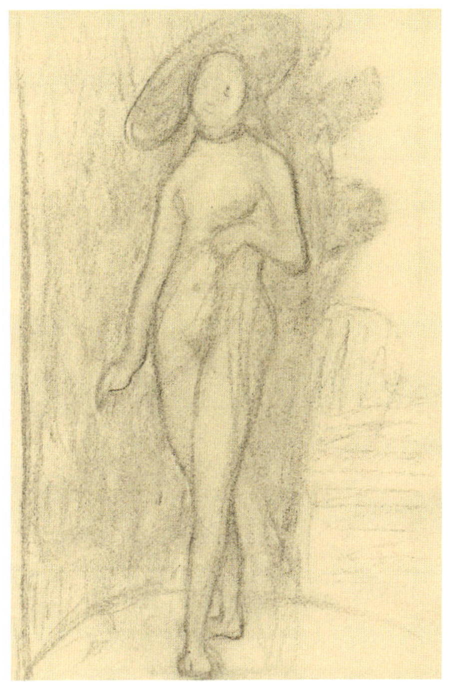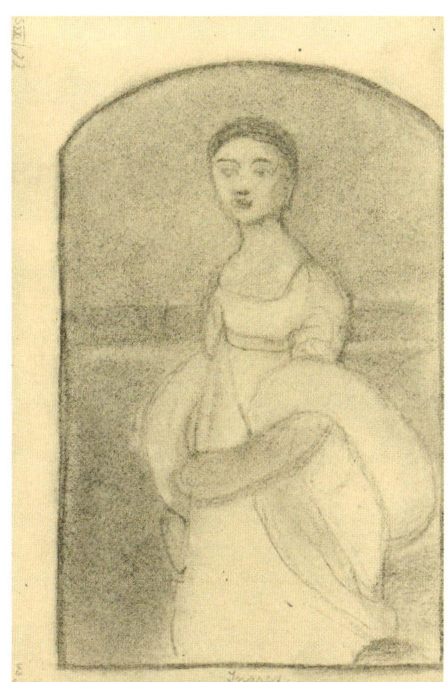

27 Sketch of Lucas Cranach's *Venus Standing in a Landscape*
in the Louvre, charcoal, 1903

28 Sketch of Dominique Ingres's *Mlle Rivière*
in the Louvre, charcoal, 1903

1901–5: The Unfamiliar in the Familiar

Modersohn-Becker was now living at 65 Rue Madame, on the corner of Rue de Fleurus, near the Jardin du Luxembourg. The art collectors Michael and Sarah Stein lived opposite her, and Michael's sister, the writer Gertrude Stein, lived at 27 Rue de Fleurus with her brother Leo. They sometimes showed their important contemporary artworks, notably the latest works by Matisse and Picasso, to people who were interested (ill. 29). At the time, Modersohn-Becker was specifically seeking out private collections in Paris and it seems likely that she took advantage of one of those opportunities. Certainly, we know that when Otto Modersohn was briefly visiting her in Paris, they went to see Gustave Fayet's large collection of works by Paul Gauguin on Rue de Bellechasse in the 7th arrondissement. Gauguin had died two years earlier, in 1903. Fayet's collection must have made a strong impression and, judging by her later work, it had a lasting effect. It was a sign of her interest in Gauguin that she kept up to date with the latest book releases: after returning to Worpswede, she sent her sister Herma – who was still living in Paris – a list of books about Gauguin that she wanted to read.

About three weeks after she arrived in Paris, she wrote in a letter to her husband: 'It's strange; this time it is not so much the old masters who impress me but mainly the most modern ones.' She wanted to visit Edouard Vuillard and Maurice Denis, feeling that you could get the best impression of an artist's work in the studio. Vuillard and Denis were key members of the Nabis, a group of artists formed in the late 1880s who shared a passion to renew the art of painting and whose individual styles, although varied, were certainly subjective. Through their work,

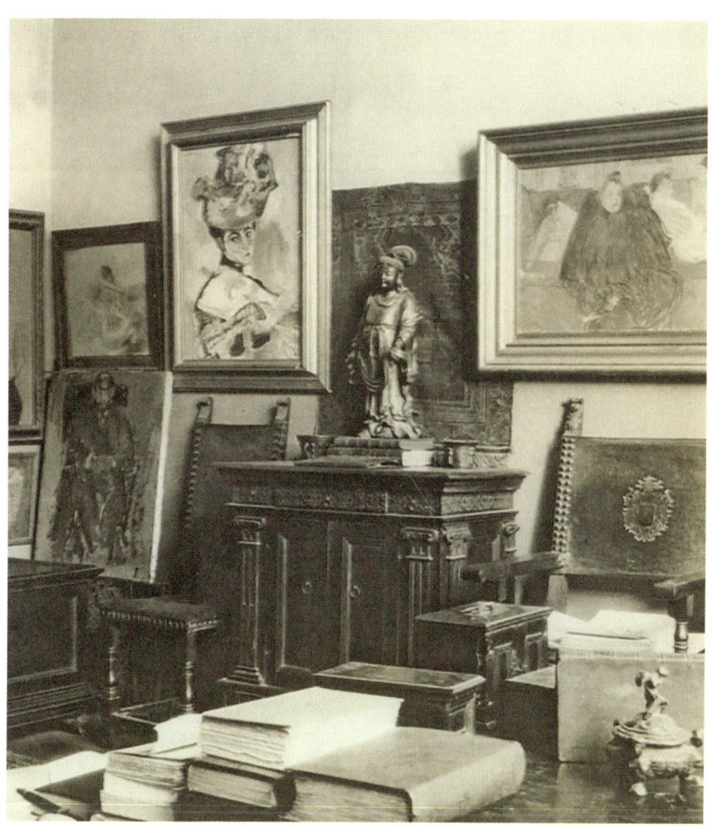

29 Collection of Gertrude and Leo Stein at 27 Rue de Fleurus, photo, *c.* 1906. Top centre: *Woman with a Hat (Madame Matisse)*, 1905, by Henri Matisse

Modersohn-Becker may have rediscovered those 'subjective sensations' that she so valued in her own art.

The first decade of the 20th century was a hive of activity in the art world, at least in Paris. The Post-Impressionists had passed their peak but were still represented in the Paris art trade and the Palais du Luxembourg. Gauguin and Cézanne were especially admired by artists, particularly after their deaths (Cézanne died just three years after Gauguin, in 1906). The leading figures of the Nabis (who had gone their separate ways in 1899) were still influential but the Fauves, centred around Henri Matisse, were attracting the most attention with their free use of colour. Spanish-born Picasso lived in Paris from 1904. It was the decade in which, in studios all over France, artists were striving to give their paintings autonomy.

In the autumn of 1905, the Fauves – key among them, Henri Matisse, Henri Manguin, Albert Marquet, André Derain and Maurice de Vlaminck – who were more or less the same age as Modersohn-Becker, shocked the art world when they showed 39 works at the Salon d'Automne with a never-before-seen intensity of colour and an unfinished aesthetic. When Leo Stein first saw Matisse's *Woman with a Hat* (1905, ill. 29), he commented that it was the nastiest smear of paint he had ever seen.[16] This was a breakthrough for the daring new art. The Matisse painting became the work of the hour and a turning point in art history. Paris avant-garde galleries were vying for sensational works by these exciting talents.

Modersohn-Becker kept abreast of what was happening in Paris at the time. She had to miss the autumn exhibition, but she did go to a preview at the Salon des Indépendants in the spring. She was not hugely impressed: 'A lot of empty talk, the walls covered with hessian and a lot of pictures with no jury, arranged alphabetically in a jumble of colours.' In March 1905, she wrote: 'You don't know exactly what is wrong, but you vaguely feel

CHAPTER 3

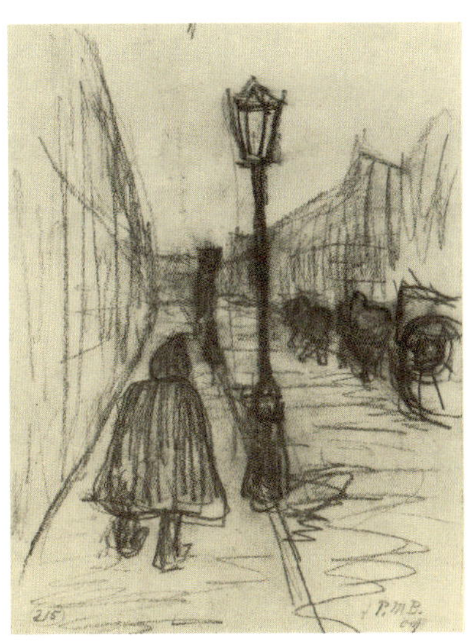

30 *Paris Street with Child in a Hood,*
Lamppost and Horse-Drawn Cart,
charcoal, 1905

there is something missing.' Nor did she find the related Van
Gogh and Seurat commemorative exhibitions all that interesting. However, she was impressed by some of the modern works
at the Salon des Indépendants. They included around eight
major paintings by Matisse (one of which was *Luxe, Calme et
Volupté* of 1904).

Modersohn-Becker worked in the same way as Franz Marc
had done shortly before her, and August Macke not long afterwards. Marc noted during a stay in Paris in 1903: 'It is
remarkable, you can learn how to draw here better than anywhere else.' Four years later Macke spent most of his time in
Paris sketching and collecting impressions.[17] During this third
stay in Paris, Modersohn-Becker did the same. She did not paint

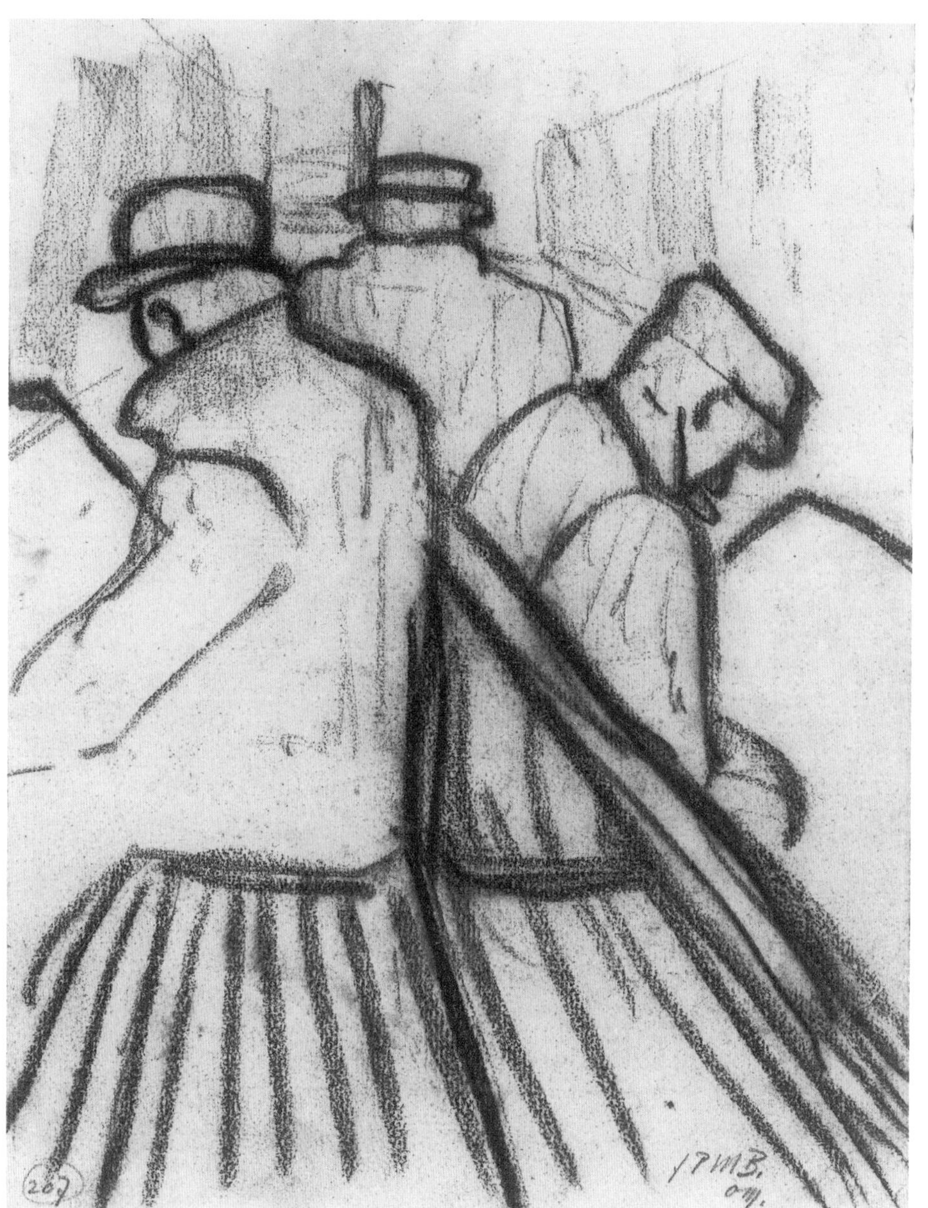

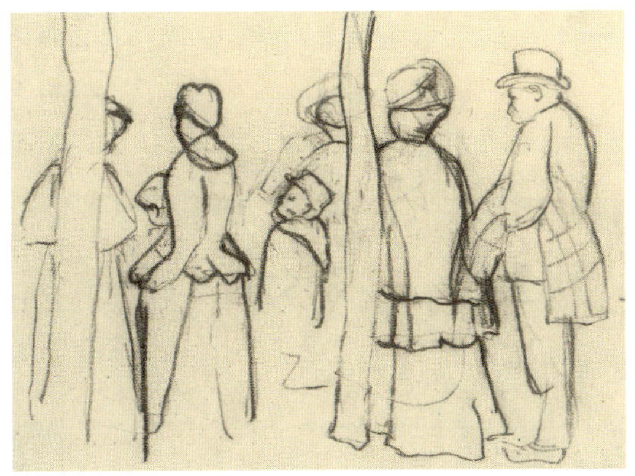

31 *Horse-Drawn Bus in Paris, Three Men Sitting
on Top of the Bus*, charcoal, 1905

32 *Group of Women and Children and a Man
between Tree Trunks*, charcoal, 1905

on the spot, but as well as the sketches in museums she did powerful charcoal drawings recording her impressions of street life (ills 30–32). Again, these are not detailed. They show observed arrangements of figures and people in characteristic positions. Since they were set in the city and touched on urban themes, they were different from the work she did in Worpswede: people waiting at a stop, passengers in a horse-drawn bus, strange-looking figures in the street, a newspaper kiosk, women at a market stall. The drawings were done quickly in outline and hatching, but the precise composition (or construction), the decisive, emphatic execution of detail and the striking use of charcoal give them a graphic quality. They make up for the paintings that she did not do in the capital at this time.

'Coloured light within shadow'

When Modersohn-Becker returned from Paris in the spring of 1905, she took up a theme that was to have a significant impact on all her work. She wrote to her sister Herma that in Worpswede she saw 'all earth tones as blackish in colour', which she really loved. In February 1900, during her first stay in Paris, she had gone on an excursion to the surrounding countryside and had noticed that when the sun was shining, the earth seemed much too light to her: 'then I want every colour to be deeper and fuller and I get quite annoyed at that lightness'. Five years on, despite her admiration for the leading lights of the Nabis, to her mind the lightness in their pictures was as wrong as the Impressionist approach to light. She told her friend Clara Rilke-Westhoff that she now had a relationship with the sun – not the sun 'that divides everything and casts shadows everywhere and breaks the picture up into a thousand parts', but the sun 'that is oppressive and makes things grey and heavy and ties them all together in that grey heaviness in which they are as one'.

That aim of making things 'as one' had important implications for her colour aesthetic. For her, the way ahead lay not in pure localized colours or in the breakdown of colours in Impressionist and Neo-Impressionist works but in the 'coloured light within shadow' connecting objects and tones, 'in which they are as one'. She had already said on her first visit to Paris in May 1900 that 'what is most beautiful for me, the depth, the fullness of colour, I do not see here'. She considered Monet superficial. Her equivalent to French *plein air* painting, her concept of dark light and full colour tones, was rooted not in Paris but in provincial northern Germany.

CHAPTER 3

In this regard, it is understandable that she felt drawn to the Bande Noire artists, especially Charles Cottet and Lucien Simon, who painted melancholy pictures of the harsh aspects of simple Breton life in muted dark tones. Her admiration for the work of Hans von Marées is equally understandable. 'Marées uses extraordinarily deep colour, like the old masters,' she remarked after visiting Schleissheim. People commented on his characteristic 'colourful darkness' and the fact that his male figures belonged on the one hand to the light and on the other to the dark.[18] The impenetrable dark colours, in particular, gave Marées's imagery a melancholy tone that clearly touched Modersohn-Becker.

The Promise of Modern Life

Around 1904–5, Modersohn-Becker painted a small group of new pictures of children in Worpswede (ills 33–35). The heads are now depicted up close, and are much more strongly defined and characterized than before – personal yet remote, but at the same time expressive. Sometimes the subjects are looking out of the picture. In one painting, a girl stares down at the ground, her expression closed (ill. 34). In another, the subject looks the viewer straight in the eye but makes a mysterious gesture with her hand, creating a sense of distance (ill. 33). While the children in earlier pictures were archetypal, these paintings marked the start of a serious exploration of humanity, which is direct and unusual, portrayed through individual figures. There is nothing like it in the art of the time. The sparse colours are kept in a dark palette, lending the isolated heads in their stillness an air of melancholy – making the familiar seem unfamiliar.

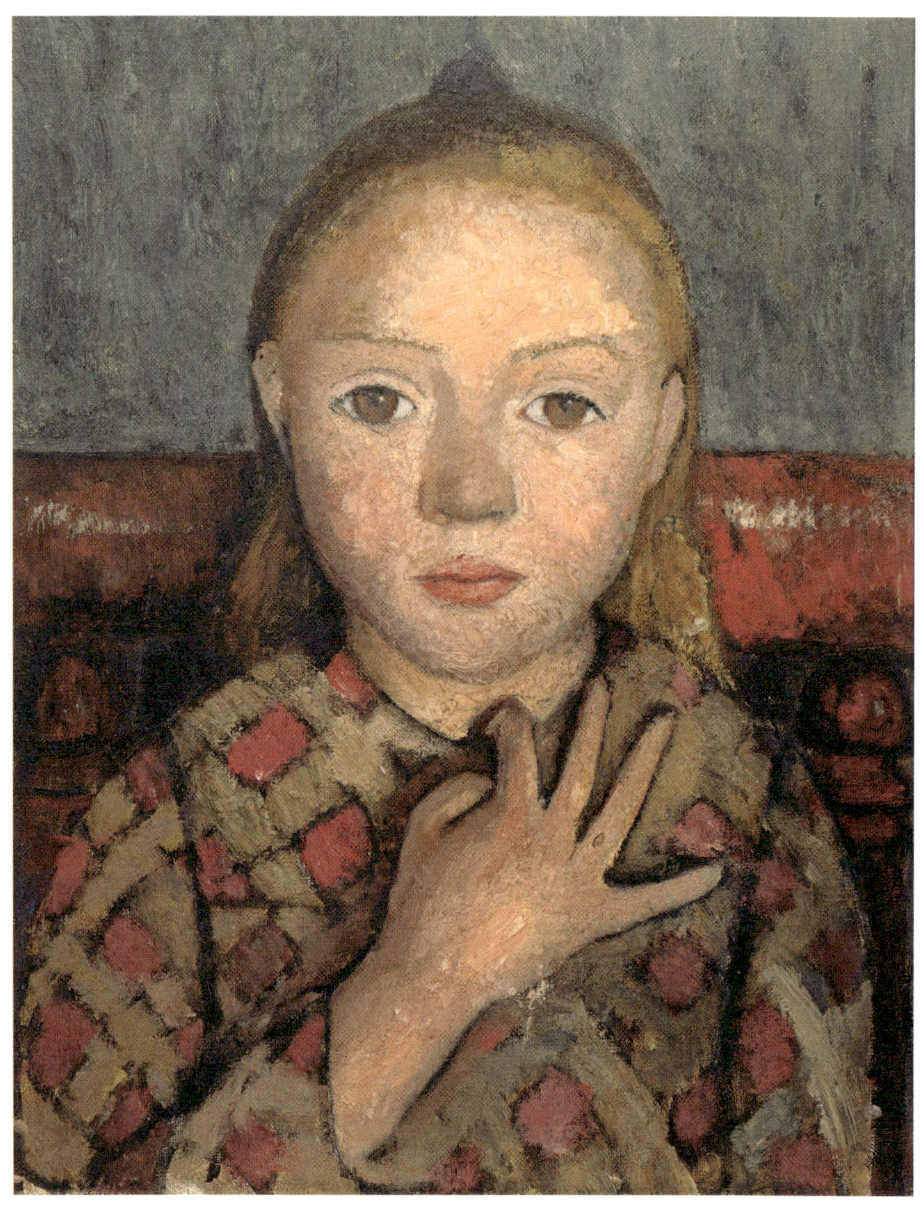

33 *Portrait of a Girl with Hand Spread across her Chest, c.* 1905

                    CHAPTER 3

The symbolic nature of these works is suggested in an earlier entry in Modersohn-Becker's journal, probably from 1898. Perhaps talking about a cousin, she wrote: 'How this girl fascinates me! She creates a powerful and beautiful world from within herself. A world like that of a youngster starting out in life with great plans… She hates pettiness in women… She is still waiting to develop. She doesn't know what will happen, but she waits for it with a beating heart… I love that simple greatness. It is refreshing, soothing, like classical antiquity. And yet much more natural, more exciting. Because it is reality. It is life, modern life.' These words might be seen as a manifesto. This girl, on the cusp of awakening, with ambitions beyond the socially set female boundaries, embodies the transition into modern life, and its 'refreshing' and 'soothing' greatness. It is a theme that runs throughout these pictures of children, which also serve as a kind of self-portrait – a call for women in this

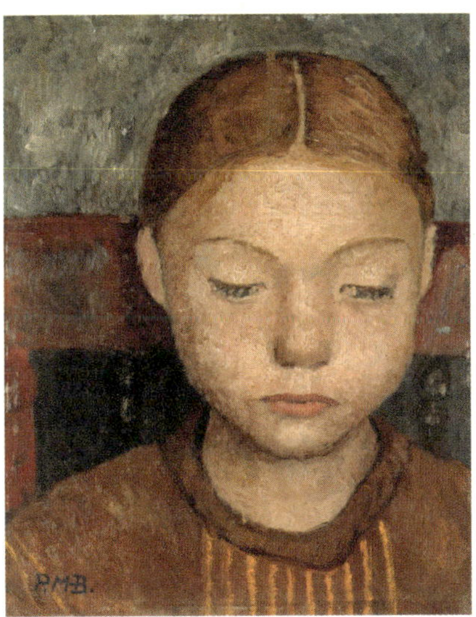

34 *Head of a Girl Sitting on a Chair, c.* 1905

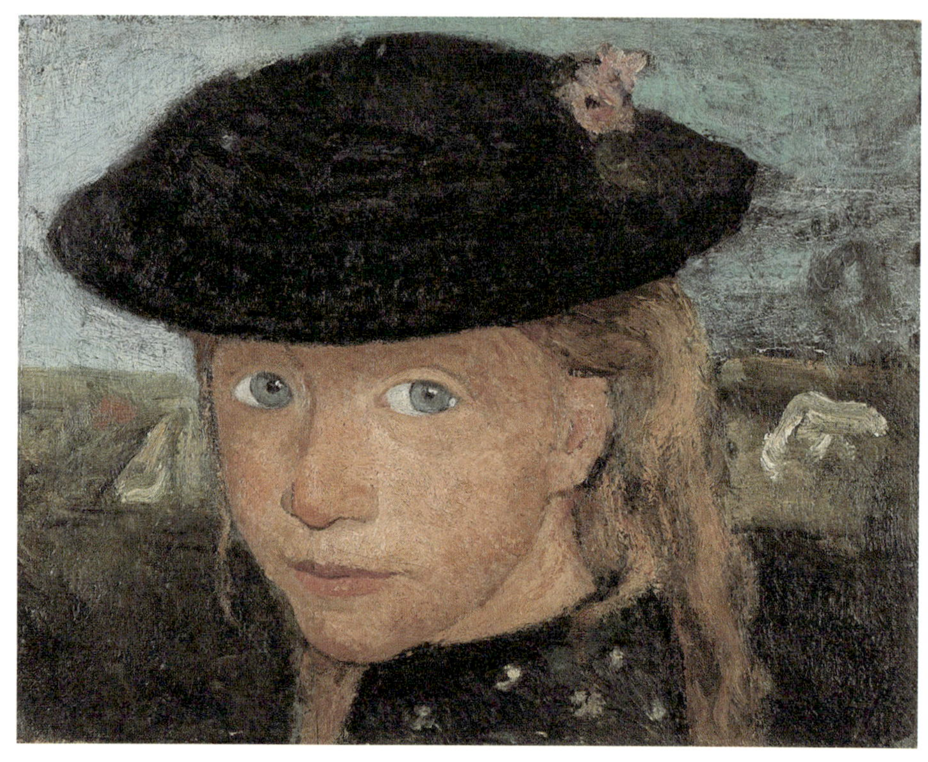

35 *Head of Blonde Girl with a Straw Hat, c.* 1904

                    CHAPTER 3

male-dominated world to independently draw on this 'more natural, more exciting' quality in order to bring their ambitions to life.

Layers of Varnish

In recent years, when some of Modersohn-Becker's small-format works were restored and the old varnish removed, it became clear that the colours used by the artist do, in fact, stand out as strongly from the dark as she had dreamt of. The restorer Angelica Hoffmeister-zur Nedden noted that the 'muddy' appearance frequently found in Modersohn-Becker's paintings was often nothing more than shiny, yellowed varnish that had been applied by later owners of the works; the artist had not added varnish because she had specifically wanted to avoid that effect.[19] As in the pictures of children, Modersohn-Becker was looking not for smoothness but for a porous, textured, often relief-like surface.

Here a technical artistic process – varnishing – takes on a crucial and even a symbolic role. Normally it was used to give the image a sheen and protect the picture. At the turn of the 20th century, many artists did not want a glossy finish. Gauguin feared that Vollard would ruin his pictures 'with the dirty varnish loved by dealers which is so common',[20] and when Munch went to the Sonderbund exhibition in Cologne in 1912 one of his main observations was that with the young artists you hardly saw any varnished paintings; applying varnish was tantamount to 'vandalism'.[21] Modern paintings should not be glossy; instead, they should be direct and raw in effect. The same was true of Modersohn-Becker's work.

1906: A Turning Point

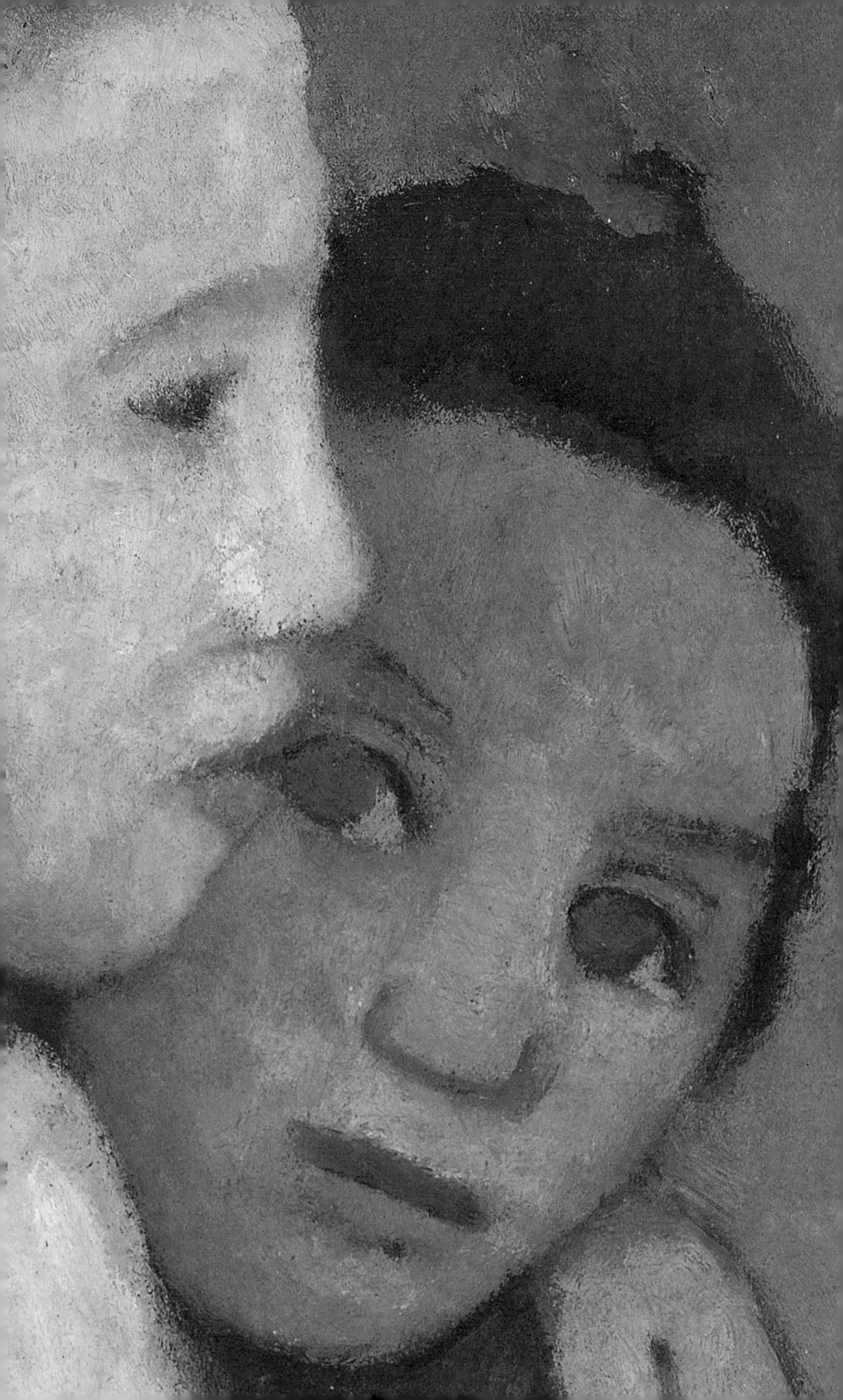

'Between my old and my new life'

In 1906, at the age of 30, Modersohn-Becker moved to Paris for good. She had quietly made preparations and travelled by train at night, waiting until after her husband's birthday, when her mother and brother were away in Italy and it was too late for them to intervene. She took the mail coach to Bremen ('Worpswede was still the same remote place with its slow mail coach,' wrote Rilke in January 1906[22]) and from there travelled on to Cologne before arriving in Paris. She had said several times that by the time she was 30 she wanted to have become someone in the art world. Just as her first journey to Paris at New Year 1900 was a symbolic departure, so too was this one: the start of a new artistic life.

She arrived in the city on 24 February, having separated from her husband: 'Now I have left Otto Modersohn and am between my old and my new life,' she wrote in her journal in the same month. 'He is a philistine and not free in any way,' she wrote later. The marriage had left her unfulfilled and deeply

Detail of ill. 38

frustrated. Their different artistic aims drove them further and further apart and, while he was content with the simple provincial life, she longed to be out in the world: 'Even other relationships in Worpswede do not satisfy me. It is too narrow for me.' She needed the freedom to live. Clara Rilke-Westhoff described how important it had been for Modersohn-Becker to go 'out in the world again, to go back to Paris'.[23] Worpswede was introverted silence and the archaic 'wonderland' of other people; Paris was everything else – the world.

Modersohn-Becker had rented out her Ostendorf studio, and that changed the parameters of her art. Her criteria and her actions were no longer defined by the German scene, and certainly not by the regional artists' colony. Now she was only interested in what was happening in the capital of art: 'You'll see, now I am free I will make something of myself.' In Paris she first moved into a studio at 14 Avenue du Maine and then, in October 1906, into another studio nearby, at 49 Boulevard du Montparnasse, where there was enough room for larger paintings. There she would produce her most important works.

It was common for artists to spend time in Paris, to study the latest developments in the world of art and immerse themselves in old masters, and to participate in the artistic freedom if not to marvel at foreign cultures. The artists Max Beckmann, Käthe Kollwitz, Wassily Kandinsky, Franz Marc, August Macke, Paul Klee, Lyonel Feininger, Alexej von Jawlensky and Max Pechstein were all attracted to the city. Marc wrote about his stay in 1907: 'These eight days are among the most fantastic in my life – and very worthwhile. I looked at very little apart from the two great new masters, Van Gogh and Gauguin, as well as Egyptian and medieval sculpture and Rodin. But above all "la belle Seine"...'[24] In the middle of the first decade, a group of German artists around the same age as Modersohn-Becker would meet at the Café du Dôme, on the corner of the Boulevard du Montparnasse. They included Friedrich Ahlers-Hestermann, Rudolf Levy and Franz Nölken, together with Hans Purrmann and Albert Weisgerber, and were sometimes joined by art dealers such as Paul Cassirer (who was based in Berlin), Alfred Flechtheim (Düsseldorf) and Heinrich Thannhauser (Munich). Writers on art, such as Carl Einstein (Berlin), also dropped by.

For all of them, these were temporary stays for inspiration. The enterprising painter Ida Gerhardi and the sculptor Bernhard Hoetger were among the few who stayed longer in Paris (Gerhardi lived in the city from 1891 to 1913, and Hoetger from 1900 to 1910). Paula Modersohn-Becker, who also planned to stay, was not part of the German painter Maria Slavona's circle, nor did she join the Café du Dôme circle. That might also have been because, as Purrmann says in his memoirs, even there women 'were not readily admitted'.[25] So she largely kept to herself. However, even the artists who met in the Café du Dôme for mutual support did not manage to establish themselves in the Paris scene.

A First Taste of Recognition

After a visit to Worpswede, in January 1906 Rilke finally expressed surprise at the 'quite extraordinary development' of Paula Modersohn-Becker: 'painting relentlessly and purposefully, things that are very typical of Worpswede and yet no one had ever been able to see and paint them before'.[26] This was a remarkable endorsement, defining what was unique about Modersohn-Becker's artistic position when she had not yet produced her major work in Paris.

Not long after, Modersohn-Becker met someone in Paris who was to have a unique impact on her work. On 13 April 1906, she wrote: 'Was at Hoetger's today.' The sculptor Bernhard Hoetger was two years older than her. As a student, he too had been to the 1900 Paris Exposition. He had been particularly impressed by the Rodin exhibition staged at the same time in a special building on the Place de l'Alma. He had then settled in Paris and married the pianist Helene (Lee) Haken. In 1927, the entrepreneur Ludwig Roselius commissioned Hoetger to design an Expressionist building to house the Paula Modersohn-Becker Museum on Böttcherstrasse in Bremen, a space devoted to her work. The museum is still there today, displaying works from her estate and from the Roselius collection.

Before their meeting, Modersohn-Becker had been impressed by some of Hoetger's works shown at the International Art Exhibition at the Kunsthalle Bremen and in the Salon des Indépendants. She visited the sculptor and his wife at 108 Rue de Vaugirard, near the Palais du Luxembourg, without at first disclosing that she was an artist, and they became friends. Rather by accident, she opened up to them.

Hoetger persuaded her to show him her work, and in mid-May she wrote to Worpswede: 'He came to my studio and he thinks I am very talented.' This was clearly an understatement. Recognition and genuine admiration from a respected artist was something she had never experienced before and provided a crucial impetus.

A letter sent to Hoetger three weeks after their first meeting shows just how momentous this encounter was for her: 'You have given me myself. I have courage. My courage was always barricaded behind gates and was unable to get in or out. You have opened the gates.' She wrote emphatically to her sister Milly: 'I am experiencing the most intense happiness of my life.' 'In the past few weeks, I have worked as I never worked before,' she wrote to Heinrich Vogeler, adding confidently: 'I think I am getting somewhere.' It was a turning point, leading to a period of intense activity in which she produced her most incredible works: portraits and more pictures of children, numerous still lifes and, above all, her groundbreaking self-portraits – works that reveal her own pictorial world.

Archetypes of Human Experience

For the 1906–7 portraits of children, Modersohn-Becker again chose subjects from humble backgrounds as her models. Looking for naturalness and simplicity, she selected Italian models from the Monday 'model market' at the nearby intersection of Boulevard du Montparnasse and Rue de la Grande Chaumière. The portraits share a characteristic that ran through the work she was doing in Paris: the motifs and colours, especially in their heaviness, their seriousness, their dark tones and air of melancholy, were still rooted in Worpswede.

The pictures of children from this period are formally reduced. The figures cannot be linked to a particular period, place or background. They are lifted out of their time. Unlike the artist's early pictures of children, in these compositions there is social interaction, mostly between two children. They are shown in different positions in relation to each other, with a mere indication of their gestures. In one painting, a younger child stands close to a kneeling older child, and each holds an offering of fruit (ill. 36). In another example, two girls put their arms around each other affectionately, the older child appearing to offer comfort (ills 37–38). Intimately connected, the children in these paintings are as one, forming a unit. In explorations of social contact of this kind, the archetypes of human experience can be perceived: Otto Modersohn described them as great, free and self-contained.[27]

In this third group of pictures of children, the motifs are repeated but they are given new forms. Compared to the pre-conscious Worpswede children (ills 20–22) and the individual portraits of girls awakening to the possibilities of the future (ills 33–35), these children are emerging social beings in their own world, each in a particular guise. They mark the beginning of a shift to a new iconography.

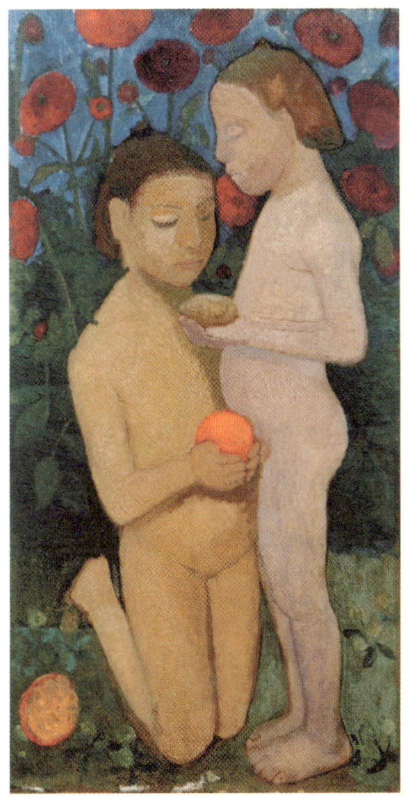

ABOVE

36 *Standing and Kneeling Girls Nude in Front
of Poppies II*, May–June 1906

OVERLEAF, LEFT AND RIGHT

37 *Two Girls in White and Blue Dresses*,
May–June 1906

38 *Two Girls in White and Blue Dresses
with Arms Around Each Other's Shoulders*,
May–June 1906

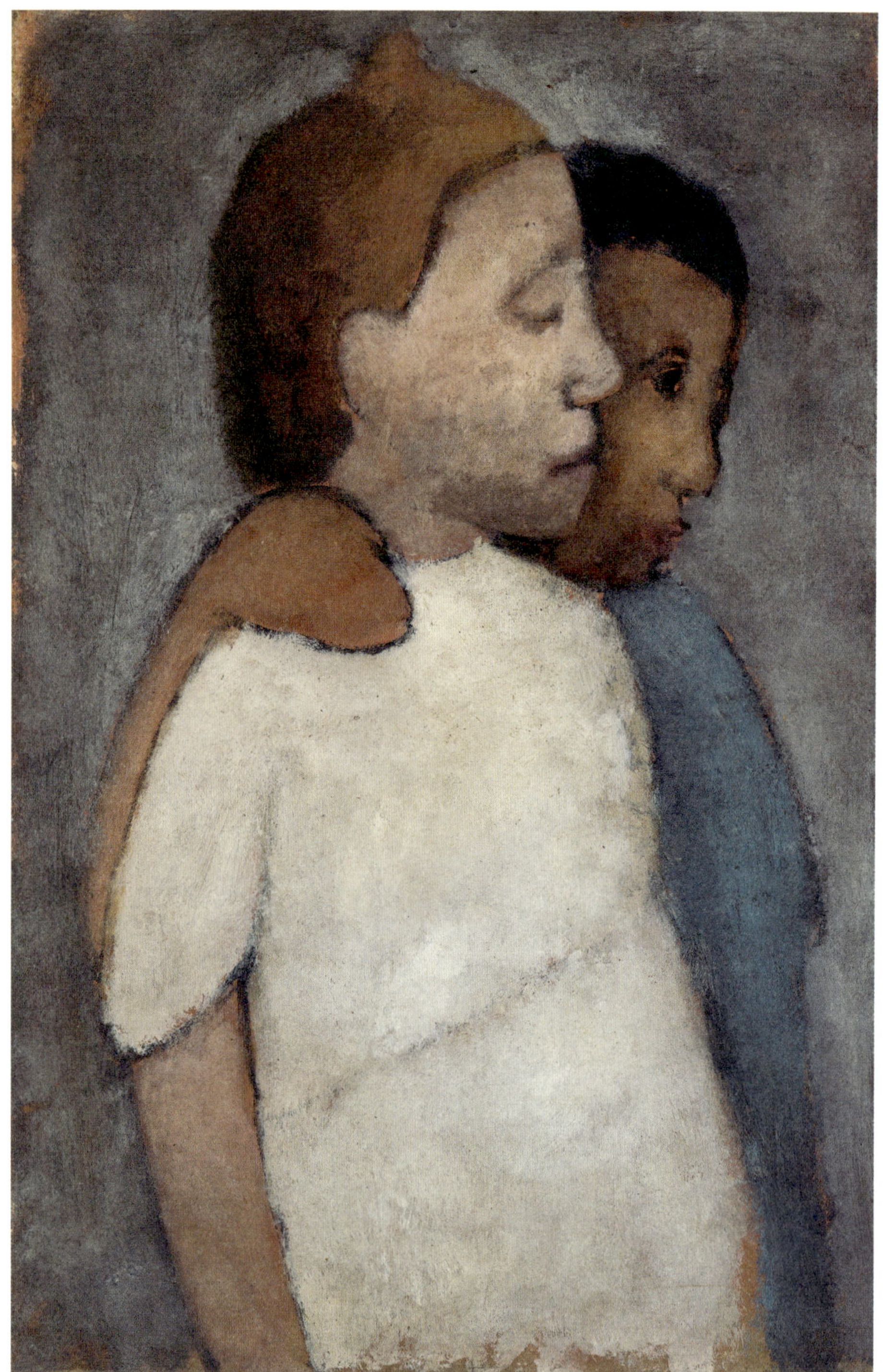

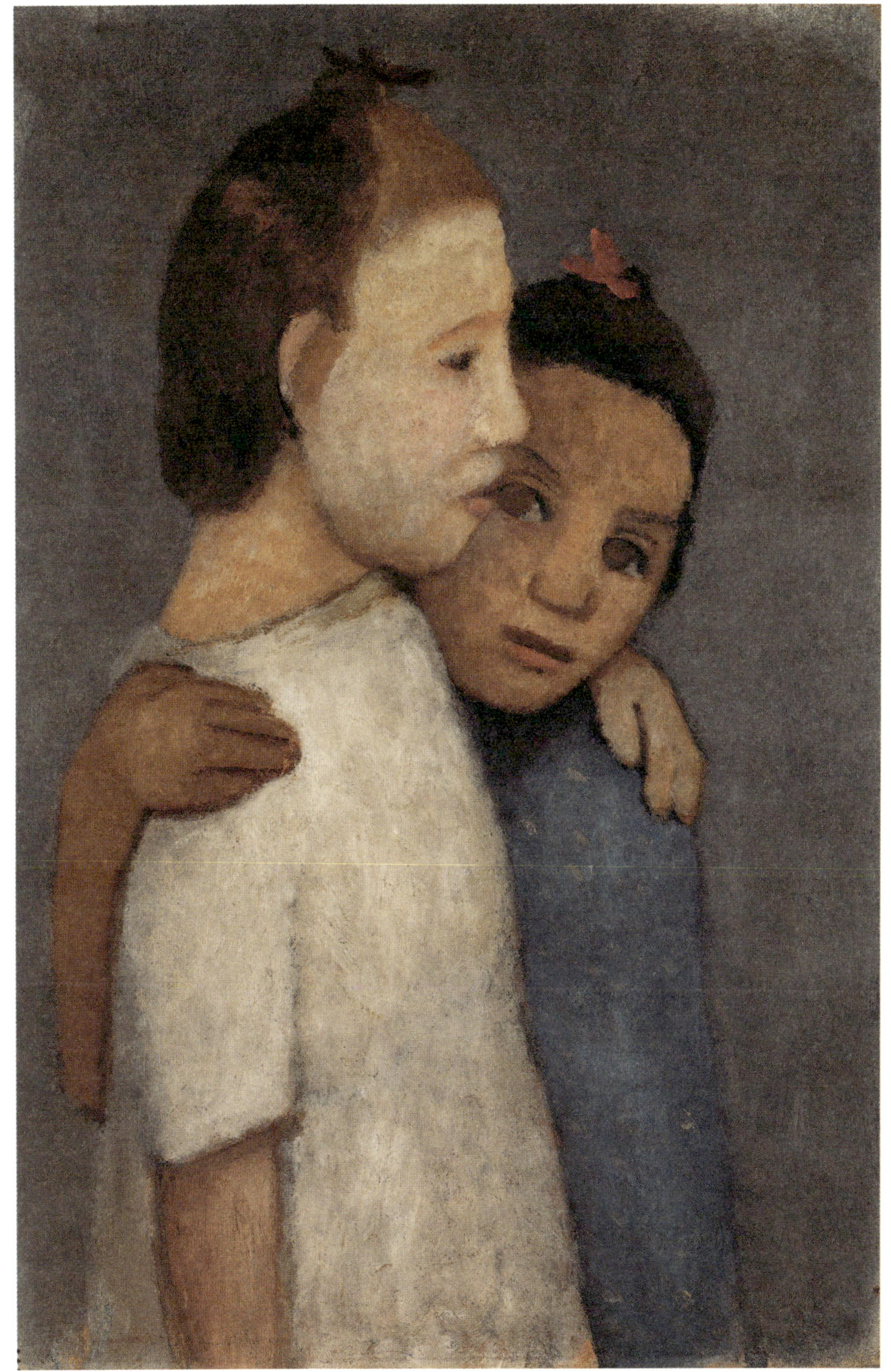

Balance and Confusion

Still life is arguably more open than other genres. Artists need only have access to everyday objects: a jug, a bowl or some fruit, and a suitable backdrop such as a table, a chest of drawers or a cloth. Paula Modersohn-Becker made full use of that freedom in the still lifes she painted in Paris, experimenting with contemporary techniques more consistently than in other genres.

Like Cézanne she explored perspective, painting the backdrops and objects – plates, jugs, fruit – from different angles. In Modersohn-Becker's case, this was a deliberate pictorial strategy designed to give the image autonomy. Whereas the stylistic structure in Cézanne's work is mainly uniform, Modersohn-Becker experimented with different brushstrokes. Sometimes her painting style was full of brio, with an expressive use of contrasting colours; at other times, she chose softly modulating, muted tones. In some works she simply observes, as in *Still Life with Asters and Tomatoes* (1906, ill. 40), in which both the motif and the simplified forms bear similarities to Picasso's *Green Bowl*

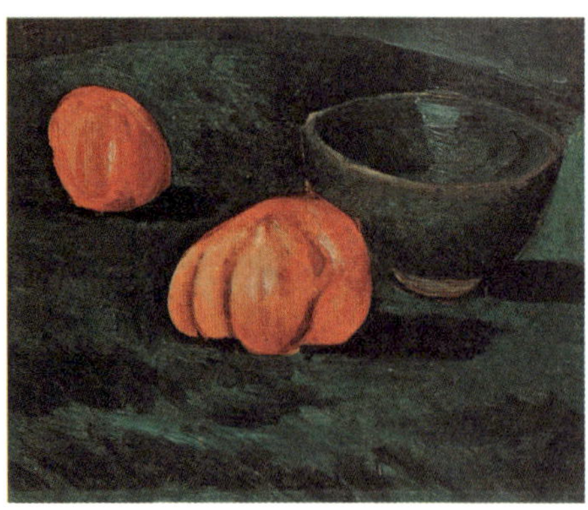

39 Pablo Picasso,
Green Bowl and Tomatoes,
spring to summer 1908

OPPOSITE

40 *Still Life with
Asters and Tomatoes*,
August 1906

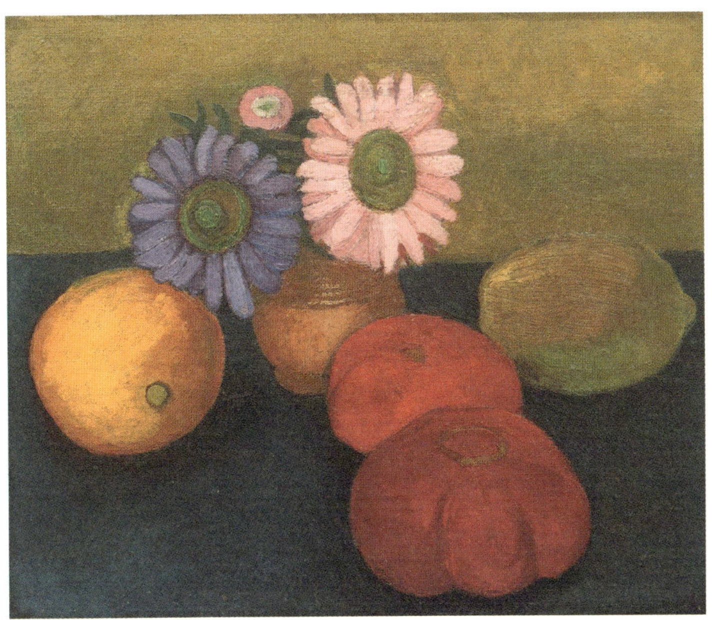

and *Tomatoes* (ill. 39), painted two years later. With Modersohn-Becker the fruit and objects are secondary to the colours. It is the materiality of the colour that matters, not the materiality of the fruit. She saw another ten of Cézanne's paintings, including two major still lifes, *Still Life with a Chest of Drawers* (1887–88, Bavarian State Painting Collections, Munich) and *The Sideboard* (1877–79, Museum of Fine Arts, Budapest), when visiting the Salon d'Automne at the Grand Palais in Paris in the autumn of 1906, after first discovering his work at Vollard's gallery in 1900.

Whereas Cézanne tried to reflect the characteristics of the different fruits, dishes and materials with appropriate pictorial means ('Art is a harmony parallel with nature,' he once said), those structural differences are absent from *Still Life with Asters and Tomatoes*. The fruit has been dematerialized into semi-

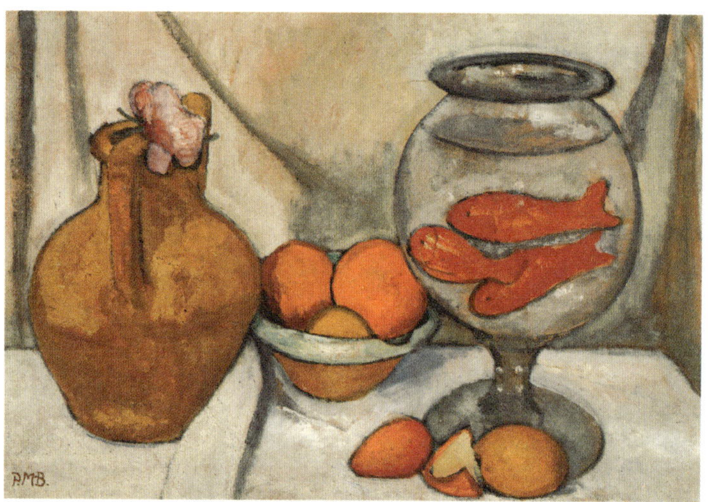

ABOVE

41 *Still Life with Goldfish Bowl*,
May–June 1906

OPPOSITE

42 *Still Life with Terracotta Jug,
Peonies and Oranges*,
May–June 1906

abstract forms. The stylized flowers also appear abstract. Only the horizontal grooves on the vase have a precise structure. In breaking down the materiality of the objects and reducing them to flat forms on a neutralized ground, without a clear compositional structure, Modersohn-Becker brings this still life closer to Cézanne's work.

In *Still Life with Goldfish Bowl* (1906, ill. 41), the spatial structure is unclear and the background so muted that the colours take on a life of their own. Between the reddish-brown jug and the bright red goldfish, the red and orange tones of

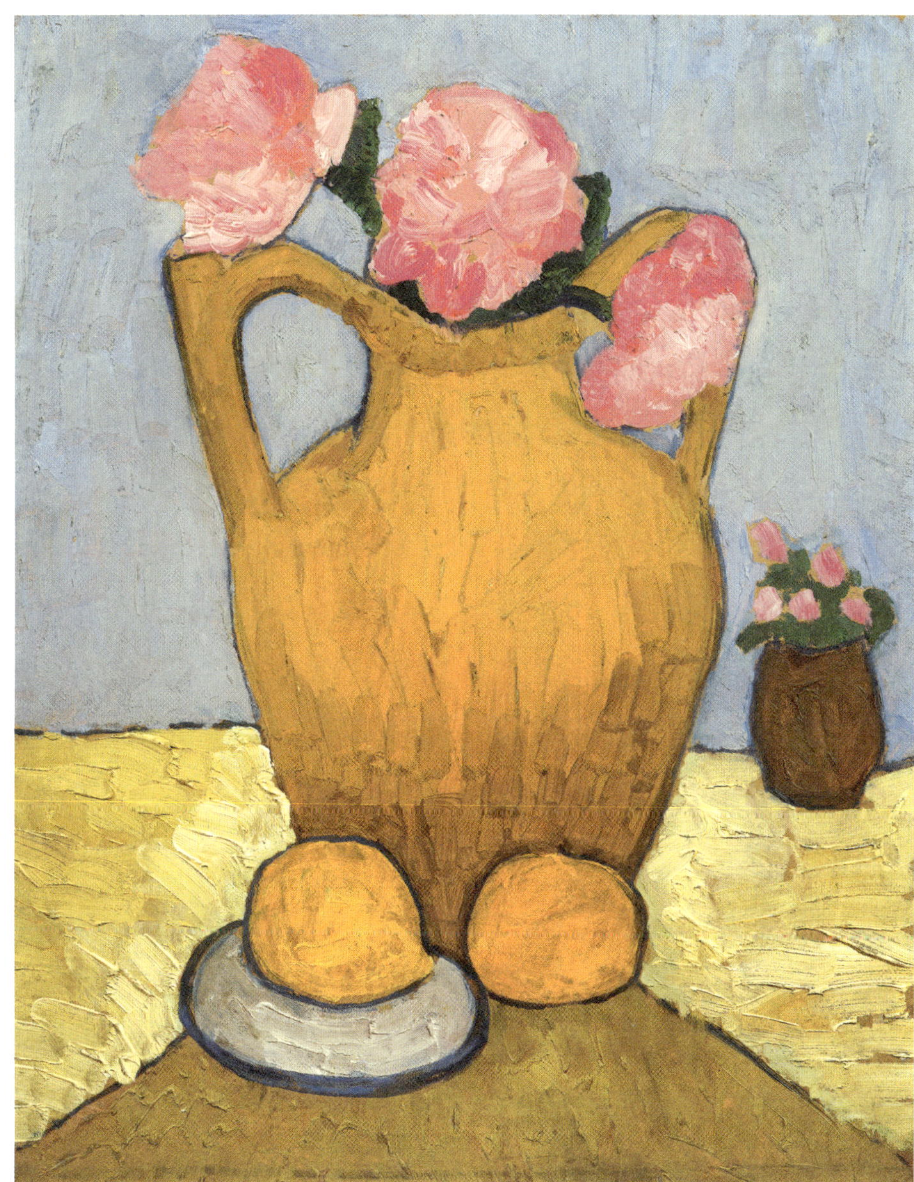

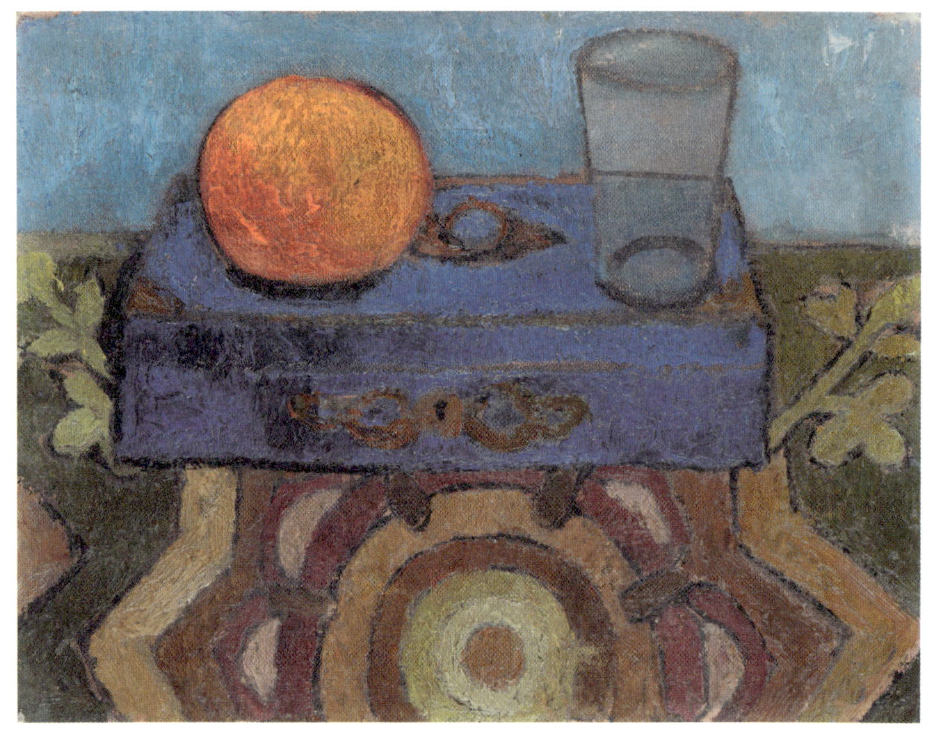

43 *Still Life with Blue Box*, 1907

                    CHAPTER 4

the fruit and the bowl do not create a complementary contrast. The large forms are offset by the unusually powerful colours. As Rainer Stamm has pointed out, Modersohn-Becker's goldfish foreshadowed Matisse's own use of the goldfish as a motif.[28]

In *Still Life with Terracotta Jug, Peonies and Oranges* (1906, ill. 42), the strong, light colours are applied with such a broad brush that each impasto stroke is visible and speaks for itself. The flatness of the painting is accentuated. The objects are outlined in a way that turns them into abstract forms, so that the surface on which the jug rests, viewed from a somewhat disorientating angle, becomes difficult to grasp. This allows for a different composition. The low-angle view, further underlined by the perspective of the surface, elevates the jug, topped by the fiery reddish-pink of the flowers. The smaller jug adds depth. With this unorthodox and experimental construct, Modersohn-Becker was developing her own personal pictorial language for a still-life motif.

Likewise, *Still Life with Blue Box* (1907, ill. 43) is characterized by an imbalance. The brightly coloured, flat orange and the transparent glass effectively offset the mysterious blue box in the sombre overall tone and radiate a peaceful beauty, but the decorative base on which the box appears to be sitting is tilted, making it look like the box is floating. For the viewer, the stability becomes disturbingly unstable, the beauty now uncertain.

From an art-historical perspective, it is interesting that Modersohn-Becker's pictures tended to be very different in style. It has become clear that this was a fundamental principle for her. She was not seeking a single style but exploring the many artistic possibilities available to her.

No More Copies

In the particularly productive year of 1906, Modersohn-Becker painted more self-portraits than anything else. She also did a small series of extraordinary paintings of people she knew and was especially fond of, including her sister Herma (April–May), the sociologist Werner Sombart (spring), Rainer Maria Rilke (May–June) and Lee Hoetger (August). They are intimate head-and-shoulders portraits. These works would soon develop in a surprising direction in parallel with French modernism.

In modern art, spontaneous portraits often had quite different functions and meanings that took precedence over their resemblance to the subject. Degas wanted to make portraits a study of modern experience,[29] so his portraits of artists and art critics are a snapshot of intellectual and artistic life and its revival in the Paris of the 1860s and 1870s. Edvard Munch, on the other hand, painted an idealized picture of himself as a rebellious artist in his 1880s portraits, while his life-size portraits of sympathizers in the first decade of the new century were effectively a gallery of modern art patrons in Germany. Around 1910, the young Oskar Kokoschka surrounded himself with a phalanx of defenders of the new ideas and the new art with his portrayals of friends, patrons and other like-minded people. Picasso's portraits of his four Parisian art dealers in his Cubist period were an inward expression of the solidarity of the Paris avant-garde in its attitude to Cubism and an outward expression of their collective strength on the art market. So what about Paula Modersohn-Becker?

Portrait of Sister Herma with Artichoke Flower in her Raised Hand (1906, ill. 44) is extremely simple. It looks like an experiment with its own set of rules: the elimination of three-dimensional

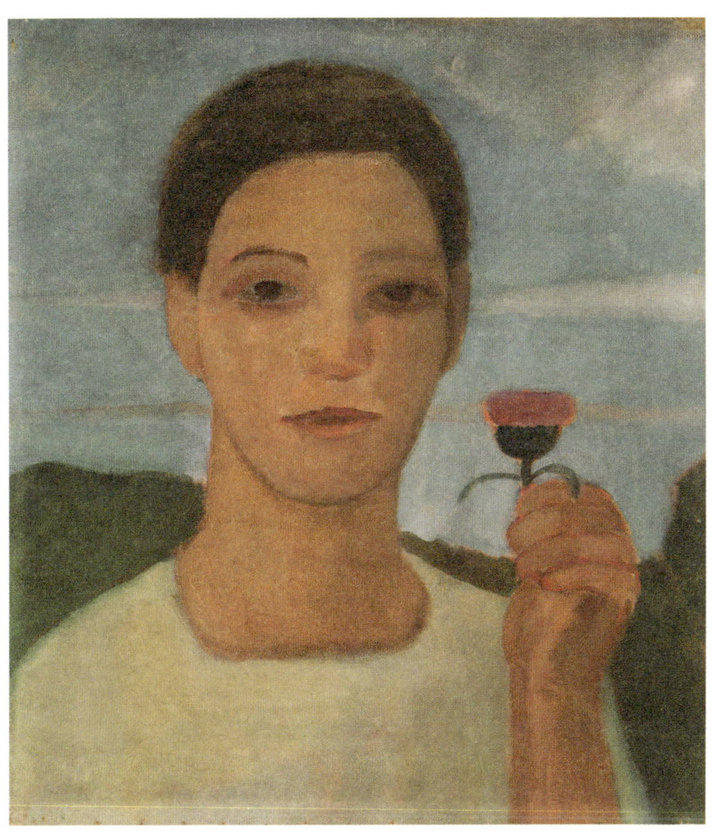

44 *Portrait of Sister Herma with Artichoke Flower in her Raised Hand,*
April–May 1906

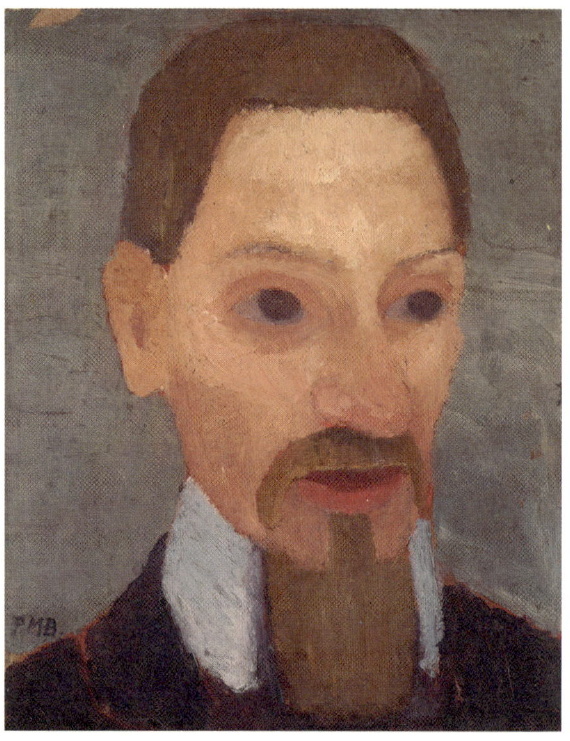

45 *Portrait of Rainer Maria Rilke*, May–June 1906

forms, the composition made up of vaguely defined areas, the blurring of the colours (including the colour of the flower), the downplaying of individual features. The figure's expression is neutral in keeping with the formulaic nature of the composition. The gesture made with the hand, as if the subject is reaching out to the viewer, gives the simplified, pared-down face of the half-length figure an unusual, hieratic appearance. The single artichoke flower curiously heightens the effect.

A similar blurring of colours and forms can be found in *Portrait of Rainer Maria Rilke* (1906, ill. 45). The poet and the

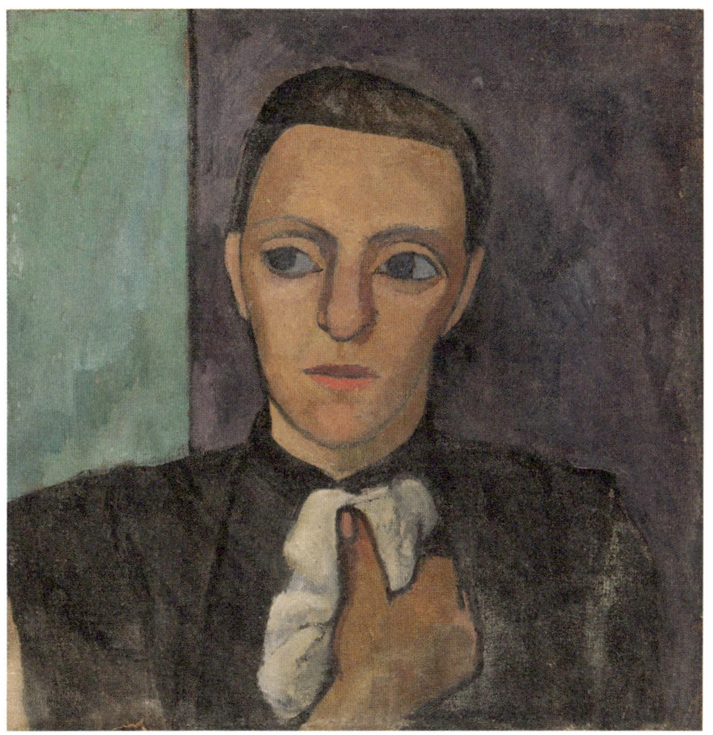

46 *Half-Length Portrait of Woman in Black with Handkerchief,* spring 1906

painter were friends in the early days in Berlin, but they drifted apart when Rilke married Clara Westhoff. They eventually grew close again in Paris in 1906, when Rilke had stopped working as private secretary to Rodin and Modersohn-Becker had left her husband. Rilke sat for the portrait in May of that year. Otto Modersohn arrived for a visit on 2 June, and Rilke stopped coming for sittings (he also shaved off the beard he still has in the painting). Modersohn-Becker then had to finish the portrait without her model, which must have significantly affected the final result.

The stiff collar forms a base above which the head looks sombre, indeterminate, opaque. The viewer is left wondering what kind of person this is. The lifeless black eyes stare into the distance; the mouth is slightly open as if on the point of saying something. The lack of colour contrast and the flat structure also give the figure an undefined quality: although he is depicted in close-up, he seems remote. The open expression can be interpreted in different ways. It is not known what Rilke thought about this picture. Could he have shaved off his beard and stopped coming for sittings because he was disappointed with the result?

The composition of *Half-Length Portrait of Woman in Black with Handkerchief* (ill. 46), painted in the spring of 1906, is impressively large and wide. The head, with its broad, stylized eyes, sharp hairline, schematic hair and clearly defined nose, shows a clear Proto-Cubist influence. The use of similar pictorial elements can be seen in the related portrait of *Half-Length Portrait of Lee Hoetger with Flower* (1906, ill. 48).

The portrait of Werner Sombart (1906, ill. 47) is done in a different style. The artist had met the sociologist while visiting Gerhart Hauptmann's brother, the writer Carl Hauptmann, in the Silesian town of Schreiberhau (now Szklarska Poreba). They met again in Paris in 1906 and became close. Sombart had been teaching at Breslau University, and after that had gone to the Berlin Business School. The portrait is very different from photographs of Sombart and reveals a strong focus on form. For Modersohn-Becker, the most important thing was not to create a true likeness but to produce a coherent work that followed its own rules. A red outline demarcates the broad head from the green background. This is the red primer, which has been left and then highlighted, a deliberate artistic device to separate the pictorial elements. The angular section of the face – framed by the dark areas of the hair and beard – is like a mask. The lack of

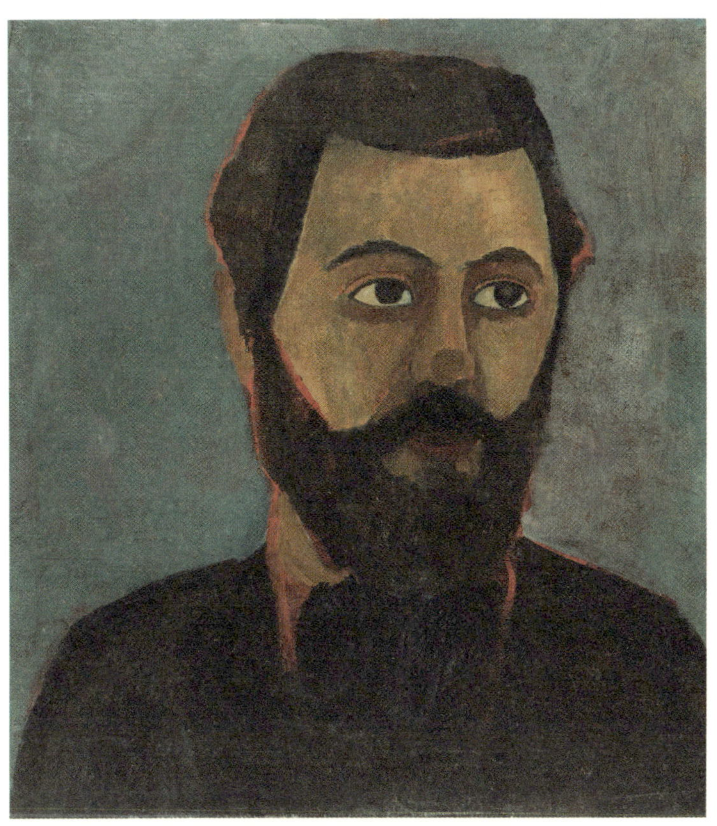

47 *Portrait of Werner Sombart,* spring 1906

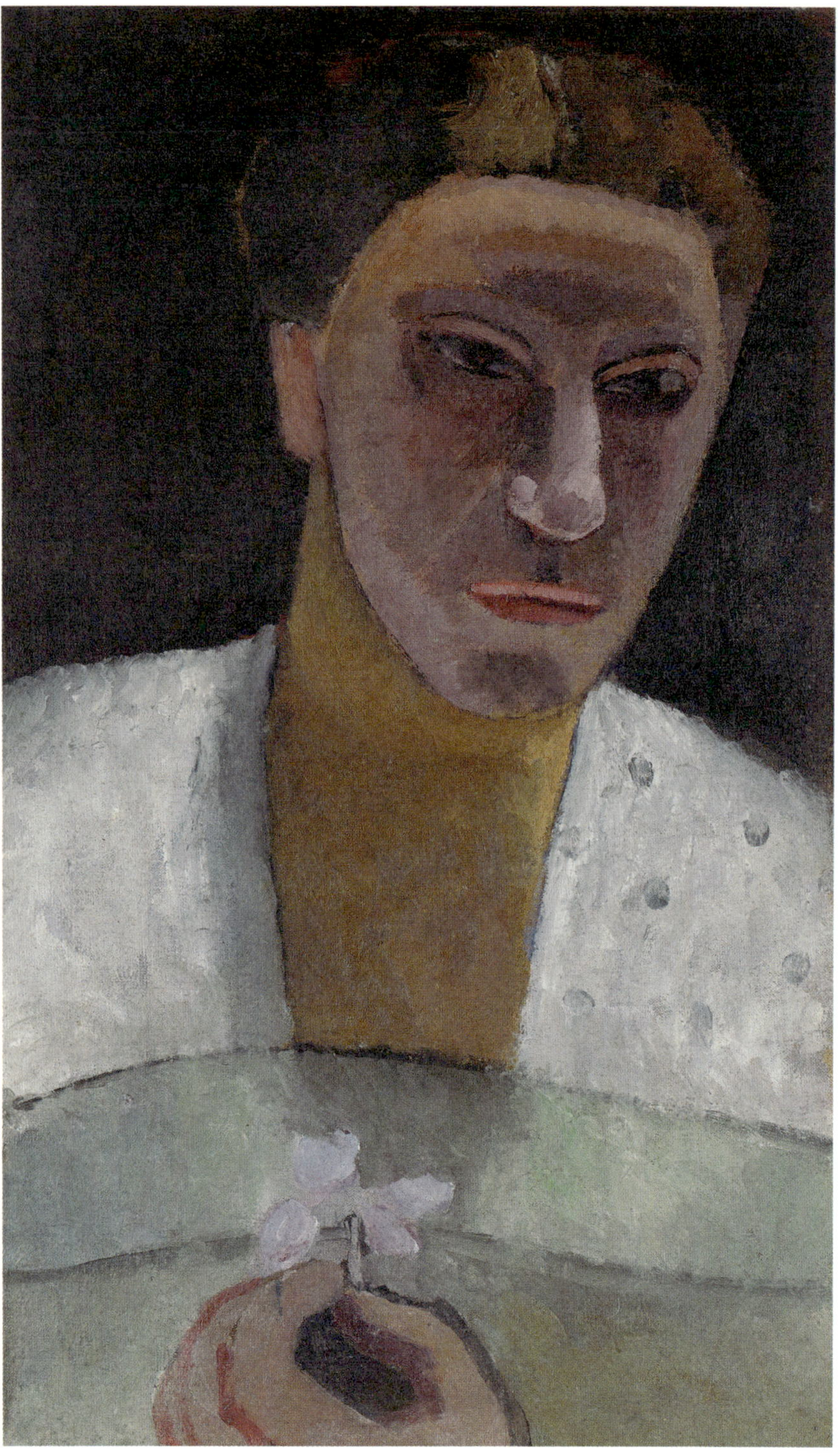

distinction between the pupils and the dark iris adds to the overall effect, creating a sense of distance.

It has rightly been pointed out that the stylization evident in this picture bears similarities to the Egyptian mummy portraits from Fayum that Modersohn-Becker had so admired in Paris in 1903 (ill. 61). However, while the Fayum subjects seem alive, looking out defiantly at the viewer – the living reaching out from beyond the grave – Sombart's head is turned to the side, his eyes fixed firmly on an unknown point. What makes this portrait striking is not an expressive look but the physical presence of the head, which is further heightened by the red outline, as if to emphasize the figure's intellectual abilities.

At the beginning of August 1906, Modersohn-Becker told her husband she had been enjoying working again and had just started a portrait of Hoetger's wife, the pianist Lee Hoetger. 'There is something grand about her. And she is really wonderful to paint,' she wrote, repeating later, in a letter to Heinrich Vogeler, that Lee Hoetger could 'look magnificently grand … with an enormous crown of hair, blonde, incredibly well-shaped'. Of the two versions she painted, the cohesiveness of the second, in particular, *Half-Length Portrait of Lee Hoetger with Flower* (ill. 48), made it an artistic landmark. The head is Cubist in shape and reminiscent of African tribal art. The full red lips are accentuated by the dark tones of the hair, face and neckline. Hoetger looks away, outside the picture, with black, expressionless eyes. The strikingly large hand at the bottom edge of the picture is clasping a sketchily painted, delicate flower, which she is holding up like an offering. These pictorial elements infuse the portrait with a classical intensity.

48 *Half-Length Portrait of Lee Hoetger with Flower*, August 1906

Parallels with Picasso

It was often said that, artistically, Modersohn-Becker's brilliant portrait of Lee Hoetger is closely related to Picasso's *Portrait of Gertrude Stein* (ill. 49) of 1905–6. During the autumn or winter of 1905, the writer Gertrude Stein had sat for Picasso many times. In the spring of 1906, Picasso suddenly gave up and painted over the head. Having spent much of the summer in the Catalan village of Gósol, where he was fascinated by ancient Iberian sculpture, in the autumn of 1906 he resumed work on the portrait, this time without his model, painting only from memory. Stein is depicted with dark, heavily lidded eyes and a waxy, smooth face, giving it the appearance of a tribal mask; her body has been reduced to simple masses, with just a few details picked out in the background. Picasso's portrayal of Stein was described as an iconoclastic decision and a turning point in modern portraiture.[30] The use of the mask as an alienating art form was a strategic act – in Picasso's words, a 'rejection of any imitation'.[31] The mask challenges conventional ideas of identity and evokes the unfamiliar. The portrait's revolutionary rejection of the need for a likeness is characteristic of modern art.

The timing is striking: Modersohn-Becker finished her painting in August 1906, while Picasso completed his in September. Neither was emulating the other. They simply produced similar artistic results at the same time. And there are clear differences, of course: with Modersohn-Becker, the body is flat and disembodied, and her use of pale colours in the combination of green and purple stands in stark contrast to Picasso's muted tones. In the Picasso painting, the break between the old way of depicting a body and the new kind of head is visible. Soon after, Picasso would develop the principle of Analytical Cubism

– characterized by a fragmentary appearance of multiple view-
points and a monochromatic use of colour – while in her final
period Modersohn-Becker would resist all the current trends
towards fragmentation and work on the construction and recon-
struction of the figure and the content as a whole.

Art was moving in a radically new direction at this time,
particularly in Paris. The story goes that Maurice de Vlaminck
showed his fellow painter André Derain an African mask, saying
it was almost as beautiful as the Venus de Milo, and Derain
replied that it was just as beautiful. When Picasso saw it, he
went even further, remarking that it was even more beautiful.[32]
It is reported that in the autumn of 1906 Matisse was on his way
to visit Gertrude Stein and, probably with the sculptor Aristide
Maillol's encouragement, he bought a statuette from the
Congo.[33] Picasso saw it at the Steins' and soon afterwards happened to be in the Museum of Ethnography at the Trocadéro

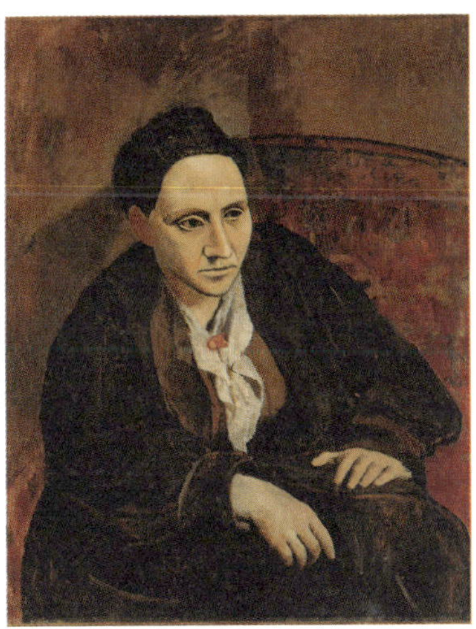

49 Pablo Picasso, *Portrait of
Gertrude Stein*, 1905–6

(its collection is now in the Musée du Quai Branly). He saw the masks there not just as sculptures but as magical objects.[34] The following year marked a radical change of form for Picasso with the landmark painting *Les Demoiselles d'Avignon.*

In 1906 – the key year for the arrival of so-called 'primitive art' in Paris[35] – African sculpture was associated with stereotypes of non-Western cultures and was seen as different, untamed, mysterious. While he was living in Paris, in 1907, August Macke enjoyed a morning visit to a 'colonial exhibition',[36] and in the afternoon he returned to the Louvre. In 1912, Franz Marc told Kandinsky that he had been deeply impressed by the museums, such as the Trocadéro with negro sculptures.[37]

Wolfgang Werner, the administrator of Modersohn-Becker's estate, has pointed out that Bernhard Hoetger was one of the few people who visited the Trocadéro.[38] The fact that Hoetger and his wife often went to places with Modersohn-Becker suggests that he may have visited it with her. The sketches by Bernhard Hoetger, Paula and Otto Modersohn on the back of a letter (ill. 50), dated 29 November 1906, when Otto was in Paris, would certainly seem to support this argument. Among the portraits and caricatures, the head in the top-right corner of the letter is particularly mask-like. Picasso made a very similar record after his encounter with African art at the Trocadéro. It could therefore be argued that they had a common source of inspiration, resulting in artistic innovations that were closely connected but independent of each other.

Modersohn-Becker's small-format portraits are, above all, personal expressions of friendship. They are populated by family and close friends, people recognized for their own achievements or striving for recognition. They inspired Modersohn-Becker to experiment in new ways, and within a few months she had undergone a remarkable development in

CHAPTER 4

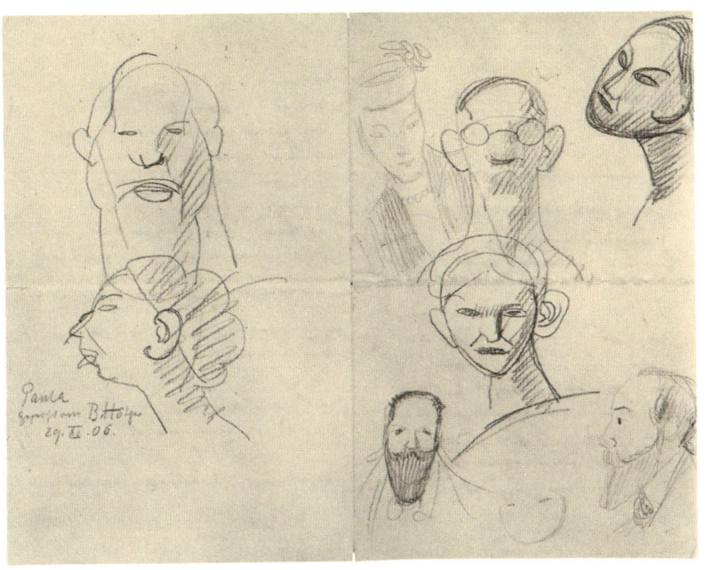

50 Sketches in pencil (on the back of a letter)
by Bernhard Hoetger, Paula and Otto Modersohn,
with portraits of Bernhard and Lee Hoetger
and of Paula and Otto Modersohn,
29 November 1906

her art. From her initial experience in autonomizing the pictorial means, based on the rejection of imitation (in other words,
not looking for a direct likeness), and stimulated in particular
by African masks and sculptures, she succeeded in formulating
her own special style: one that encapsulated the 'great simplicity of form' that she had so admired in the mummy portraits
from Fayum. By focusing on the development of a diverse and
form-conscious pictorial language that nonetheless chimed with
the innovative trends of the era, she had found an independent
path to modernity.

The Studio as Exhibition Space

Modersohn-Becker had no opportunities to exhibit her Paris works to the public, although a sketch she did on the back of an envelope (ill. 51) at Christmas 1906, while she was visiting her family in Bremen, gives an idea of her situation. It is a glimpse into her studio on Boulevard du Montparnasse. There is a couch, a cupboard, a cooker and a ladder to a small, raised recess but no easel, and the table, chairs and large mirror that she sometimes included among the contents are not shown. Instead, three of her paintings are hanging on the walls: a portrait of Lee Hoetger, a lost work known as *Woman with Cat and Parrot* and, on the right, the large canvas of *Reclining Mother and Child*, all painted in 1906. Whereas in studios the works are usually hung close together, covering the walls, or are stacked on the floor, here we see only three paintings, spread out. It looks more like an exhibition space than a studio.

We do not know whether Modersohn-Becker was simply putting an idea to paper or whether she actually hung those paintings. It is possible she was planning to attempt to show her work to the public. She did consider taking part in an exhibition in the spring of 1907, possibly at the Salon des Indépendants where there was no jury. She would have found herself in the best company: in the spring of 1906, she had seen works by Bonnard, Braque, Denis, Derain, Matisse, Munch, Signac, Vlaminck and Vuillard there – as well as Hoetger – among the 5,500 submissions in the large greenhouses on the Cours-la-Reine. She might also have been encouraged by the involvement of many international female artists, including the French painter Marie Laurencin, the Norwegian Marie Hauge, and Maria Slavona and Jelka Rosen from Germany. The works in the sketch would have been representative: a portrait, an allegorical scene, and the sensitively painted mother and child motif reduced to its simplest elements, which was a frequent theme for her at that time.

Modersohn-Becker's systematic way of creating an image is again evident from the preliminary sketches she did for *Reclining Mother and Child II* (ill. 54) in the summer of 1906. She daringly took a common religious motif and depicted it in a completely new way. In a series of charcoal drawings, she tried out possible arrangements for the two naked, lightly sketched figures: the mother lying on her side with her arms in different positions; the child held close (ill. 53), propped up or unsupported; the child semi-hidden in the folds of its mother's arms, leaning against

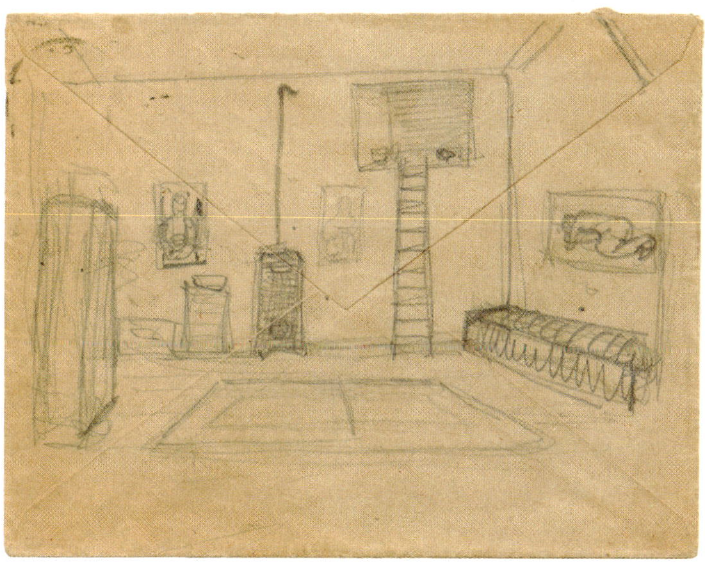

51 Pencil sketch of Paris studio at 49 Boulevard du Montparnasse,
on the back of an envelope, 1906–7

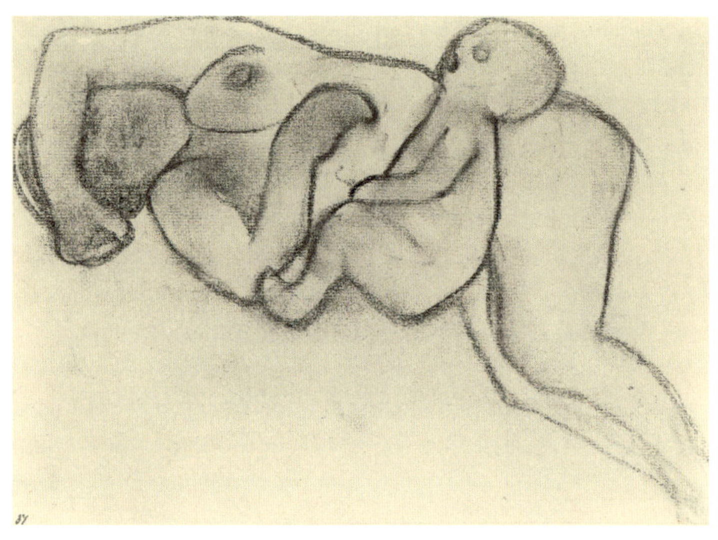

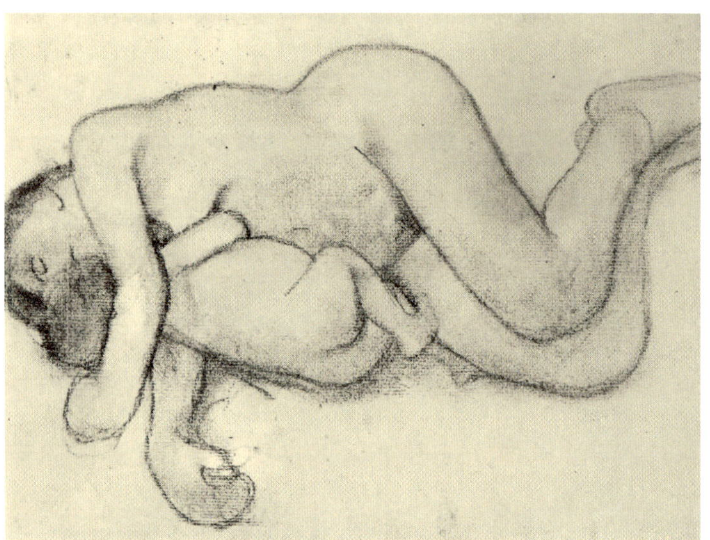

52 *Mother and Child*, charcoal, *c.* 1906

53 *Reclining Female Nude with Child*, charcoal, *c.* 1906

     CHAPTER 4

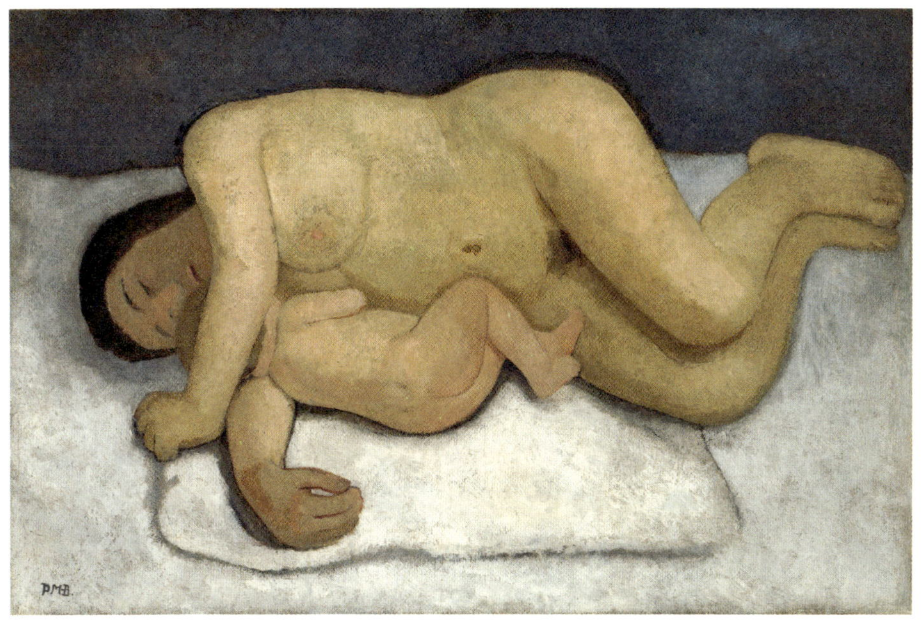

54 *Reclining Mother and Child II*, summer 1906

her or even leaning back in a resting position (ill. 52). The natural relationship between mother and child is explored unsentimentally with a precise observational skill and a sensitive eye. The artist is always looking for a characteristic arrangement and the one from which she can develop the final picture. Heinrich Vogeler remarked in amazement when he saw the painted version after the artist's death: 'An archetypal image of maternity. Exciting in its monumentality, arranged with impressive simplicity.'[39]

At the same time, Paula Modersohn-Becker was also creating a series of extraordinary self-portraits.

Self-Portraits: The Many Faces of Modersohn-Becker

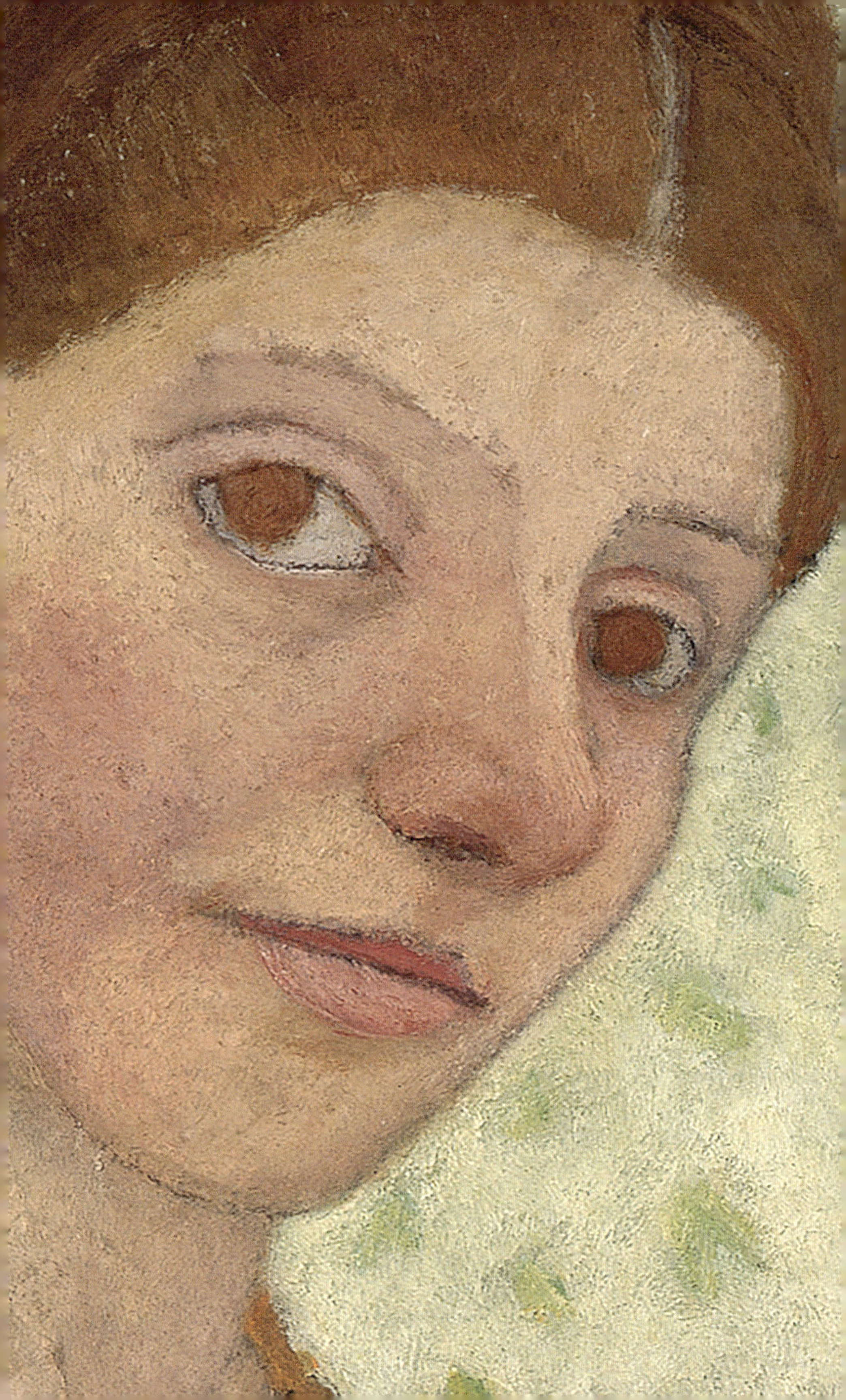

The Most Complex Genre

Of all the modern art genres and sub-genres, the self-portrait is perhaps the most complex. It tells us – sometimes in exaggerated or staged form – something about the artist: their appearance, their age, their physical posture. At the same time, a self-portrait can provide an insight into the artist's approach and artistic development, since it is a special opportunity to use pictorial media more freely than with other subjects. Finally, it can often be self-revelatory, reflecting how artists view themselves and their relationship to the art of the period. Sometimes, as in the case of Paula Modersohn-Becker, a self-portrait can have other functions as well.

For personal, artistic and sometimes purely practical reasons, modern artists painted themselves over and over again. The Finnish painter Helene Schjerfbeck (1862–1946) said that many artists, from Vincent van Gogh onwards, could not afford a model or could not find one when they wanted one. Self-portraits were a natural choice, she said, because then your model was always available, although it was not a pleasure to

Detail of ill. 66

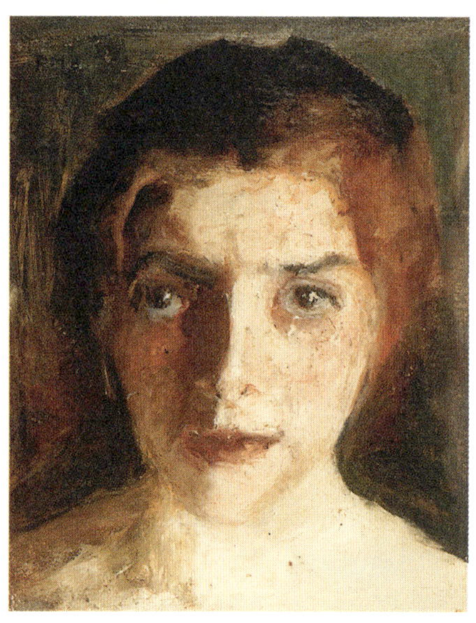

keep staring at yourself.[40] The German artist Lovis Corinth admitted that painters were 'the best and most willing model' for themselves. According to Corinth, painters always preferred to use themselves as the subject of studies because of the freedom it gave them.[41] When she was young, Modersohn-Becker did a portrait of someone and the person was so unhappy with it that 'she left wanting revenge', she noted in April 1893: 'Since then, I have been drawing my own dear reflection and at least that is patient.'

This work of self-examination has sometimes proved critical at a particular stage in an artist's life. When Lovis Corinth decided, at the age of 40, to paint a portrait of himself every year on his birthday, he regularly took stock of his state of mind and appearance. After the artist suffered a stroke in his early fifties, the physical and psychological changes he experienced were documented through his self-portraits. The Swiss painter Ferdinand Hodler's many self-portraits have been specifically

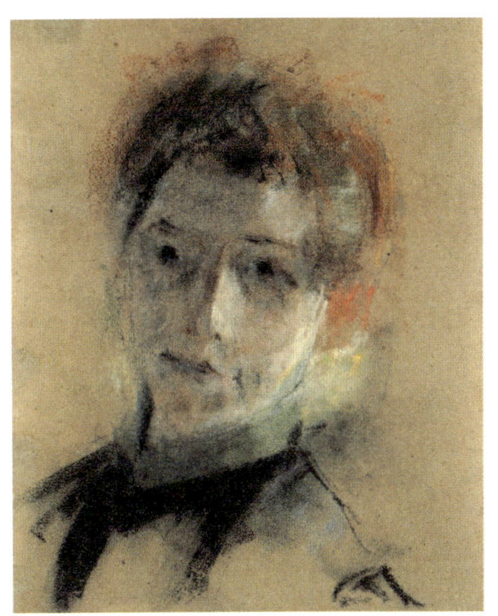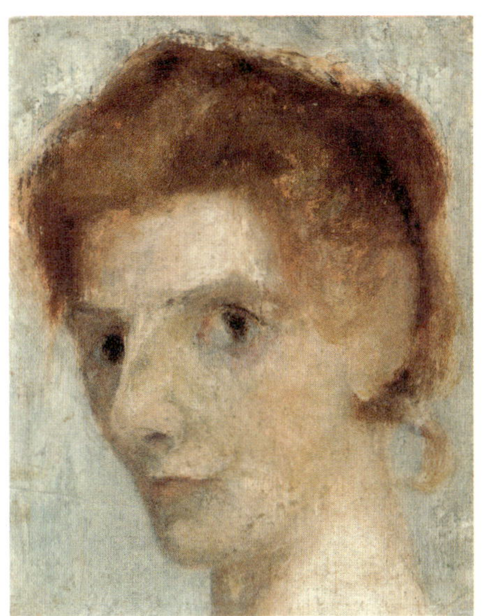

described as painted autobiography.[42] Edvard Munch, on the other hand, called his long series of self-portraits, centred on the theme of the artist's conflicts with society, 'self-examinations in difficult years'.[43]

Modern artists tended to have a difficult relationship with the world. Often they did not attach any particular value to being an artist, using the traditional tools – palette, easel, brush – relatively rarely. Some, like Van Gogh, presented themselves as lonely and angst-ridden; others, like Egon Schiele, as rebellious and ostracized by the local community, or, like Edvard Munch and Oskar Kokoschka, as latter-day martyrs in the fight for modern art. The German Expressionist Ernst Ludwig Kirchner, having signed up during the First World War, subsequently suffered dependency on drugs, mental breakdown and illness. Max Beckmann was an exception. Even when times were hard, he presented himself as self-confident.

A 'patient reflection'

'It is evening. I am alone and I have painted myself again,' Paula Modersohn-Becker wrote in a letter from Berlin in March 1898. Her early self-portraits are frontal views, with a simple composition, no props and no references to occupation, place or time (ill. 1). In most years she produced at least one self-portrait. There were many more in her last period in Paris, but unlike Corinth's they did not function as a journal; nor did they have an autobiographical purpose, like Hodler's, or form an expression of dissent from the world. She produced over sixty paintings and drawings in all, but why? Self-reflection? Self-assertion?

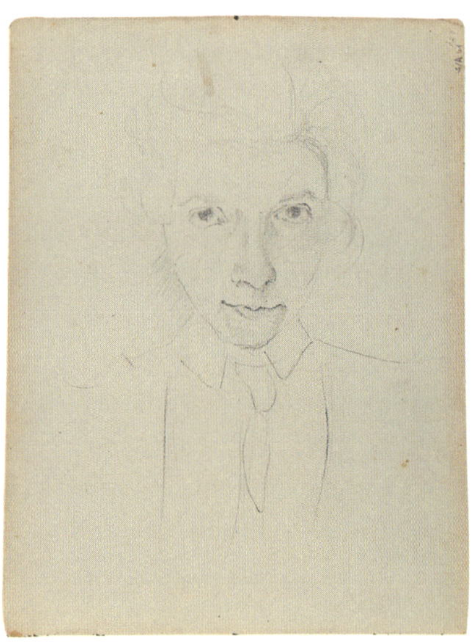

58 *Self-Portrait*, pencil, *c.* 1897

                    CHAPTER 5

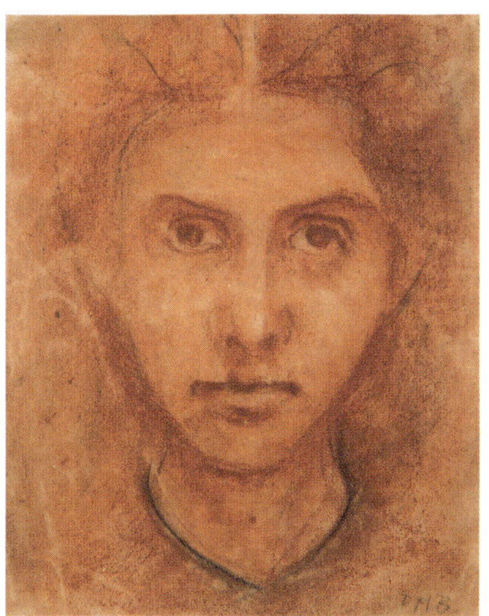

59 *Self-Portrait*, red chalk and
charcoal, 1897

The early Berlin works (ills 55–59) look like studies. They use every available technique: red chalk, charcoal, pastels and coloured pencils, watercolours, pencil, oils and gouache. The results are varied: a classic outline, an experimentally smudged creation in chalk, a study in oil or gouache. The artist is often unrecognizable in her pictures when compared with photographs taken at the time. The facial details are interpreted very freely. The head can range from narrow to well-proportioned to broad; the nose is sometimes crooked and at other times straight, short or long, of different widths – recalling Modersohn-Becker's description of her reflection in the mirror as 'patient'. Among the identifying features that frequently recur are the centre parting and – as she said in a letter in August 1903 – 'my one droopy eye'.

These disparities show that Modersohn-Becker, rather than observing or examining herself through her self-portraits, was exploring artistic techniques, using the closest, most readily available model she had to hand: her own reflection. The same was true of Van Gogh. When he was living in Paris (1886–88), before going to the south of France, he wanted to practise painting people but had no money for models, so he painted himself. His focus was not on achieving a likeness, but on trying out and adapting the latest experimental techniques used in Paris studios. His style was so varied that his self-portraits took very different forms.

The figures in Modersohn-Becker's self-portraits fix us with a penetrating, searching gaze. They stare out at us – sceptical, gloomily downcast or self-assured, often with an intensity. The facial expressions, the moods, even our impression of the person we see, can vary according to the technique. Female faces and expressive possibilities are explored, and in the process we see a glimpse of the artist 'as another person'.

Modersohn-Becker often spoke of the 'extraordinary' in the context of a picture or pictorial techniques, expressing her resistance to anything that was familiar and conventional. By 'extraordinary', she meant the different, the unfamiliar, the new, the magical effect of colours and forms not seen before. In February 1903, she wrote in her journal: 'I must learn to express the gentle vibration of things, the natural roughness,' explaining: 'Going back to the "natural roughness" again, that is what makes old marble and sandstone sculptures that have been exposed to the weather so pleasing to me, that uneven surface.' To create a rough, textured surface, particularly in the self-portraits around 1903 (ill. 60), she experimented with

60 *Self-Portrait with Necklace, c.* 1903

   CHAPTER 5

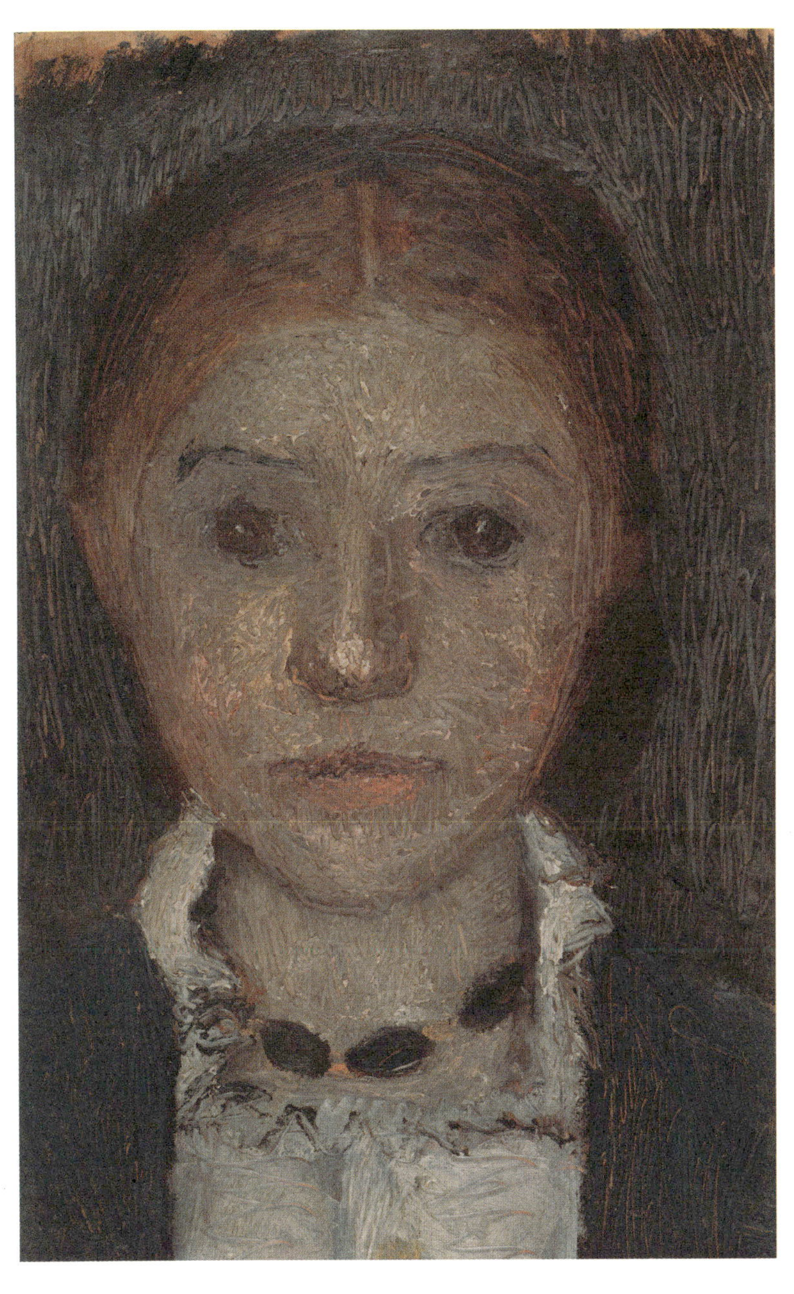

colour, media and tools. Otto Modersohn wrote: 'To make the flat surface uneven, she worked the paint often with the brush handle.' She also dragged the 'very thickly applied paint after drying' with a knife or spatula 'and then painted over it again, gradually achieving the result she wanted in several layers, one on top of the other'.[44] Like Hans von Marées, she tried to develop a particular style of textured brushstroke to create autonomy.

Vibration, roughness: those were qualities that fascinated her in the textured surfaces of Rembrandt's paintings. Similarly, Vincent van Gogh had talked of a plan for a 'rough' picture. He told his fellow painter Emile Bernard that the personal should be visible in the pictorial media themselves, for instance through 'impastos, uncovered spots of canvas – corners here and there left inevitably unfinished – reworkings, roughnesses'.[45] The goal was to get away from the conventional picture,[46] to depict 'modern sentiment', and thus to give appropriate expression to 'raw modernity'.[47]

This reflects the challenge to popular academic art that began in the late 19th century, among painters who argued that only 'rough', spontaneous work could be truthful. Modersohn-Becker deplored the perfect gleaming boots in Anton von Werner's history paintings, as she noted in February 1903. Her porous, textured surfaces and figures, even in the self-portraits, were a reaction against them.

Different Aspects of Character

The few contemporaries who spoke of Modersohn-Becker said very little of significance about her personality. She was reportedly modest and yet lively and full of self-confidence, open but reserved, of slight build and energetic. Emil Nolde, whom she met in Paris in 1900, summed her up briefly: 'small, full of curiosity, vivacious'.[48] But according to her sister Herma, her character was 'not at all straightforward'. In fact, she had 'depths and labyrinths' in her 'in which she could have lost herself'. In her art, however, she was uncompromising, and according to her sister, 'there she could look tough and ruthless'.[49] In her letters she sometimes sounds light-hearted and witty, while at other times she had a melancholy tone. Despite her self-doubt she remains confident and single-minded, always focused on the right formulation and independent thought and action. Even when she goes into flights of fancy, she always seems thoughtful and realistic. She worked for herself and was dedicated only to art. Apart from Hoetger, she found no one with the authority to critique her work; nor were her fellow artists in provincial Germany and the French capital a source of lasting support. At any rate, worldly success seemed unthinkable.

In her self-portraits she took on many different forms. The severe style of *Self-Portrait, Half Figure Facing Left, Holding a Bowl and a Glass* (c. 1904, ill. 65), made up of flat areas of broad brushstrokes, could have opened the way to a figurative Constructivism, but it remained an experimental exception. She produced a series of modest, simply executed but nonetheless charming self-portraits around 1905–6 (ills 62–64). In these head-and-shoulders portraits, she again looks out at the viewer, often animated by a slight turn of the head. She is not identified as an artist. The influence of the Egyptian mummy pictures from Fayum is again evident in these portraits. Paula's sister Herma said that 'in the past few years the artist has decorated her tiny dining room at head height with a frieze of Egyptian grave portraits'.[50] Reproductions of two portraits once owned by Modersohn-Becker have survived. According to Heinrich Vogeler, their impasto painting technique 'is also found in other works by Modersohn-Becker; she used it to try to give an

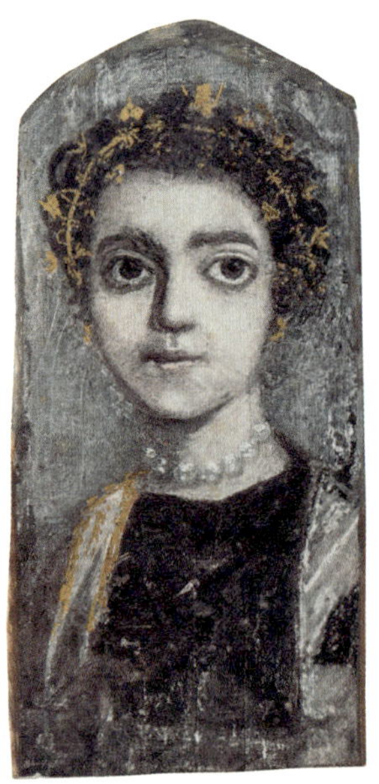
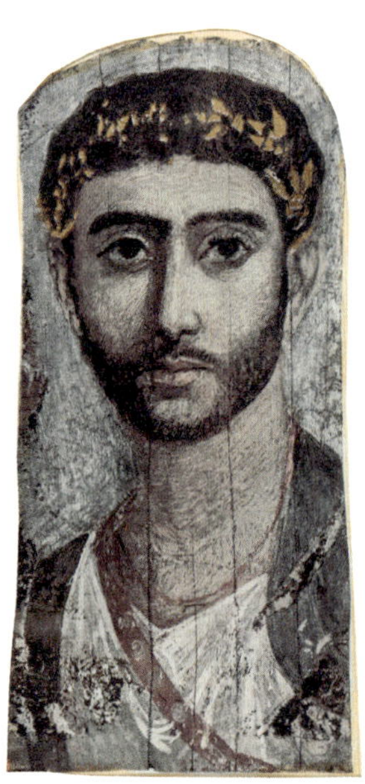

61 Two mummy portraits from the Fayum oasis,
c. 120–130 CE. Gold-highlighted reproductions
from Paula Modersohn-Becker's studio

62 *Self-Portrait in Front of Green Background with Blue Iris, c.* 1905

                         CHAPTER 5

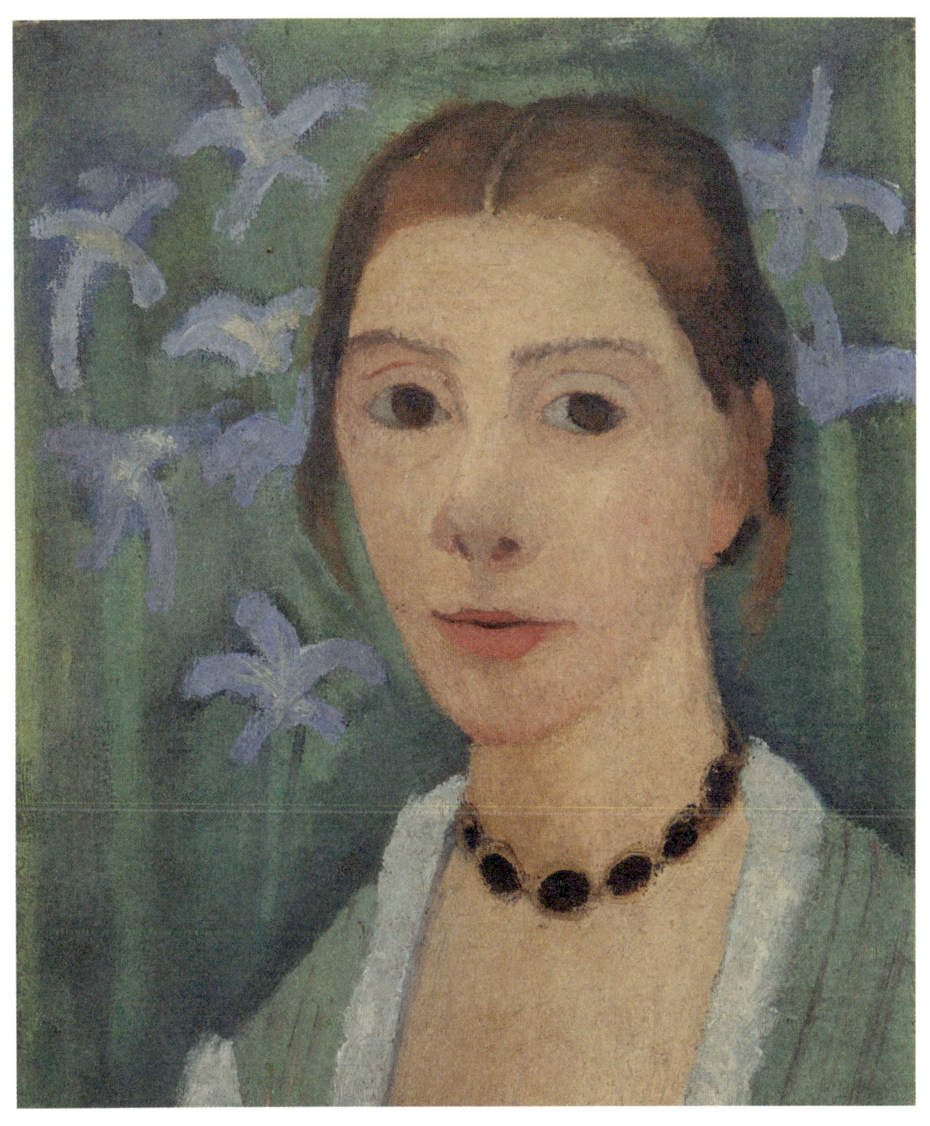

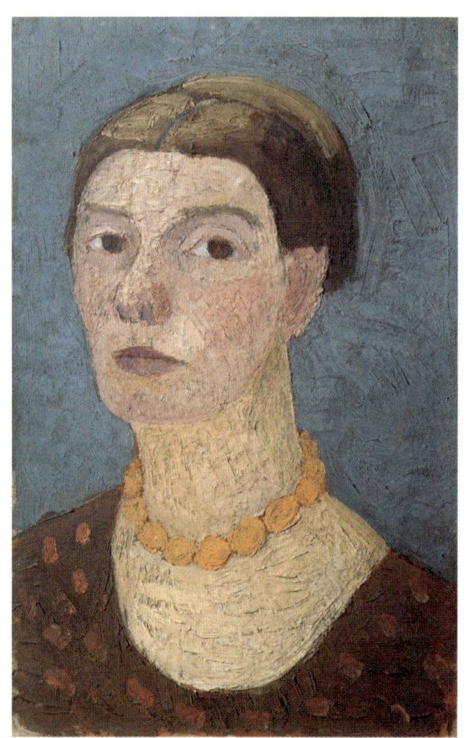 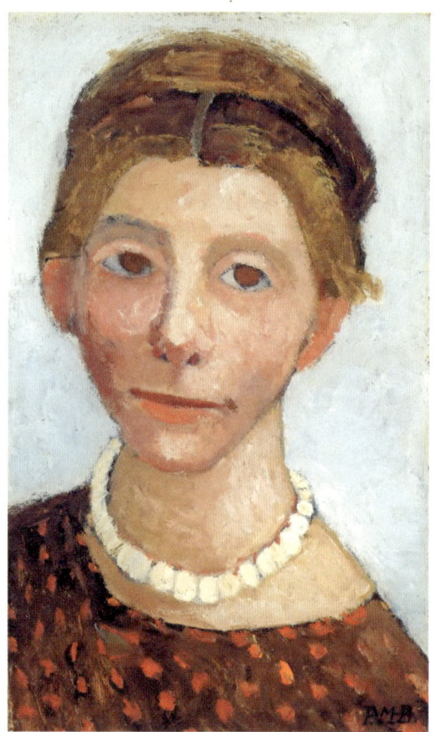

63   *Self-Portrait in Front of Blue-Green Background*, 1906

64   *Self-Portrait with White Pearl Necklace*, 1906

OPPOSITE

65   *Self-Portrait, Half Figure Facing Left,*
Holding a Bowl and a Glass, c. 1904

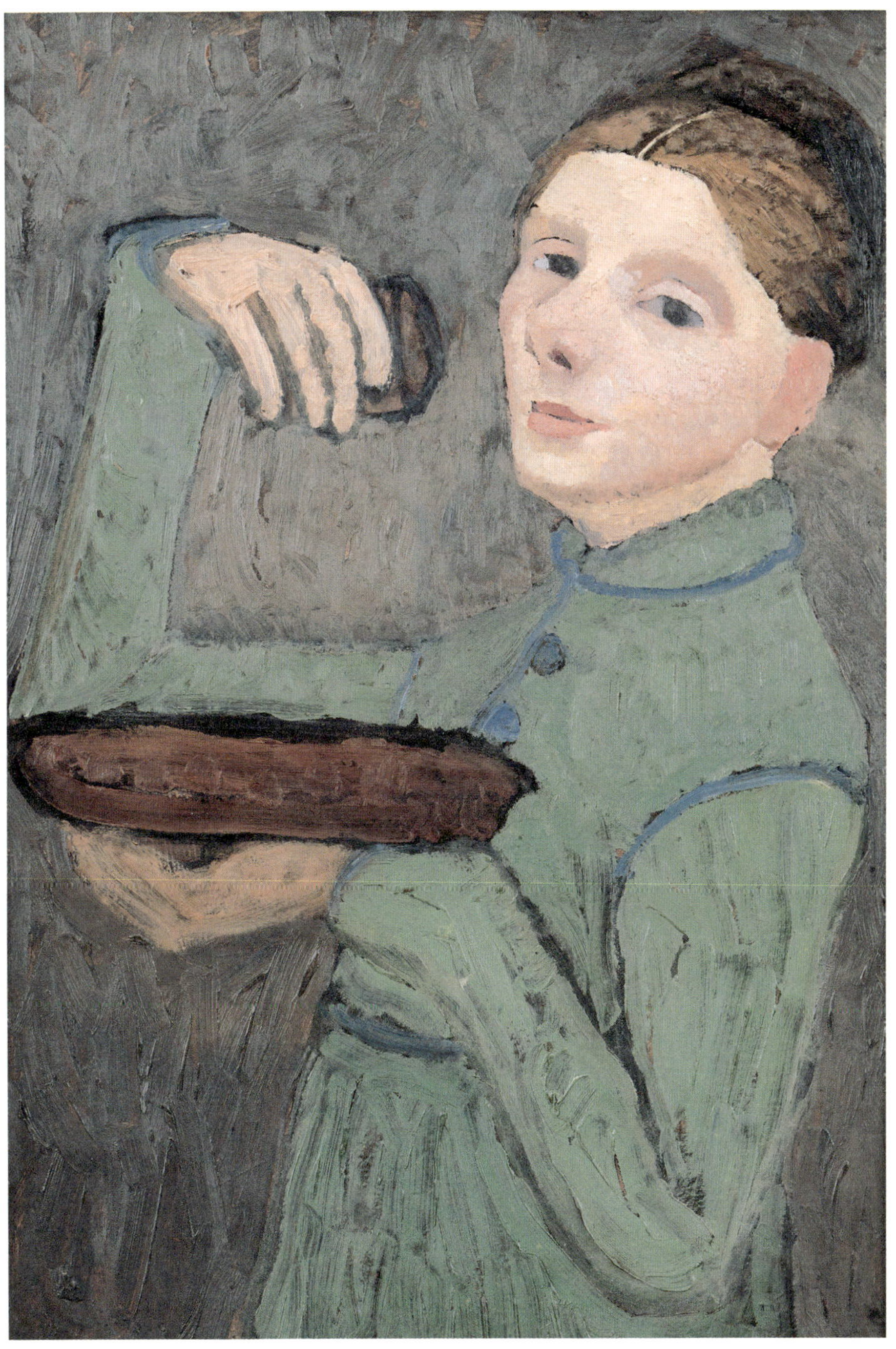

impression of life and movement, without having to sacrifice anything of the simplicity and clarity of form and colour.'[51]

Modersohn-Becker must have found it fascinating that the Fayum paintings breathe life into the dead. Her self-portraits are also suspended between presence and absence, an effect heightened by the unreflective dark, often black, pupil-less eyes, making the gaze, and therefore the person, remote and enigmatic. This empty and impersonal gaze is also found in portraits by Cézanne, Gauguin and Matisse, and in the Proto-Cubist heads painted by Picasso in 1906 – suggesting it was characteristic of the period to use this device to explore the individuality of the sitter and at the same time to mask it, make it more generalized.

This again raises the question of likeness. In Modersohn-Becker's self-portraits, the figure presented to us appears in various forms, one might even say archetypal figures: a country girl, a self-confident young woman, a melancholy figure encircled by a garland of flowers, a self-assured older woman. Indeed, when the influential German art patron Karl Ernst Osthaus bought *Self-Portrait with Camellia Branch* (ill. 78) in 1913, having met the artist when she visited Hagen in 1905, he wrote in a letter that he saw a strong resemblance in it, but 'I would not even have recognized her from the other pictures'.[52] Unlike Max Beckmann, however, who used self-portraiture to slip into different roles with suitable settings, Modersohn-Becker made only slight shifts to present different aspects of her character to others.

The Symbolic Self-Portrait

Modersohn-Becker took a significant step in 1906 with *Self-Portrait on the 6th Wedding Anniversary* (ill. 66). Until then, she had preferred small formats, but in this painting she depicted herself as an almost life-size, three-quarter-length figure, and it was the first self-portrait in art history of a pregnant female nude. On seeing the work in 1921, the conservative art critic Karl Scheffler wrote disgustedly in the magazine *Kunst und Künstler*: 'extremely tasteless, naked as far as beyond the navel, at an advanced stage of pregnancy'.[53] One can only imagine the taboos that would have been broken in the German Empire had the painting been shown during the artist's lifetime.

The composition is simple, with no great colour contrasts or experimental brushstrokes. The content and a telling inscription in the lower right-hand corner are what sets it apart. The inscription, scratched into the wet paint with the brush handle, reads: 'I painted this when I was 30 on my 6th wedding anniversary', signed 'P. B.' The message seems clear: Paula Becker, having separated from her husband and asserting her independence, has reverted to her maiden name and is determined to go her own way and ignore social rules. In fact, she was not pregnant at the time.

Various references have been cited for the specific narrative. In his *Self-Portrait during Illness* in the Kunsthalle Bremen, Dürer depicts the naked artist's physical pain with a pointing finger and an inscription. The nude pose is reminiscent of the self-portrait by the half-naked Victor Emil Janssen, with shirt pulled down and prominent stomach (*c.* 1828, ill. 67), which Modersohn-Becker could have seen at the centenary exhibition in Berlin in 1906. There are other allusions: Dürer is pointing to the wound; Janssen shows himself in front of a mirror, painting at the (barely

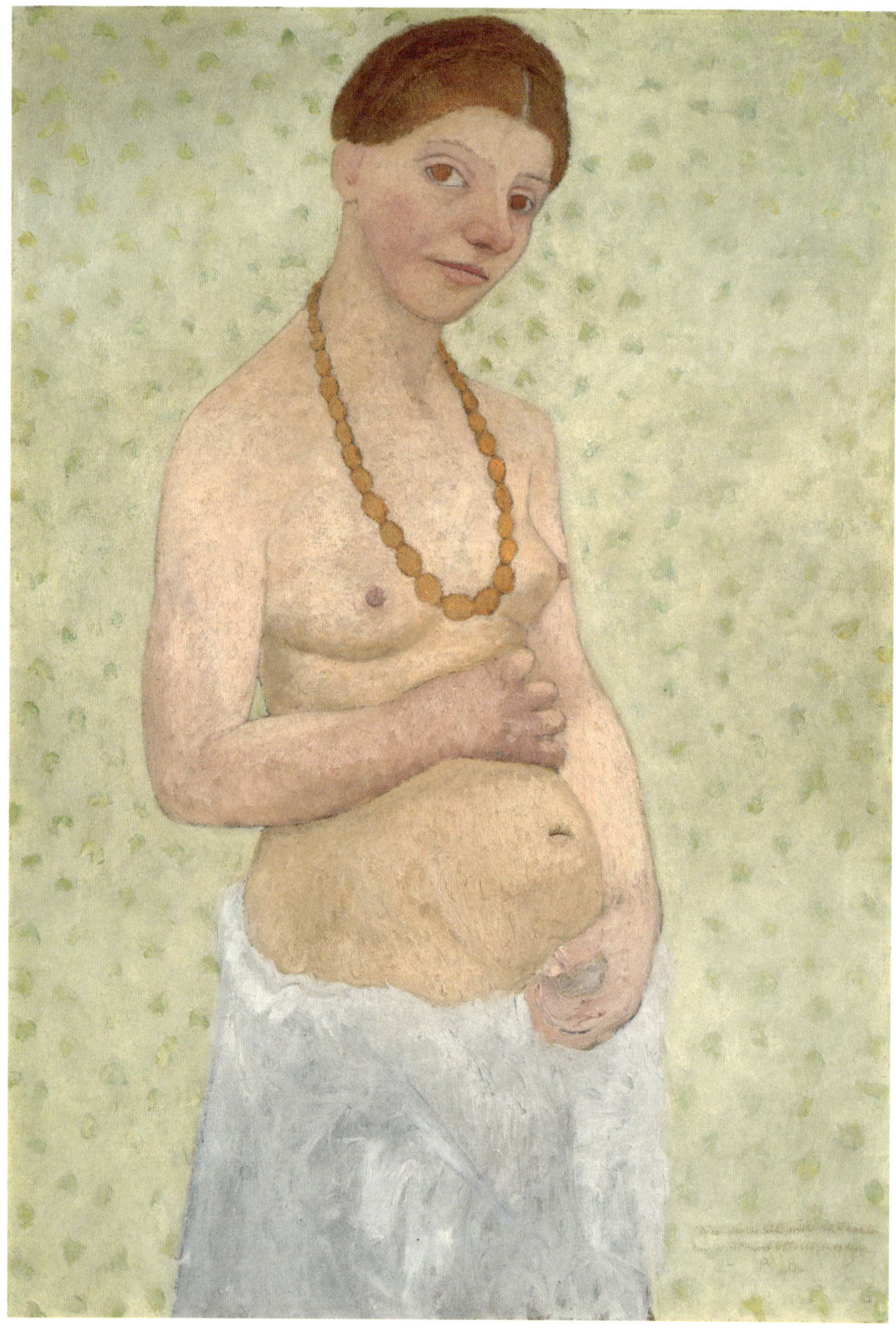

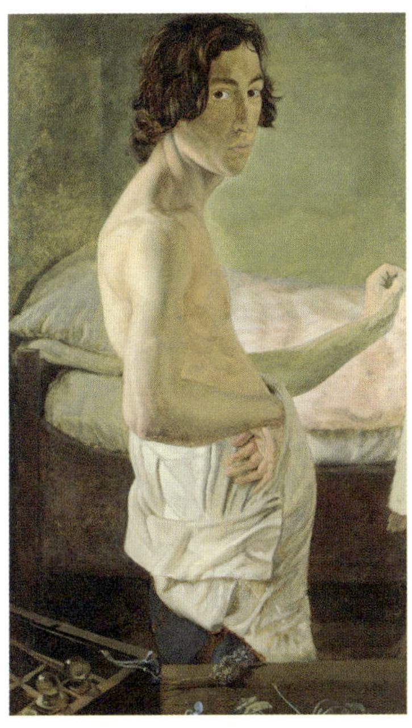

indicated) easel. Like Janssen, Modersohn-Becker's gaze is
directed at the viewer and, as if standing in front of a mirror, she
rests one hand above the rounded stomach and the other below
it, encircling the important element of the picture.

The gestures in these works reveal the theme: in Dürer's
case, the self-confident artist who in illness calls to mind images
of the Passion; in Janssen's, as Sebastian Giesen has shown, the
act of creation by a free artist.[54] But what of Modersohn-Becker?

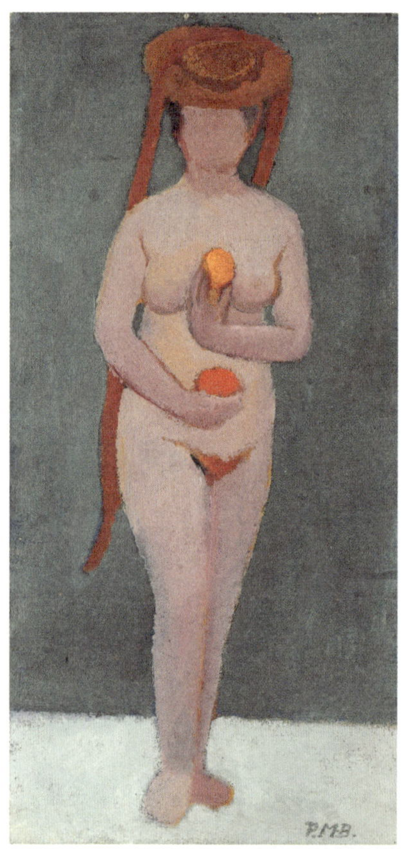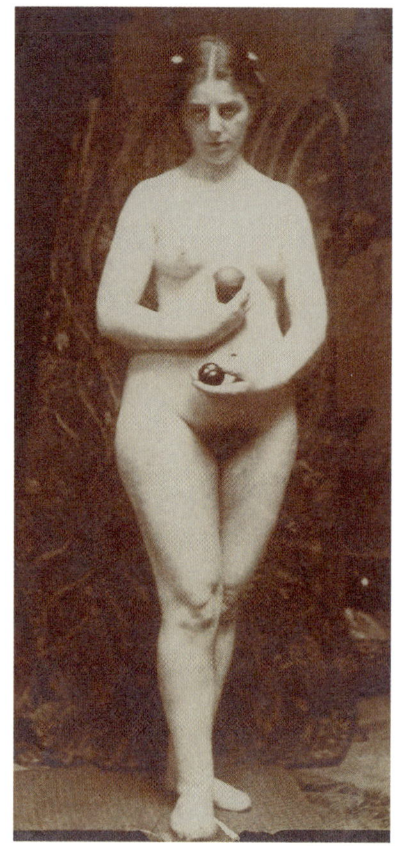

68 *Self-Portrait as a Standing Nude with Hat,* summer 1906

69 Paula Modersohn-Becker in her Paris studio, May–June 1906.
Photo by Herma Becker (?)

          CHAPTER 5

Thinking about the husband she had left, was she drawing attention to the fact that she was still not pregnant after several years of marriage? Was this perhaps wishful thinking: she was pregnant in the picture but not in real life? Or did she, as Rainer Stamm asks, want to show herself and future generations that she had finally managed to liberate herself, that she could make something of herself outside the trappings of marriage?[55]

A symbolic element is surely present. The pregnancy becomes a metaphor for how she feels about her art: fertile and free, she is pinpointing her thirtieth year as the threshold of artistic maturity – the year she brings her mature, artistic self into the world. Her nakedness widens the theme to the resolutely independent new art that was emerging and, in this sense, the painting might be seen as a unique personal expression of the position of the female painter asserting herself in a radically changing world. 'I am starting a new life now,' she wrote in May 1906, when she was working on the painting. Shortly before completing it, she said emphatically, 'You will see, now I am free I shall become something.'

In the summer of 1906, while still in Paris, Modersohn-Becker produced more nude or semi-nude self-portraits. This time they were based on nude photographs, probably taken by her sister Herma in the Paris studio. In one photo, with arms bent, she holds one piece of fruit between her breasts and another in front of her stomach (ill. 69). In the later painting (ill. 68), the pieces of fruit become vague, round shapes of different colours, the face is unfinished and the body has few details. The only accessory is a tilted hat. The composition is all about form. The Cubist style suggests that, in this painting too, she used herself as a model purely for an experiment in form. In the words of Wolfgang Werner, this was 'certainly one of the earliest Proto-Cubist paintings in the history of art'.[56]

Iconization

Another way of developing her own pictorial language was to make the facial features in her self-portraits so schematic that they became almost mask-like. This could already be seen in the portraits of friends in the summer of 1906. One example is a series of works that reflect the development of her ideas. They start with *Self-Portrait with Blue, White Striped Dress* (ill. 70). The use of distinct areas of colour in the skin, applied side-by-side or layered one on top of the other, creates a conflicting result: an animated, pleasantly familiar face that is at the same time enigmatic and remote, not least because the eyes have no pupils. The position of the hand in front of the chin is odd. What could it mean – a moment of reflection? Hesitation? Concealment? The form is reminiscent of her portrait of Rilke, completed not long before, particularly in the blurring. A shadow under her lower lip recalls the shape of Rilke's beard. Was she drawing a direct parallel with the Rilke portrait, or is this a broader expression of the concept of masculinity or even an attempt to use a work of art to portray an ideal male–female image?

In any case, the pictorial form she discovered was so important for Modersohn-Becker that she used it to carry out an experiment. She pressed a piece of newspaper – the financial section of a French paper – onto the picture while it was still wet, making an impression (ill. 71). She partly reworked it and, while continuing to work on the original painting, made another copy, this time on the back of a letter (ill. 72). In the initial copy, all that remained of the face was a partially transparent mask which,

70 *Self-Portrait with Blue, White Striped Dress*, summer 1906

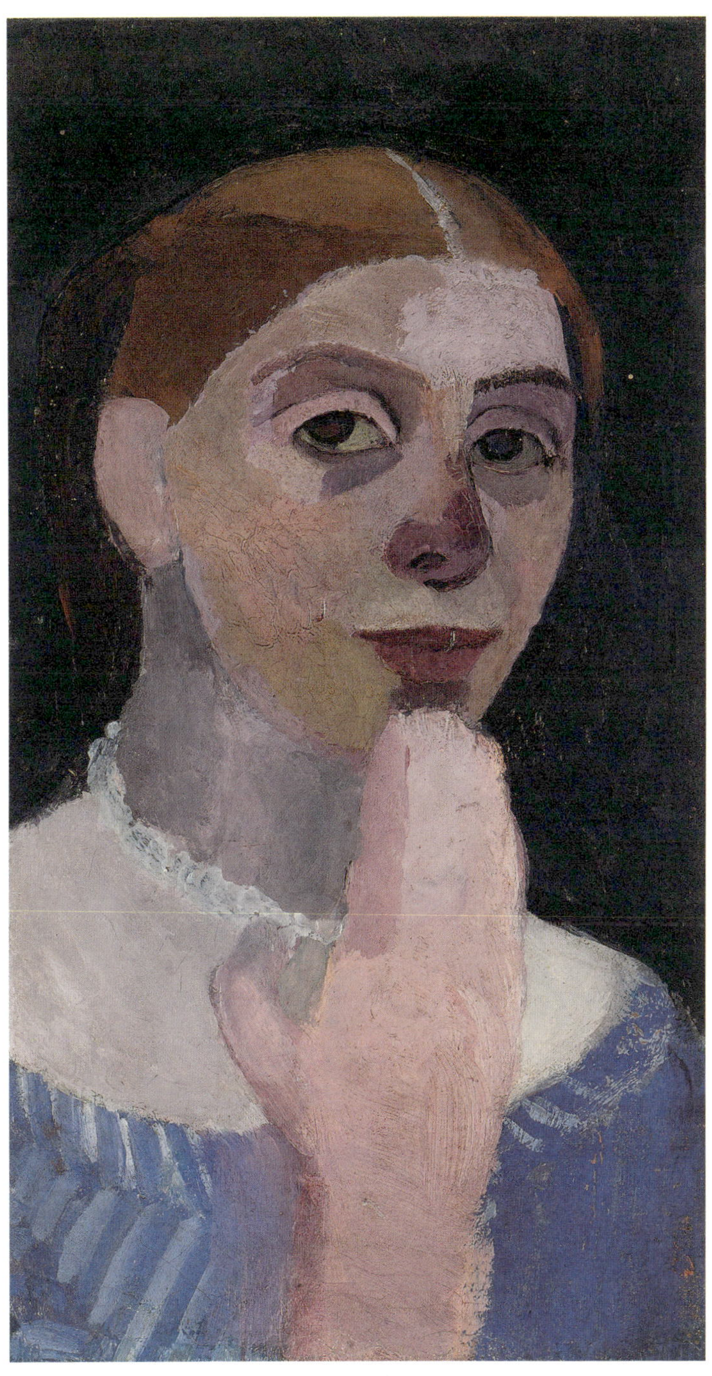

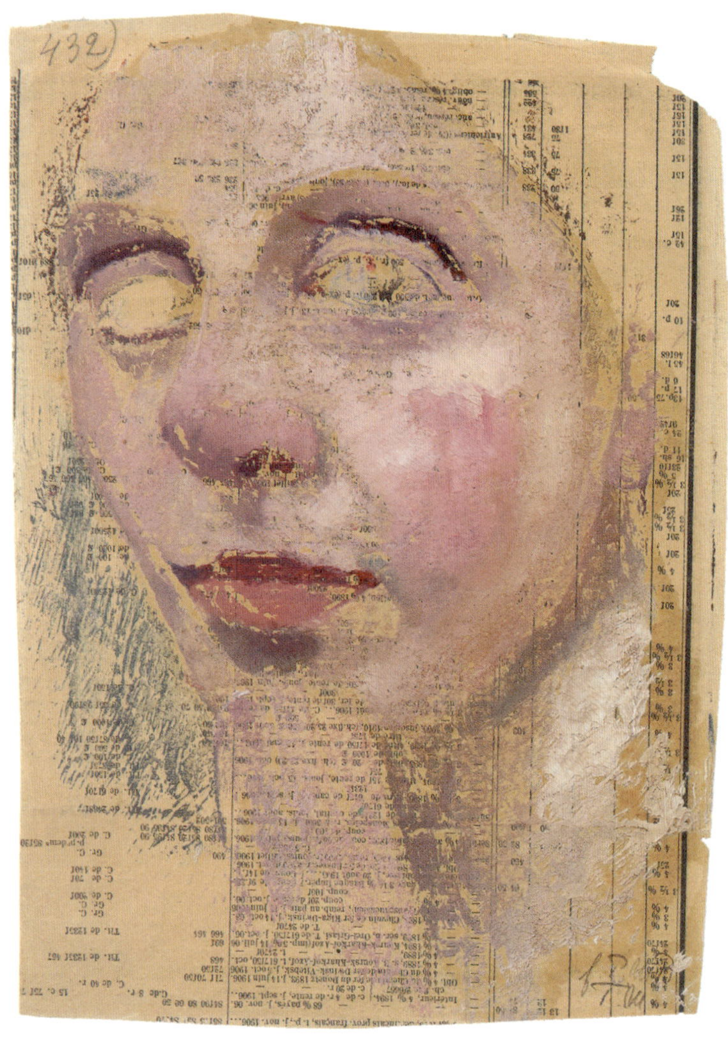

71 *Self-Portrait, Right Hand on Chin,* monotype on newspaper,
partly overpainted, summer 1906

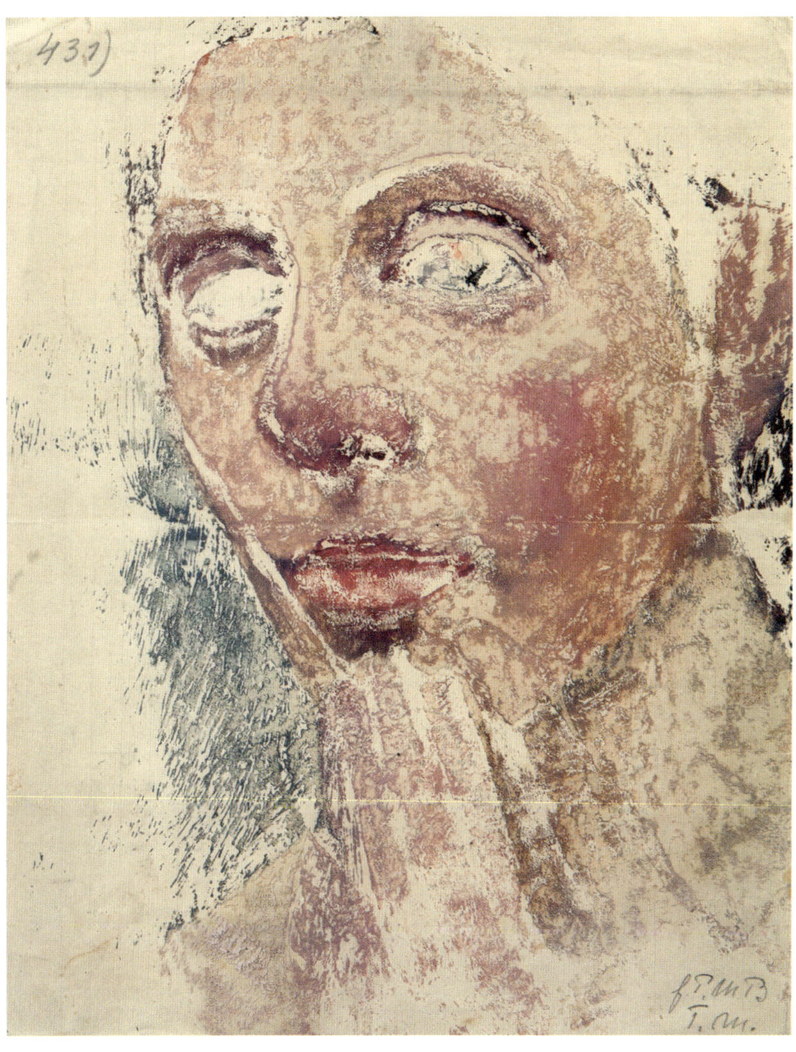

72 *Self-Portrait, Right Hand on Chin,* monotype
on lined paper, summer 1906

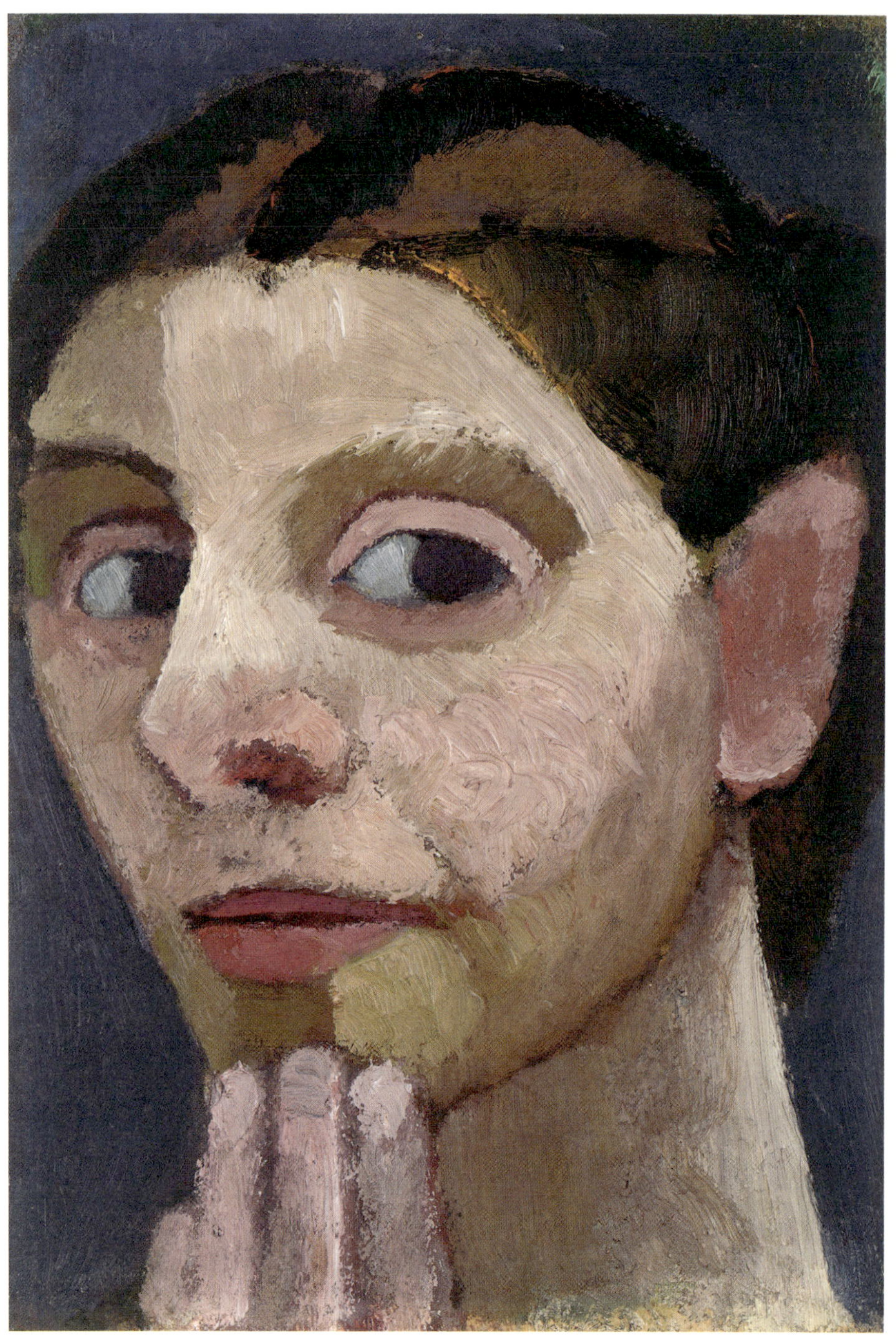

with the application of white and pink, became so alive that it looked like a living person. In the second copy, although the mask retained a suggestion of individual features, it took on a more distant look, especially since the detail in the eye was mostly lost. While only a faint outline of the iconic hand gesture is evident in the impression on newspaper, in the case of the latter it is reinforced by the composition of the fingers.

In the summer of 1906, Modersohn-Becker experimented with this concept further. In *Self-Portrait Facing Left, Hand on Chin* (ill. 73), she depicts herself close-up, humanized, with a knowing look. The upper half of the face is distinctly brighter than the lower half, and the compelling hand gesture is repeated. She followed the painting with another contrasting variation, *Self-Portrait Facing Right, Hand on Chin* (ill. 74). This work no longer relates back directly to the monotypes but takes the motif of the original picture a step further. The face – now distinctively mask-like – is brought even closer. The Primitivism of the sim-plified forms and the exclusively sombre colours make the image disturbingly radical. Again, the dialectic of closeness and dis-tance is characteristic. The features are close enough for us to study, but the face is turned away, formally distanced and decid-edly abstract, giving it a remote and mysterious air in a similar way to a tribal mask.

For Modersohn-Becker, the mask-like nature of the faces makes them into icons and turns lived reality into an invented, constructed image. Anything personal and individual is stripped away; the familiar is discarded in order to create a generalized and decisive new form, which nonetheless contains hidden ref-erences to the original subject. So here again the mask-like appearance is part of a strategy to avoid a mere likeness and

73 *Self-Portrait Facing Left, Hand on Chin*, summer 1906

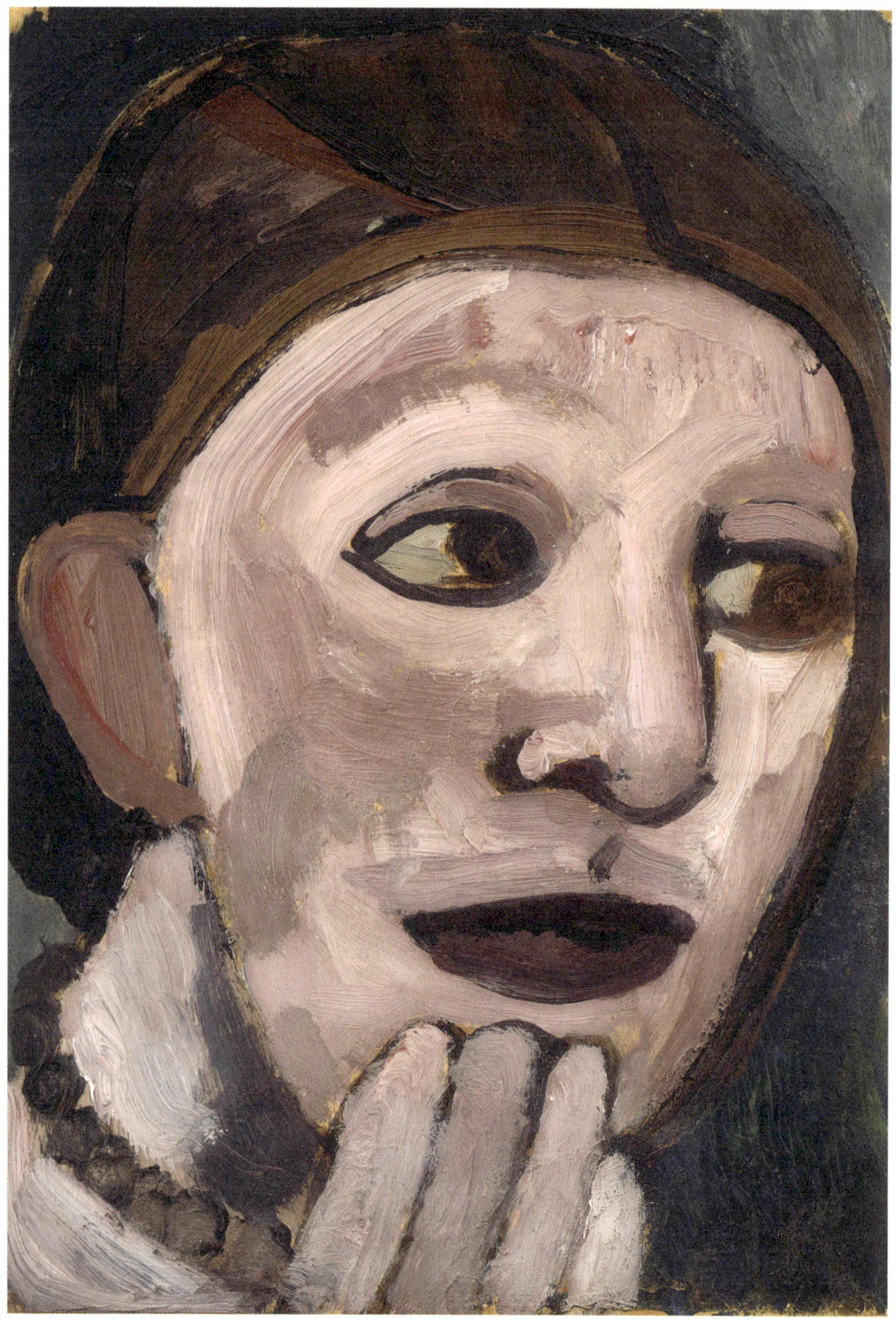

direct identification – 'the great simplicity of form'. Modersohn-Becker's aim in her constant experiments with pictorial techniques was to keep discovering new artistic possibilities. One need only compare the portrait of Lee Hoetger (ill. 48) with the self-portraits facing left (ill. 73) and right (ill. 74) to see the apparent change of style in 1906 alone.

Ritual Power

Between the summer of 1906 and 1907, which was to be her last year, Modersohn-Becker created another series of outstanding self-portraits that are unique in the history of modern art. Painted in Paris, they bring together her experiences of modern art in the great museums of Central Europe and in the French capital in particular.

Although it may not be apparent from the magnificently simplified and intensified forms of *Self-Portrait as a Half-Length Nude with Amber Necklace I* (ill. 76), this painting from the summer of 1906 was also based on a photograph (ill. 75). In the half-length photographic portrait, the artist wears no more than an amber necklace and holds small flowers in her hands – one against her chest and the other between her breasts. Her head is tilted, and she is looking at the camera. Simone Ewald wrote that in her distinctive new art – 'self-portrait as nude' – Modersohn-Becker explored every possible composition with the aid of photography, establishing 'her own view of the female body in a genre that had been dominated by the male

74 *Self-Portrait Facing Right, Hand on Chin,* summer 1906

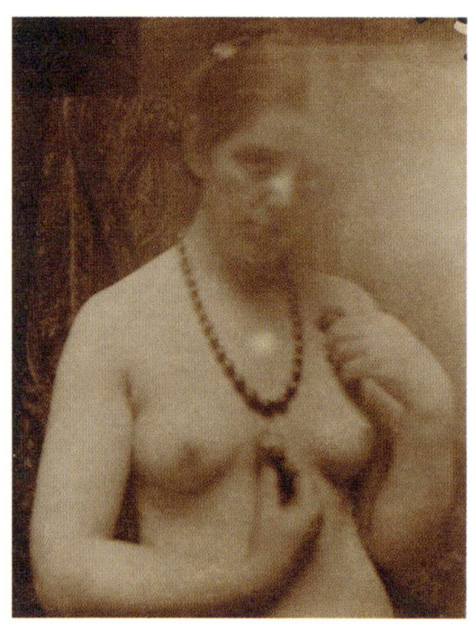

perspective.'[57] She changed the model as she wished in order to express her own ideas.

That change added a specific element of content to the work. A more meaningful figure evolved from the photograph. The simplified forms gave the gestures with the two flowers a ritual air. The eyes, nose and mouth stand out from the rest of the features, so that the face resembles a living mask. Finally, the lush, thick vegetation behind the figure looks as if it is protecting, embedding, covering or enclosing her. This was rightly seen as a link to the work of Henri Rousseau, known as Le Douanier ('the customs officer'), whose work she had seen in the studio with Bernhard Hoetger. The setting and the arrangement of the figure have classical connotations: the naturalness of the female body, the cultural references in the pose and the heightened 'artistic' background. During the summer months of 1906, Modersohn-Becker was clearly working on a figurative cohesion that Van Gogh had earlier abandoned for fragmentation and that a few years later would be largely lost in abstraction.

The narrow, large-format *Self-Portrait with Lemon* (ill. 77) of 1906–7 is even more simplified. The figure is cropped at the sides. The elements of the picture, as well as the hand holding

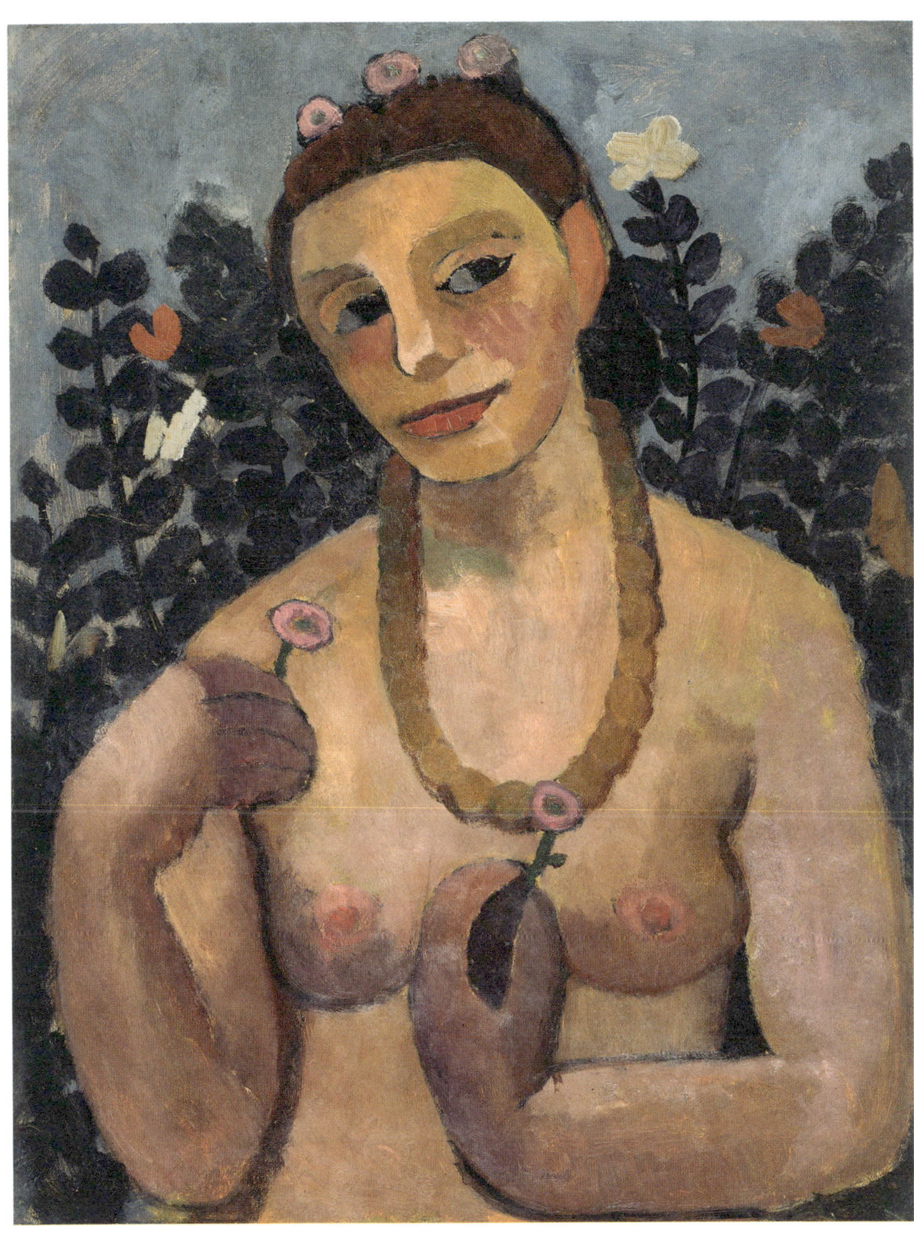

the lemon, are in the central axis and are indicated with rapid brushstrokes. The German art historian Carl Georg Heise, who acquired the painting in 1916, noted in the catalogue raisonné that the neck was completely unpainted, leaving only the grey board visible, and the intention was for the section to be covered with a neutral tone at a later date.[58]

In *Self-Portrait with Lemon* the reference to the natural – the reinforcement from nature – is an important motif, but it is the integration of the lemon into the structure of the picture by the ritualized gesture in the central axis that is essential to the content. The lemon plays a strategic function as an attribute: it grants autonomy to the image. The painting can no longer be judged by its resemblance to reality; it must be judged for its artistic truth, according to its own rules. In this way, fruit has a similar pictorial function to masks – the difference being that fruit comes from nature and the autonomization of the picture is less conspicuous, less emphatic and therefore more natural: a further step towards modern art.

Like many of Modersohn-Becker's women and children in her late period, the figure in this painting has dark skin. Although the dark tone of some of the figures in her works is sometimes attributed to her use of Italian models, this is a self-portrait. It is possible that it was a deliberate visual technique to make the familiar seem unfamiliar, to take the figure into a different world. She may have been influenced by the indigenous figures who populate Gauguin works, which she had seen in the Fayet collection in the spring of 1905 and at the major retrospective in Paris in the autumn of 1906. She was also inspired by the indigenous performances at the 1900 Paris Exposition. The dioramas at the State Museum of Natural

77 *Self-Portrait with Lemon*, 1906–7

  CHAPTER 5

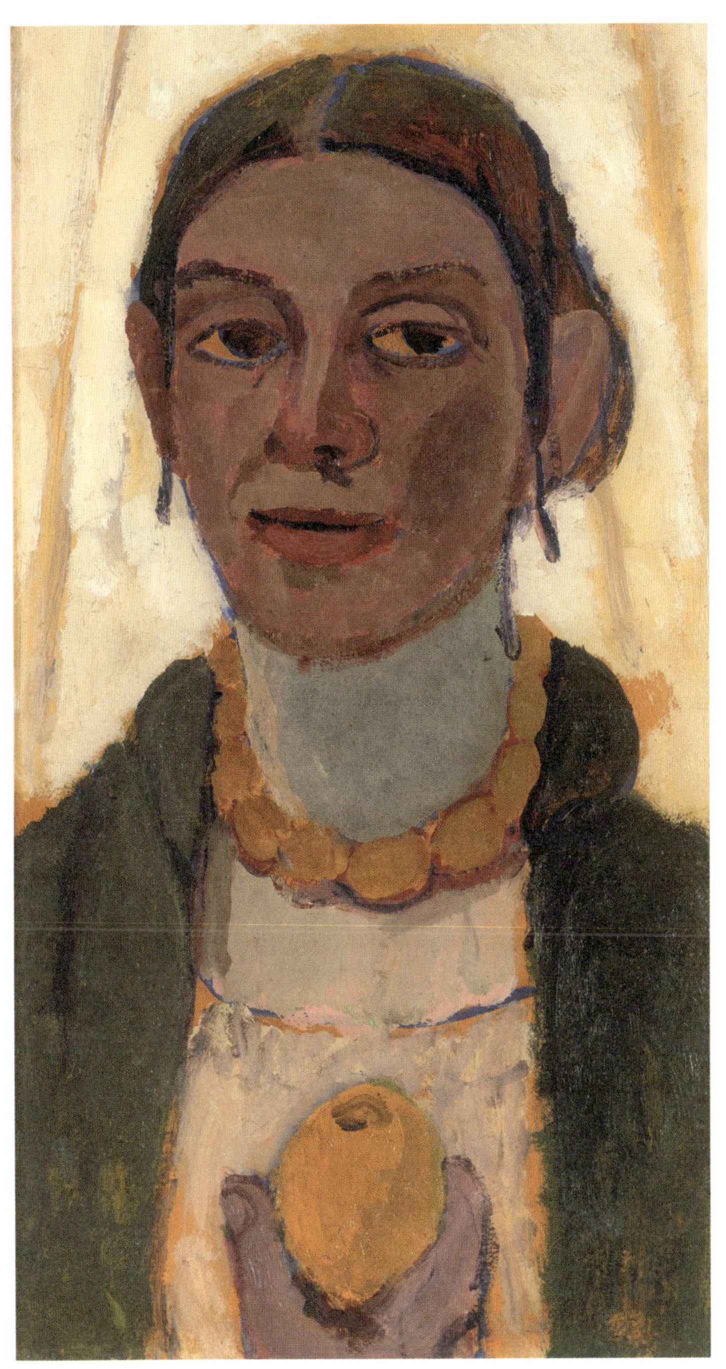

History, Ethnology and Trade in Bremen (now the Overseas Museum) were another possible source.

Fruit and plants play a special role in *Self-Portrait with Lemon*, *Self-Portrait with Camellia Branch* and *Self-Portrait with Two Flowers in Raised Left Hand* (ills 77, 78, 99). The objects are by no means incidental. They are highlighted, presented – not as food or decoration; nor are they a common symbol that can be decoded. Although familiar objects, they symbolize something else. They are held up as if on display, but unlike the attributes in the traditional iconography of saints (St Barbara's tower, St Nicholas's balls of gold, St Peter's key) they reveal nothing about the life of the person holding them and are no help in identifying the figures. They remain a deliberately added, mysterious element that nonetheless has a specific function: to take the familiar into a different sphere and give the figure a ritual power.

Alter Ego

The meaning of that power again comes from the artistic starting point: the self-portrait. In the portrait with a lemon, the artist paints herself as a strange classical-looking figure holding a symbol of fruitfulness, in this case creative fruitfulness. Does that also symbolize the strange dynamic power of the new art which Modersohn-Becker repeatedly urged should point to the future? She was already writing in her journal in 1902 that 'art that is rich and inventive should only look to the future'. At the time, as the historian Lucian Hölscher showed, art generally was focused, 'programmatically for the first time ever' on shaping the future. This emphasis on the future led to 'a new dimension of artistic creation' that was 'very characteristic of the 20th century', 'art emerging into the future'.[59] Modersohn-Becker's ideas and works must also be viewed in this historical cultural context.

Like *Self-Portrait with Lemon*, the famous *Self-Portrait with Camellia Branch* (ill. 78) was left unfinished. The hand holding the branch is merely hinted at, heightening the effect of the branch in front of the body. Again, the narrow vertical format of the work is reminiscent of the Fayum Egyptian mummy paintings. However, the key difference is that Modersohn-Becker replaced a naturalistic portrayal with a simplified, flatly arranged form in the style of the Primitivism that was shaking up, dominating and revolutionizing art in Paris in that period. The black, pupil-less eyes, which made the figure enigmatic, were still an important element of the painting.

In terms of a likeness, these late self-portraits are not actually self-portraits, although there are similarities between them. Characteristics such as the strong nose and large mouth, the wide eyes and the centre parting recur, but the figures are not individualized. The bodies become stronger, sometimes masculine in appearance. The artist's mother was deeply disappointed by the difference between the reality and the image: 'I find all Paula's self-portraits horrible when she is so lovely. How can you treat beauty so harshly!'[60]

Just as on her first visit to Worpswede in 1897 the pine trees had seemed an 'ideal figure for an artist' ('broad, gnarled … and yet with delicate fibres and nerves inside them'), her 'subjective sensation' was that birch trees were like 'modern women', 'as bold as men'. This idea of modern women being as bold as men recurs in the Paris self-portraits. She developed a kind of figure that was based on herself but was ultimately independent, specific to her art, an alter ego. The 'self' was no longer portrayed as another person, as in previous self-portraits. Now the

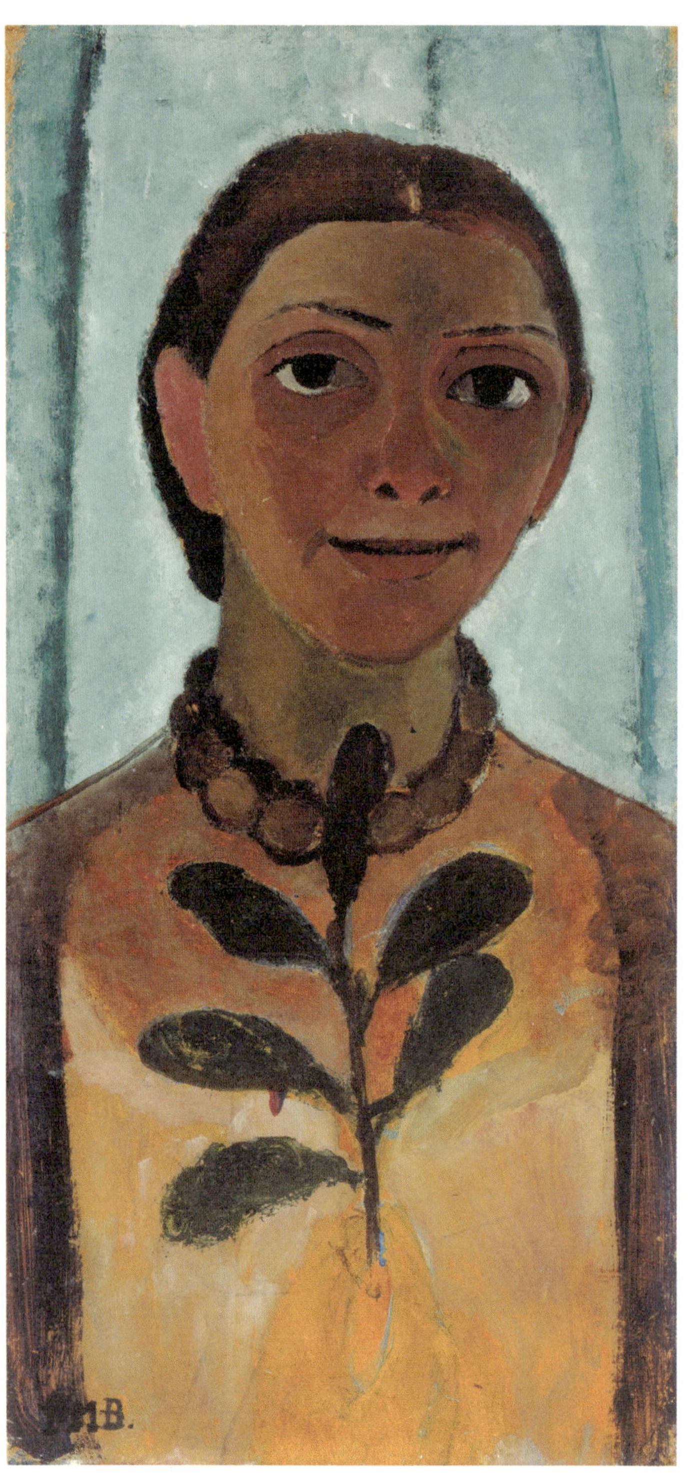

self-portraits represent a symbolic 'self', showing the artist's view of herself as being bold as a man, especially in her self-confidence as a creator with equal rights in the new art world. The artist's self-portrait becomes an image of dynamism: the self-assured female painter.

Paula Modersohn-Becker developed her own pictorial means – the creation of archetypes, the mask-like faces, the ritualization of gestures and attributes, the unusual use of colour – in order to transform the experience of reality and translate it into her own visual language. But part of the concept was that the reference to nature and the natural should be retained. As mentioned earlier, in 1902 she wrote in her journal that she believed that 'when painting a picture, you should not think about nature at all', at least not as 'the concept of the painting'. But once she had defined the structure using her own pictorial techniques, she could refer back to nature: 'Then I have to bring in from nature the features that make my picture look natural.' This was her concept of naturalism.

This approach seems unusual and striking. It is different from the division of modern art into 'great realism' and 'great abstraction' that Kandinsky observed a little later, in 1912. Instead, its goal is a new unity, the revival of the classical artistic concept of wholeness. It is a reaction against the type of stylistic specialization that had begun with the Impressionists and was continued by other avant-garde movements. The deliberately composed settings that appear in pictures painted in the last year of Modersohn-Becker's life would bring that idea to centre stage.

78 *Self-Portrait with Camellia Branch*, 1906–7

1906–7: Major Works from the Paris Studio

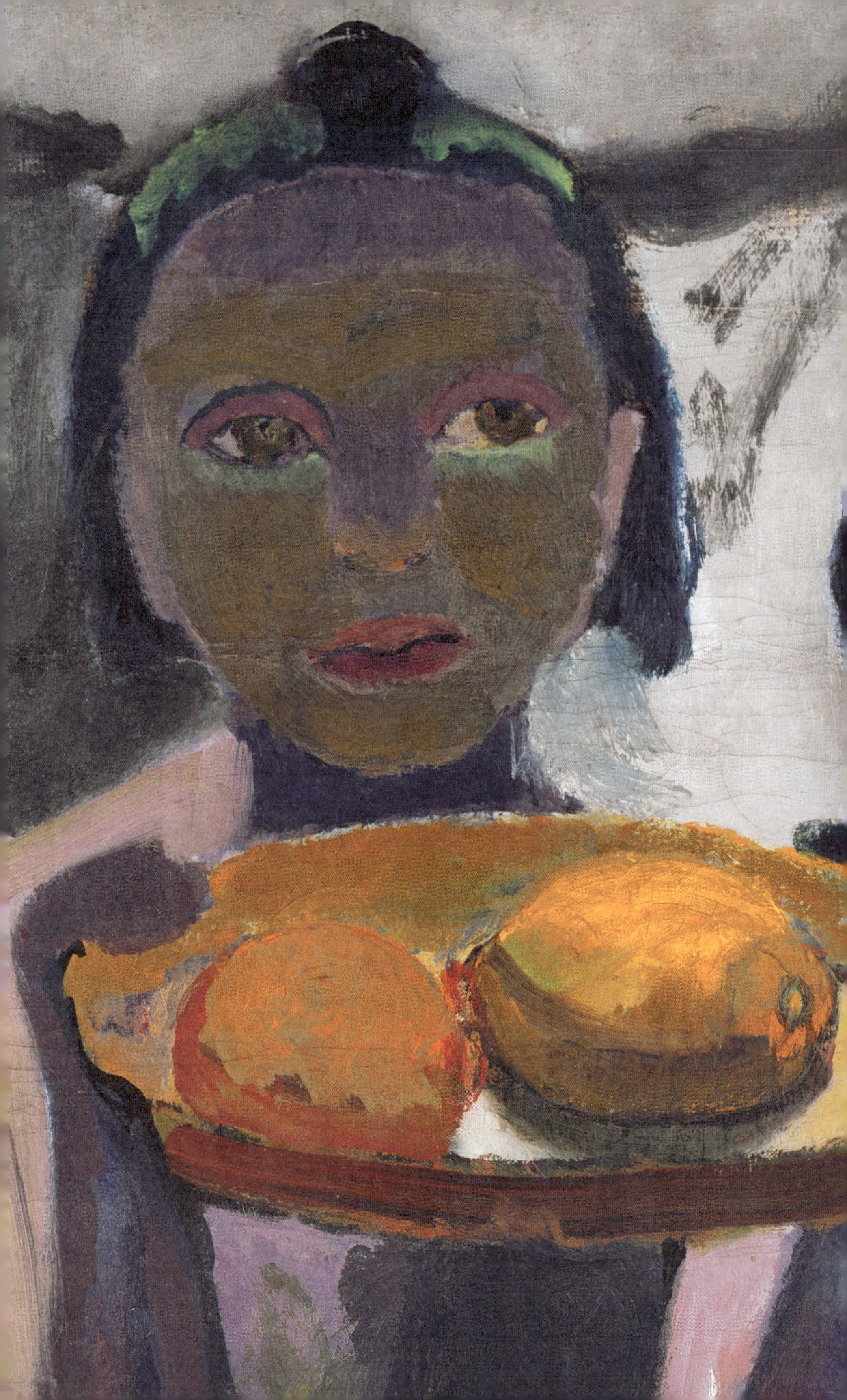

Freedom and Dependency

Paula Modersohn-Becker had been living in Paris since February 1906 and, buoyed by Bernhard Hoetger's support and encouragement, she was working harder than ever before: 'I have worked really intensively on my painting day and night, and I was fairly satisfied with everything I did.' In those 13 months in Paris, she produced about 80 paintings, mostly figurative. She was now trying specifically 'to work on things for longer' and make the form and content even stronger. After a visit to Worpswede in January 1906, Rilke had written that she was 'painting relentlessly and purposefully', creating works that 'no one had ever been able to see or paint before'. On meeting the artist again in Paris, he wrote to his wife, 'she is brave and young and it seems to me she is on her way up, on her own and without any help'[61] – although Modersohn-Becker was not entirely without help: she still received financial support from Otto Modersohn and sometimes from her sister Milly.

Detail of ill. 81

Otto found the separation difficult and urged her several times to come home, but she was determined not to go back to Worpswede. So, in July 1906, she suggested to him that he might come to Paris and take his own studio there, perhaps outside the city because she was well aware that he did not like Paris. She did write to him in the same month that she felt her life would be 'easier and better and freer' without him, but at the same time added hopefully: 'Let us see if we can work something out in the future.' However, she changed her mind about the invitation only two months later and presented her husband with the final separation. 'I am thinking at the moment mainly about myself and my life. My life is not going to be ruined.'

This raised the inevitable question of how she was going to support herself in the long term. She said she wanted to make arrangements, but she did not explain what those would be. There was little chance of her earning an independent living from commissions and sales: a market did not yet exist in Germany for very modern art, and although there was a market in Paris it was geared only to French artists. As a female artist Modersohn-Becker would have found the situation all the more difficult. Historically, male artists had often struggled to support themselves: Philipp Otto Runge had a brother who supported him all his life, so did Vincent van Gogh; Marées found a patron in Konrad Fiedler. Modersohn-Becker's friends and family became increasingly concerned. Hoetger pointed out to her that she would not be able to keep herself, especially since she was so dedicated to her art that she was unable to consider any other means of earning a living. Fritz Overbeck, a fellow artist from Worpswede, wrote to her with a realistic insight into her predicament: 'You are not going to be able to survive on your art, just because it is art.'[62]

CHAPTER 6

By November 1906, Modersohn-Becker had reached the same conclusion. 'I realized this summer that I am not a woman who can stand alone,' she wrote.

Otto Modersohn had arrived with the Vogelers at the beginning of October and stayed for the winter. Together they visited the Salon d'Automne, where they saw a major Gauguin retrospective at the Grand Palais (which was also an important inspiration for Picasso); they went on trips to see Rodin in Meudon, to St Denis, the burial site of French kings, to Versailles and Fontainebleau, and to Barbizon, the artists' colony on which Worpswede had been modelled. In March 1907 Modersohn-Becker told her mother that she was pregnant, and at the end of that month she and Otto returned to Worpswede. The desire to have a child was to be fulfilled; the desire to stay in the capital of art was not.

The Staged Image

In the extraordinarily creative period in Paris in 1906–7, as well as the portraits, self-portraits and still lifes Modersohn-Becker produced a small series of deliberately composed works with curiously intensified imagery. Following on from the paintings of two children embracing (ills 37–38), with which she had already revealed a move towards a new iconography, *Two Kneeling Nude Girls* (ill. 82) became the starting point for Modersohn-Becker's exploration of a wider range of subjects using more elaborate staging. The girls sit next to each other but apart. The one wearing a necklace is offering fruit in a bowl; from her gesture, the girl in the hat seems to be making a confession. The seriousness of the pair, the way they mirror

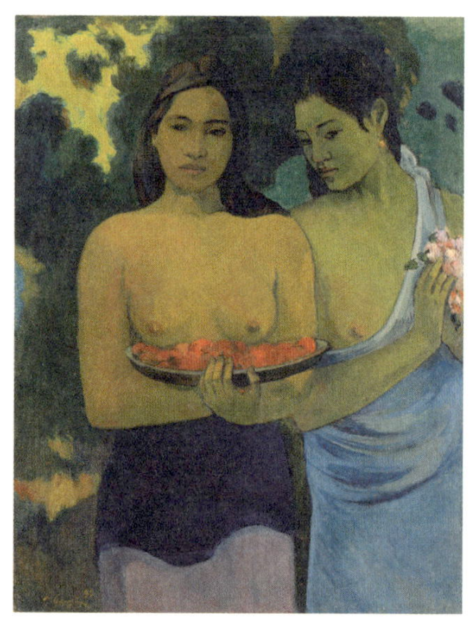

ABOVE

79 Paul Gauguin, *Two Tahitian Women*,
1899

OPPOSITE

80 *Half-Length Nude Italian Woman
with a Plate in her Raised Hand,*
autumn 1906

 CHAPTER 6

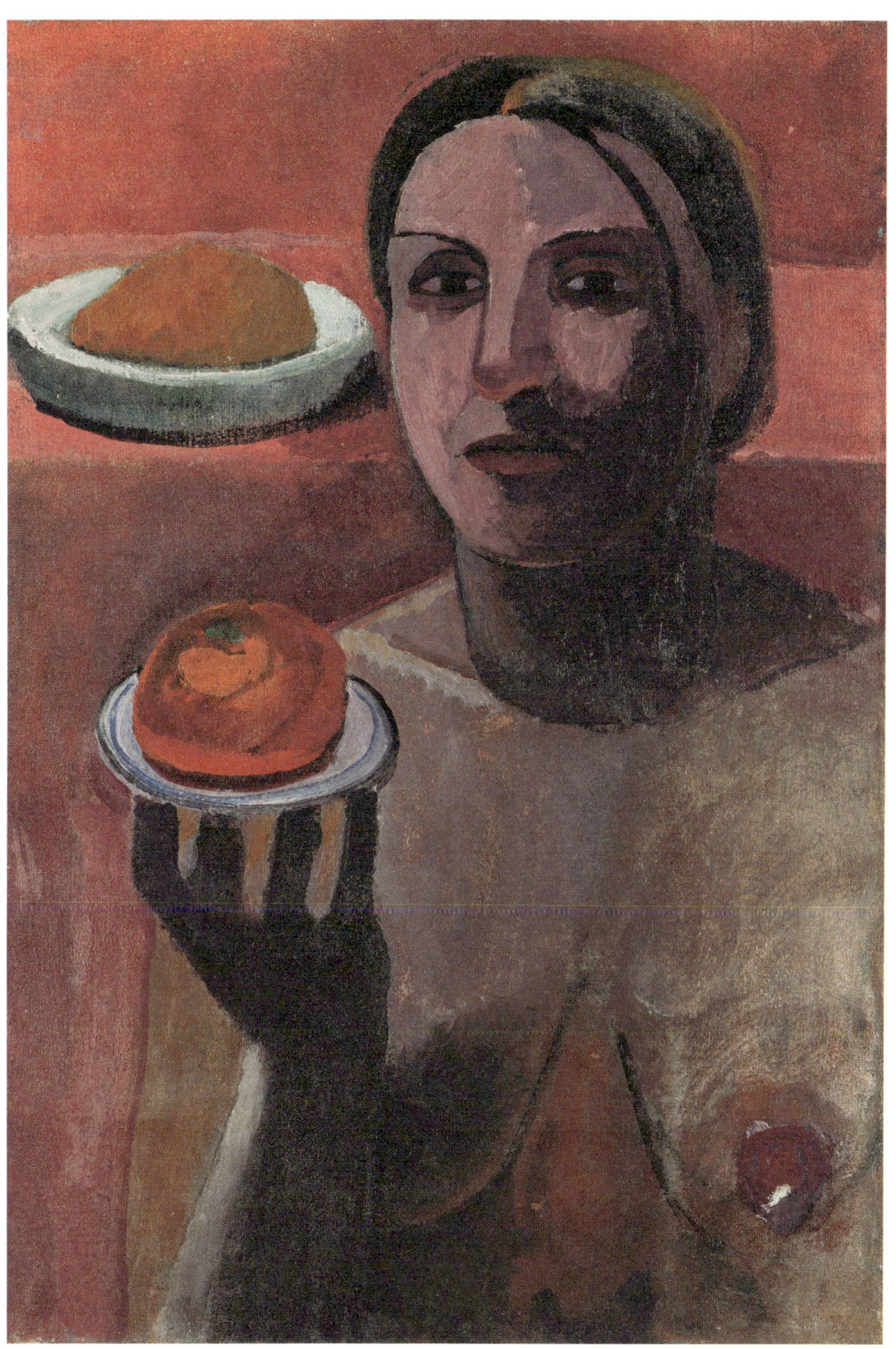

each other in position and posture, and the combination of their gestures make this look more like a ritual than a game – a ritual with an unknown origin and purpose. The children's nakedness reinforces the naturalness of these attitudes and gestures.

The ritual reflects Modersohn-Becker's desire to create a new iconography that selectively draws on traditions but opens up new possibilities for interpretation. It is not designed to be realistic, Expressionist or abstract. Instead, it is an attempt to develop her own figurative style, expressing her ideas by posing figures and objects in a deliberate fashion, and adding an unconventional element by including references to the Primitivism that was then in vogue.

In both the principle of the staged image and the Primitivist style of her figures, Modersohn-Becker was influenced by Gauguin's work in particular. She had, of course, seen Gustave Fayet's Gauguin collection in the spring of 1905 and the Gauguin retrospective at the Salon d'Automne in the autumn of 1906; when visiting Karl Ernst Osthaus in Hagen, she saw four major paintings by the French artist. She was therefore very familiar with his work. Gauguin's *Two Tahitian Women* (ill. 79) of 1899, owned by Fayet and on display in the 1906 retrospective, and Modersohn-Becker's *Half-Length Nude Italian Woman with a Plate in her Raised Hand* (ill. 80), painted in 1906, have noticeable features in common: the hieratic attitudes of the naked or semi-naked figures, the focus on the relationship between the figure and fruit, the lack of storytelling elements and the use of dark tones. Gauguin merges figures, attributes and background. In Modersohn-Becker's painting, on the other hand, the bowl of fruit held out, the large head and the bowl in the background in her reddish-brown colour range create a formal tension, an

81 *Standing Child Nude with Goldfish Bowl*, 1906–7

                    CHAPTER 6

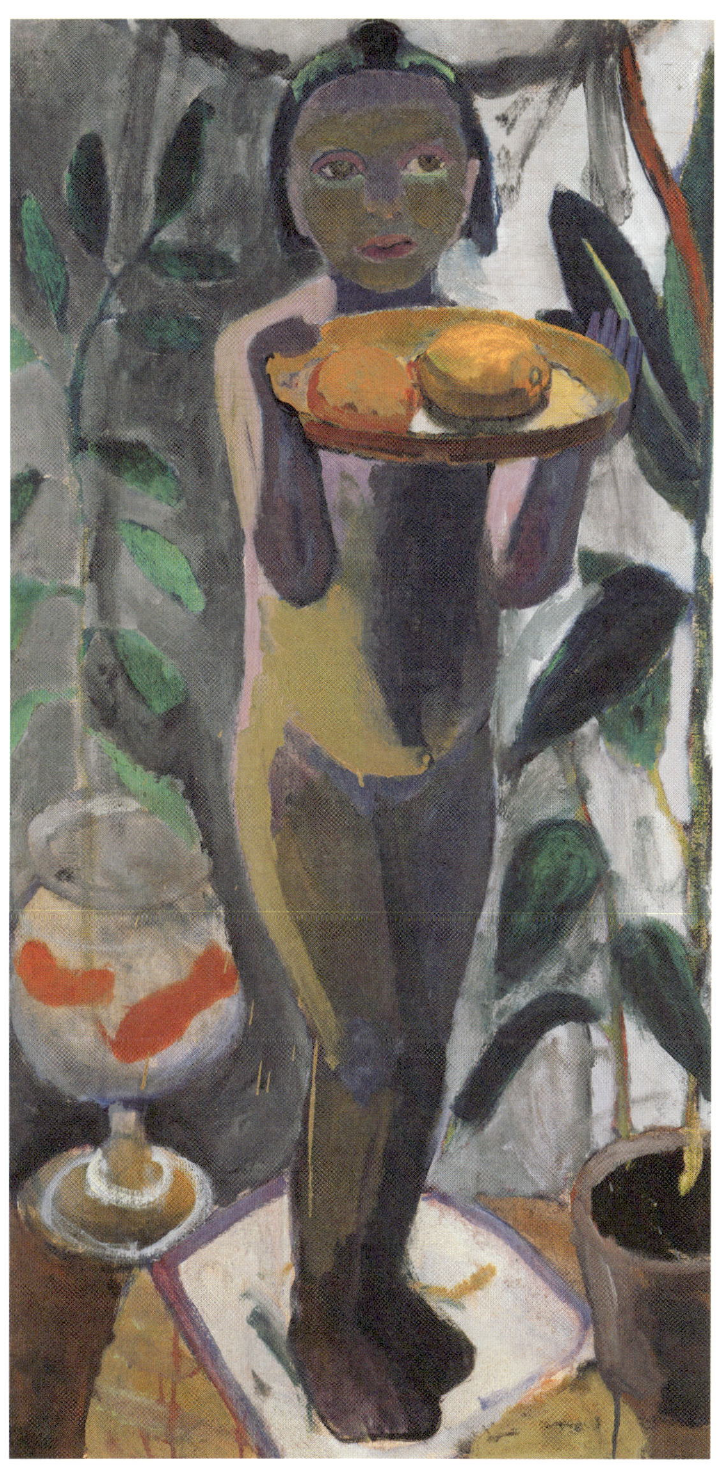

intrinsic drama, which is further intensified by the dark, flatly painted hand. Both pictures have a staged ritual content.

However, Modersohn-Becker's figures and backgrounds did not come from Tahiti or straight from Gauguin. She took figures and backgrounds from her own artistic experience and then combined them in the scene. The large *Standing Child Nude with Goldfish Bowl* (ill. 81) is an example of her gift for bringing different experiences together in a new structure. Presented in a narrow, vertical format, the painting shows a dark-skinned child holding a bowl of fruit. The composition is anchored on each side by plants that are nearly as tall as the picture, and to the left by a bowl with red goldfish. This arrangement tightens up the structure, making the composition clearer: the figure, the background with plants and goldfish bowl, and the gift come from different worlds. The hint of a curtain in the background emphasizes the staged character of the scene; the small mat on which the figure is standing provides a setting and enhances the ritual effect. In combining these elements, Modersohn-Becker developed her own kind of grandeur: strange, melancholy and sacrosanct.

In nearly all the late pictures, the main figure is standing or resting on a floor covering of this type. The art historian and curator Karin Schick has studied the genesis of this motif in Modersohn-Becker's work and concluded that, when something was laid underneath the figures, this formed a base, a reserved area, a sort of protective field. It acted as a 'place to live', a place for a metaphorical, ritual life outside the real world, a separate, closed pictorial world.[63] A similar backdrop highlighting the figure can be seen in Pierre Puvis de Chavannes's 1872 work *Hope* (ill. 84). The nude female figure is sitting on a white cloth, against a landscape that has been devastated by war, and holds a twig – a symbol of hope – in her extended left hand. Gauguin took a reproduction of this picture to the Marquesas Islands

            CHAPTER 6

and incorporated it into his 1901 still-life *Sunflowers with Puvis de Chavannes's Hope.* The later work was subsequently acquired for the Fayet collection and was on show at the Gauguin retrospective at the Salon d'Automne in 1906, indicating that the influence of Puvis de Chavannes's original motif continued to be felt.

Just as Modersohn-Becker made a point of incorporating fruit and flowers into her self-portraits in a deliberate gesture, raising questions over their function, so too in the staged arrangements of figures she draws attention to these elements. Similar displays of fruit, flowers or objects can be found in the work of Marées, Gauguin and Picasso. Around the turn of the century there was an attempt to go beyond the mere depiction of figures, to emphasize the figure and the setting via presentational means, without using familiar or mythological tropes. For Modersohn-Becker, these presentational means elevated the natural and the familiar into a different sphere and gave the figures a ritual power. By 1919 Gustav Pauli was already talking about 'a certain hieratic solemnity of the gesture' in Modersohn-Becker's work.[64]

Modersohn-Becker's figures are often wearing garlands of flowers, recalling Picasso's *Boy with a Pipe* (ill. 85) of 1905. Picasso added the two bouquets of flowers in the background and the garland of roses on the boy's head a month after painting the young working-class Parisian. The curator Raphaël Bouvier wrote that, by doing so, he had turned a normal boy with a pipe into a timeless, almost ritual figure with an ethereal appearance.[65] In Modersohn-Becker's work too, an everyday scene is embellished and becomes something extraordinary, the figure transported into a different, poetic world. *Kneeling Nude Girl with Stork* (ill. 83) and *Seated Nude Girl with Flower Vases* (ill. 86), of 1906–7, are two examples. The figures are kneeling or sitting on a base of some kind, wearing a bracelet, a necklace and a garland of flowers, and holding flowers or a sprig of foliage. The scene appears to be set against a natural background (outside), but at the same time looks like an interior (the red curtain in *Seated Nude Girl with Flower Vases*, for example) and must therefore have a symbolic meaning. The positioning of the seated figure on a small mound is reminiscent of Puvis de Chavannes, and she is surrounded with vases full of flowers and an empty bowl. Meanwhile, lemons and oranges are laid out next to the kneeling figure and in the background is a stork (Otto Modersohn's studio was decorated with stuffed birds like this).

Motifs from various contexts and with different connotations have been brought together to create a meaningful new whole. Karin Schick wrote that, in her paintings of nude girls, Modersohn-Becker consistently shaped spaces according to her own ideas and rules, and she gave the bare bodies, young souls and free spirits those things she considered most essential: nature, culture, food, protection and space. Whereas Cézanne in his landscapes looked for harmony in parallel with nature, in her portraits Modersohn-Becker – to quote Schick – 'portrayed a world parallel to reality'.[66]

Children as Personifications

Certainly the question arises as to why, when Modersohn-Becker was not painting portraits or self-portraits, she moved children to the centre of her pictorial world, in the midst of this ambitious plan to create a world parallel to reality. Could this be a paradigm shift, since that world was being created by a self-confident female artist and not a man?

 CHAPTER 6

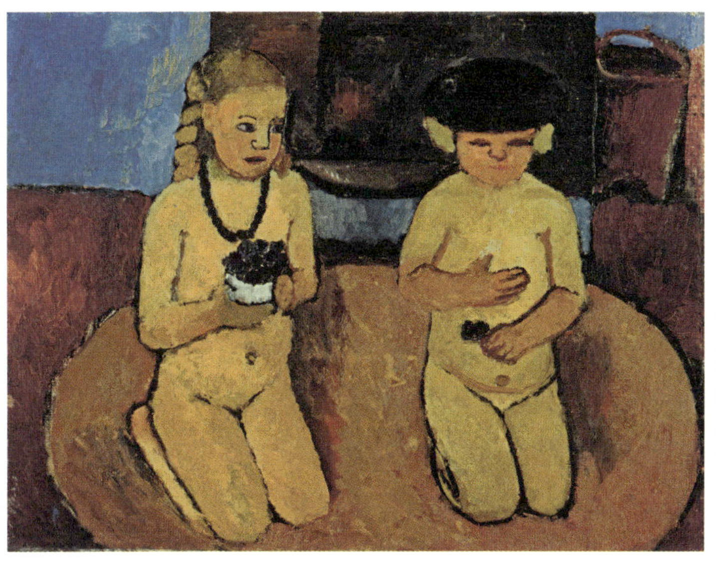

82 *Two Kneeling Nude Girls*, 1906–7

Through the centuries, the female form has been eroticized in the work of male artists. Modersohn-Becker took a different approach. She worked with both male and female subjects when she was studying life drawing. She filled many of her pictures with children and old people. Unlike some of her male counterparts, such as Edvard Munch and Max Beckmann, for whom the erotic formed an important part of their work, Modersohn-Becker was interested in subjects whom she saw as closer to nature. In children she saw a vision of the future, a life that was only just beginning. Children epitomized the promise of what was to come. Over time, the children in Modersohn-Becker's paintings became increasingly symbolic. The naked state of the children in the late paintings is in harmony with nature, but also reflects a ritualistic origin. Ultimately, the subjects of paintings such as *Kneeling Nude Girl with Stork* and *Seated Nude*

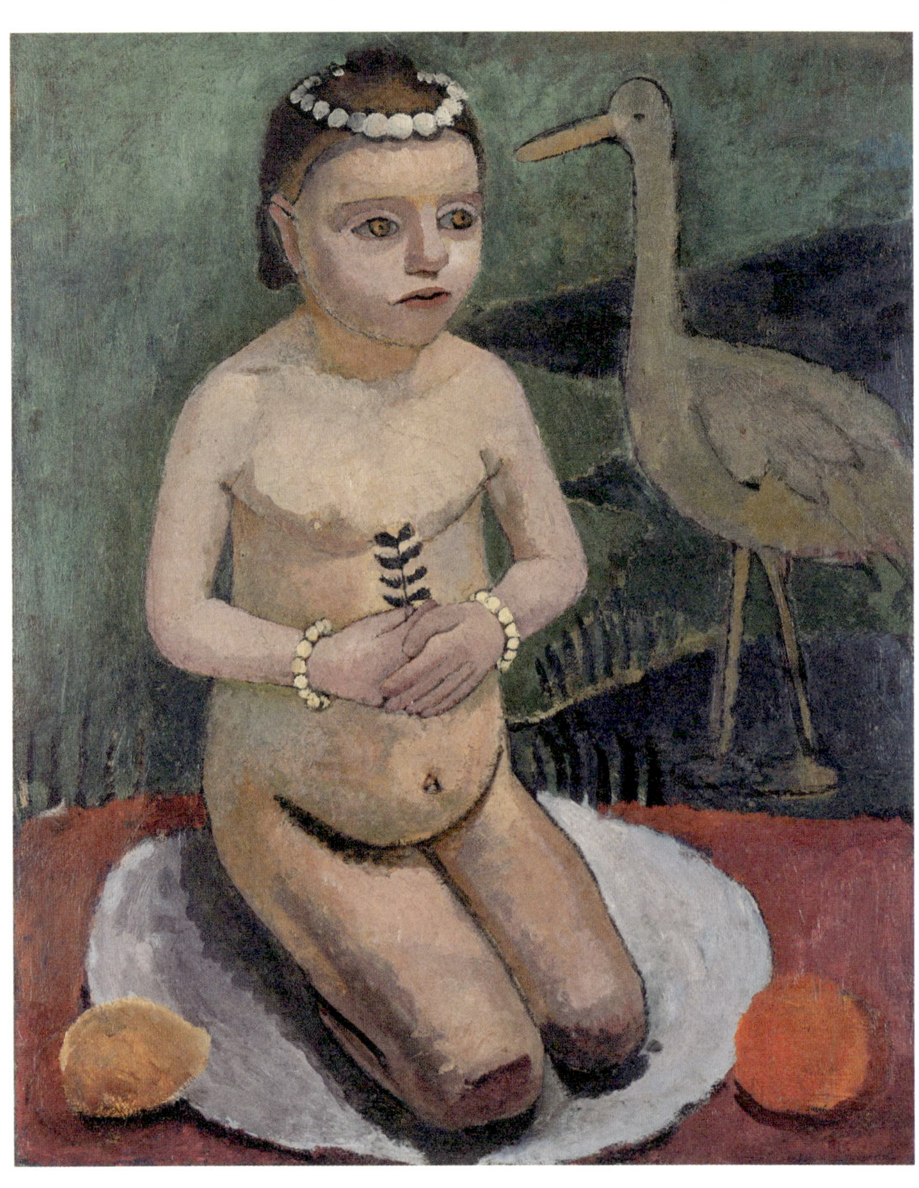

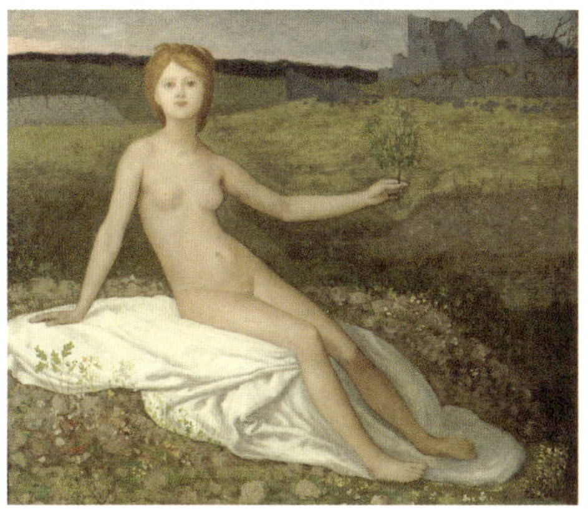

Girl with Flower Vases, surrounded by props – garland, necklace, flowers, fruit – that grant them an air of nobility, personify the hope of a better world in harmony with nature and ritual, reflecting Modersohn-Becker's belief in 'a rich, innovative art that thinks only of the future'. For her, they represented an evolving art of the future in which natural and ritual elements were combined in an idyllic world in idealized human images. At the same time, through these paintings, she was creating her own iconography.

Parallel Worlds

Creating a world parallel to reality was a truly ambitious plan. It required an artistic concept; it required an idea of content that supported and materialized that world; and it required an artistic process to build that new world.

Modersohn-Becker had sketched out an artistic concept as early as 1901, while visiting the Hans von Marées collection in Schleissheim. She and her husband were 'deeply impressed by this extraordinary person'. She explained why: 'He has managed to remain in his own world all through his life.' That was 'the only thing I want for myself and my husband'. Marées was an integral part of the world he had created for himself. The unique imagery with which he sought to give his works 'general legitimacy and meaning',[67] and which so fascinated

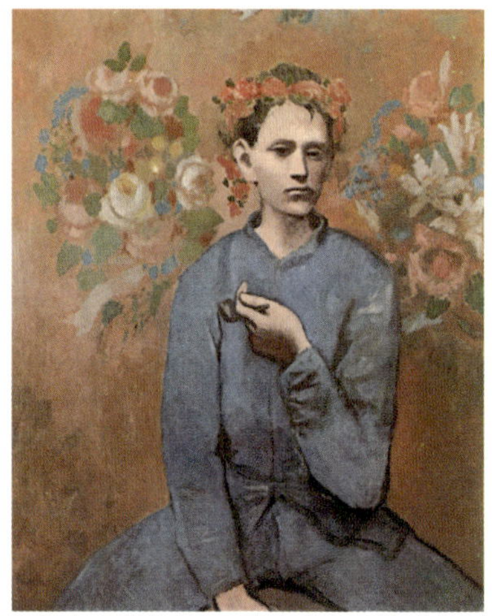

85 Pablo Picasso, *Boy with a Pipe*,
autumn 1905

                    CHAPTER 6

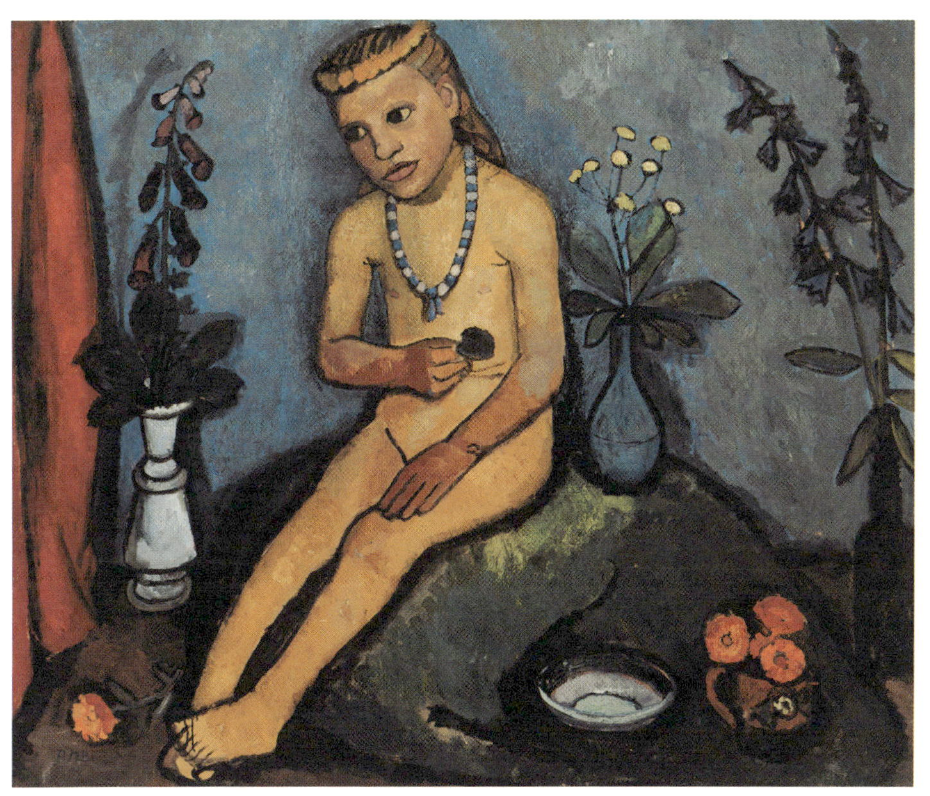

86 *Seated Nude Girl with Flower Vases, 1906–7*

Modersohn-Becker, was based on statuesque figures, contemporary links to classical themes, rigorous form, dark tones and a pervasive mood of melancholy.

Gauguin also created his own pictorial world when he lived in Tahiti and the Marquesas. He mixed Polynesian figures and myths with a knowledge of ethnographic photographs and memories of European works of art. He used, and was inspired by, reproductions of works of art from many different cultures. Gauguin used a syncretic approach, interweaving elements from different cultures to conjure up a paradise lost: an idyll in a world that he saw as debased. Modersohn-Becker must also have been attracted by the compelling notion of a cohesive, unspoiled world parallel to reality.

The same is true of Puvis de Chavannes. Although not generally seen as particularly innovative, he was a strong influence on many artists of the period – from Van Gogh to Picasso. Born in 1824, in the generation between Courbet and Manet, he chose his own path, going against the dominant trends in art. His statuesque, introspective figures stand completely motionless in arcadian fields. When Modersohn-Becker visited a number of Paris art dealers in February 1900, she wrote: 'There is much beauty and depth in Puvis de Chavannes. He is someone who suddenly stands quite alone among others.'

Vincent van Gogh's admiration for Puvis de Chavannes reflects the artistic issues of the period and is also interesting in relation to Modersohn-Becker. In 1890, Van Gogh had travelled from Saint-Rémy, in the south of France, to Auvers-sur-Oise, just north of Paris, stopping over in the French capital. There, he had come across Puvis de Chavannes's *Inter artes et naturam* (1890, ill. 87), in the Salon du Champ-de-Mars. He was deeply impressed by the programmatic title and made a special sketch of the painting for his sister Willemien. As Van Gogh wrote to his sister, 'The figures are dressed in bright colours and one

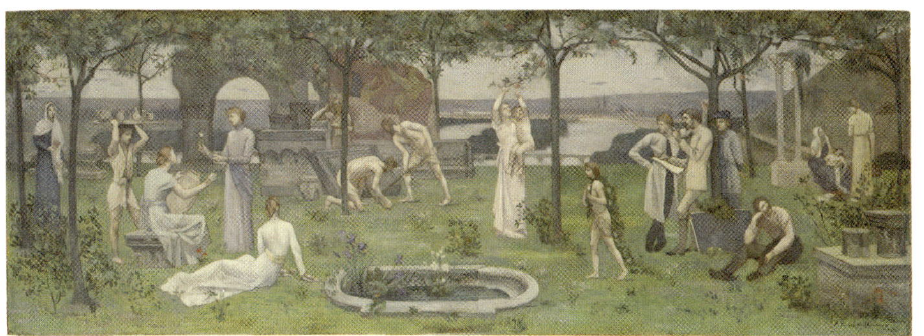

87 Pierre Puvis de Chavannes, *Inter artes et naturam*, 1890

doesn't know if they're costumes from now or clothes from antiquity.' Moved by the experience, he added that you felt as if you were present 'at an inevitable but benevolent rebirth of all things that one might have believed in, that one might have desired, a strange and happy meeting of the very distant days of antiquity with raw modernity'.[68] He analysed the painting further in another letter: it seemed 'to point to a strange and fateful encounter between an ancient world long ago and pure modernity'. Van Gogh saw a unique opportunity in that mixture of traditional and modern: 'I can see a distant possibility of a new kind of painting.'[69]

It may also have been the closed world in Puvis's work, with its mixture of classical and modern, that appealed to Modersohn-Becker, but, above all – in her conviction that art needed to be forward-looking to succeed – she was undoubtedly drawn to the personal vision of the future that it embodied.

Modersohn-Becker did not record every single meaningful experience of art in her letters and journals. For example, it was not the artist but her friend Clara Rilke-Westhoff who mentioned Modersohn-Becker seeing Cézanne's work at the gallery of the art dealer Vollard.[70] Nor did she make any significant statements or comments about Gauguin's work, despite knowing a great deal about it, partly from reading scholarly essays. We also know nothing about her impressions when she visited Henri Rousseau's studio with Bernhard Hoetger and his wife in the summer of 1906, although, as has been mentioned (see p. 154), clear parallels can be drawn in works such as *Self-Portrait as a Half-Length Nude with Amber Necklace I* (ill. 76), in which the untamed vegetation in the background is reminiscent of Rousseau.

Above all, Modersohn-Becker must have found confirmation of her own artistic approach through the likes of Marées, with his dreamlike depictions of timeless idylls, and Rousseau, whose jungle paintings are a work of imagination. According to Werner Spies, Rousseau 'found the wildness of foreign countries only at Universal Exhibitions in Paris, on visits to the zoo, in the urban jungle. He never went further than the greenhouses at the botanical gardens.' Rousseau drew inspiration from many different sources, including quotations from popular publications and works of art that he admired, to present a mysterious world of his own creation. As Spies goes on to say, the influences merged into each other 'because Rousseau wanted to produce plausible images – images in which the various sources were undetectable'.[71] These self-contained pictorial worlds expressed a desire that is also perceptible in Modersohn-Becker's late work to counteract the fragmentation in modern art.

What about the concept that Modersohn-Becker's paintings were designed to express? Marées, Gauguin, Puvis de Chavannes and Rousseau tried to combat the specialization associated with Impressionism and its rejection of ideas, and to connect with the varied experience of reality in classical art by creating rounded, complete pictorial worlds. What Modersohn-Becker created in the Paris works of 1906–7 is her own version of that approach.

CHAPTER 6

That answers the question of the artistic process by which that new world is to be created in Paula Modersohn-Becker's late works. As with Gauguin, Puvis and Rousseau, the syncretic process relies on a combination of visual elements from nature and art. However, those elements are not in a foreign environment like Gauguin's, or a mythological idyllic setting as with Puvis, or in an artistic wilderness like Rousseau's. Instead, the attributes and additions give her visual world a mysteriously ritual, exaggerated reality and, therefore, a very similar validity that is timeless.

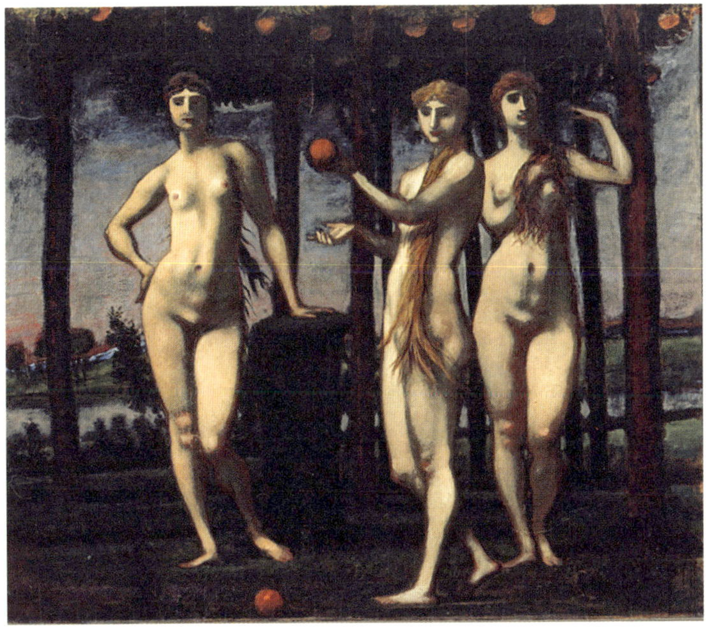

88 Hans von Marées, *The Hesperides II/Centre Panel*, 1884–87

World Art in the Studio

The syncretic process of picture-making no longer took place in nature but in the artist's studio. Modersohn-Becker was continually adding to her varied collection of pictures. The studio was soon full of reproductions that she had brought back from her travels. As well as copies of the mummy portraits from Fayum (ill. 61) and a painting by Raphael, according to Otto Modersohn his wife's collection of pictures included antique works, Persian miniatures from the Musée Guimet in Paris, reliefs at the Buddhist temple in Borobudur in Java (Gauguin had also taken photos of the same temple to the South Pacific), and reproductions from every period in art history, from Giotto, Cranach and El Greco to Gauguin, Van Gogh, Cézanne and Denis, as well as 'hundreds of postcards'.[72]

By amassing a collection of visual sources of inspiration from different cultures, Modersohn-Becker brought the art world into her studio and could draw on it at any time, not just for specific motifs but to tap into the spirit and meaning of the works she most admired. In the words of her friend, the painter Ottilie Reylaender, she needed 'contact, friction' with the work of other artists and their ideas.[73]

As Marion Ackermann has pointed out, Modersohn-Becker anticipated ideas that were only set out several years after her death, in the Blaue Reiter almanac of 1912.[74] Kandinsky and Marc published reproductions of works from many periods and cultures, juxtaposed with equal status and without the common distinction between high art and folk or tribal art. These images did not share superficial formal or stylistic relationships, but instead a varied range of cultural references to the present.

Modersohn-Becker collected pictures from other periods and worlds for just the same reason.

In the summer of 1907, in a letter to Bernhard Hoetger, Modersohn-Becker wrote that she hoped he would understand the work she did in Paris in 1906–7 was 'a reaction to a restless and superficial period and an effort to create a simple, grand impression'. In other words, her artistic concepts are not simply a synthesis of many artistic experiences; they are also direct responses to reality. The 'simple, grand impression' that Modersohn-Becker sought to create with these works was a stabilizing response to the fragmentation of the world and the superficiality of the age.

Ideas for Future Pictures?

During this final period in Paris, Modersohn-Becker also produced a small series of quite remarkable drawings. In character and function, they are very different from the systematic compositions of 1898 and 1899 (ills 3–7), the sketches she made of artworks in 1903 (ills 26–28) and the quick Paris sketches from 1905 (ills 30–32). There are no parallels in either German or French art, and one wonders about the impetus for these works and her intention – and where the ideas came from.

Only once (that we know of) did Modersohn-Becker express admiration for drawings by another artist at some length. When Rilke arranged for her to go to Auguste Rodin's studio at the beginning of March 1903, during her second stay in Paris, she described 'many, many wonderful things there'. As she was leaving, she asked the artist whether she could come to his house and studio in Meudon near Paris, where Rodin showed her numerous folders of drawings. She was deeply impressed: 'For me, these remarkable dreams of form that he throws onto the paper are the most notable aspect of his art.' She was particularly fascinated by his use of humble media, saying: 'He draws with a pencil and then colours in with extraordinary, passionate watercolours'. These pages were marked by genius 'and a disregard for convention'. Increasingly enthusiastic in her description, she uses 'extraordinary' twice – her favourite adjective for anything she found aesthetically unusual, different or even radical. She obviously admired Rodin's drawings a great deal, describing them with a term more often used for abstract art, 'dreams of form' (a term with which she may well have metaphorically captured the essence of the drawings).

Rodin's drawings were so radical that they were a source of controversy. In Germany, for example, they were notably disapproved of by the Wilhelmian authorities. In 1906 Harry Graf Kessler had to resign as director of the Grand Ducal Museum of Arts and Crafts in Weimar because of an exhibition of Rodin's drawings that was considered obscene. According to the

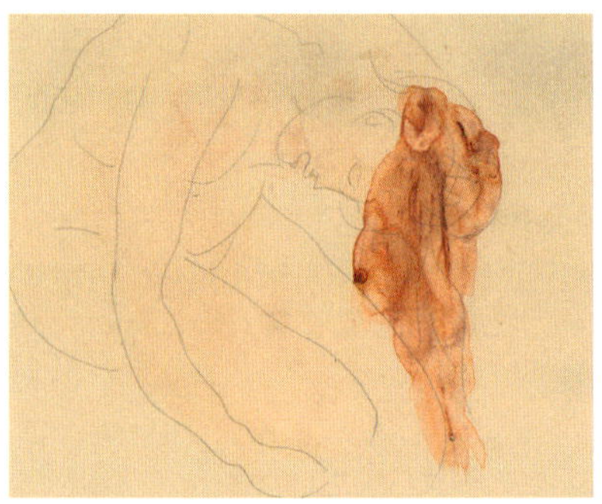

89 Auguste Rodin, *Female Nude
Bending Over with Hair Hanging Down*,
pencil and watercolour, *c.* 1900

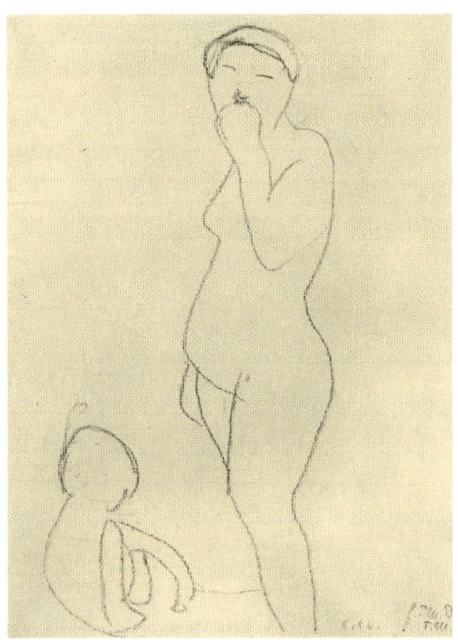

90 *Female Nude Standing with Child Sitting
on the Ground*, charcoal, May 1906

Weimarische Landeszeitung newspaper, 'women and daughters'
needed to be warned against such 'disgusting drawings': 'Shame
on their creator.'[75] However, Rodin's drawings were often praised
by German art critics as works of genius. At an exhibition in
Berlin in 1903, Emil Heilbutt wrote that they revealed 'a master
who can draw with his eyes shut'.[76] In one of the most consistent
drawings, *Female Nude Bending Over with Hair Hanging Down*
(ill. 89), a long, appropriately delicate pencil line traces the contours of a naked female figure. Rodin gives only a faint indication
of features such as breasts, bottom and legs. The rust-red hair
becomes a confusingly abstract foreign body, the artist's use of
watercolour introducing a second layer to the picture. The most
striking and, for Modersohn-Becker, probably the most

fascinating aspect of the drawing is the simplicity of the thin line that is nonetheless so expressive that it defines the whole posture of the body.

In her drawings of 1898–99, 1903 and 1905, Modersohn-Becker had already shown an interest in body postures and positions by placing an emphasis on the contours of the body rather than the details. She continued her systematic approach with the drawings of 1906–7, which have to be looked at in relation to Rodin's watercolour drawings. However, Modersohn-Becker worked in charcoal rather than pencil, which makes a significant difference. Charcoal is bolder and can suggest physicality with very few lines. The mere outline dominates. The lines are less sensitive than Rodin's, but firmly and quickly drawn. They do not differentiate further; detail is kept to a minimum. Individual features are not shown; we see only general postures and arrangements – a girl with flowers on a hill, a female nude with a seated child, a child with dog, a child in a hood (who also appeared in one of the Paris sketches) with a dog – executed with the most economical use of artistic means. When, in December 1902, Modersohn-Becker criticized Mackensen's portrayal of people as too generic, she added: 'Anyone who could, should write them in runic script.' Even at this early stage she was thinking of abbreviation, of ciphers that suggest but do not illustrate in detail. Charcoal enabled her to apply this principle to her own drawings while still creating a vivid impression.

As can be seen from a comparison between *Seated Nude Girl with Dog* (1906, ill. 91) and *Seated Nude Girl with Flower Vases* (1906–7, ill. 86), which was painted from the sketch, these ciphers recorded observations and suggested ideas. They were preparatory work for possible paintings. In this respect, the drawings differ from Rodin's, which were intended to stand alone. Modersohn-Becker had a different way of

CHAPTER 6

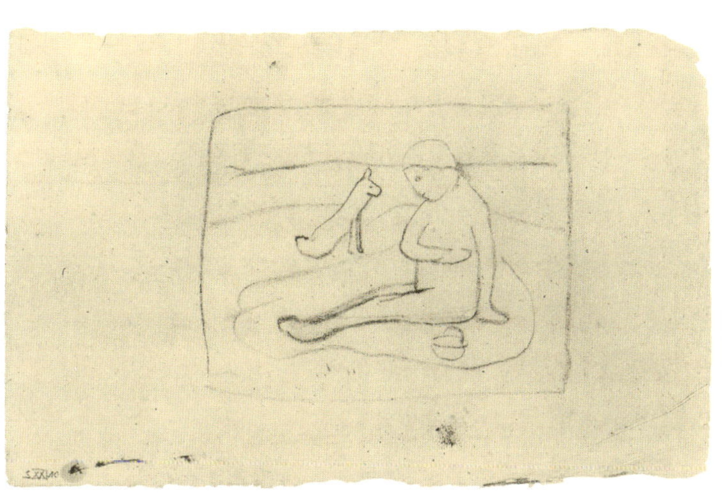

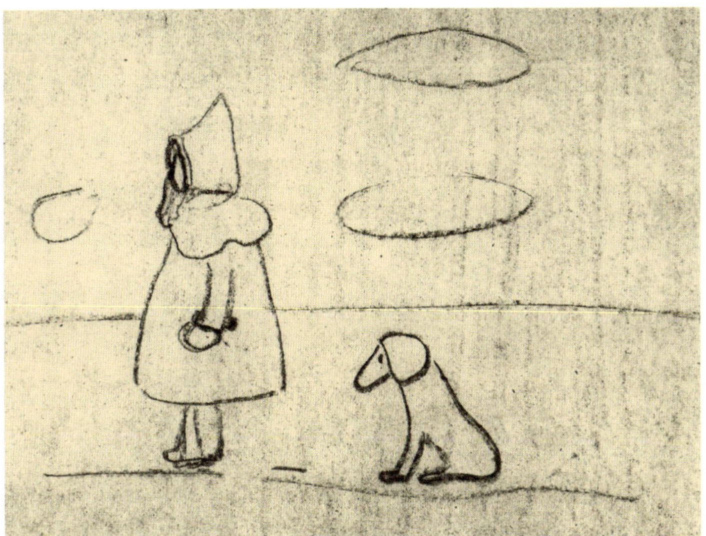

91 Compositional study: *Seated Nude Girl with Dog*,
charcoal, 1906

92 *Child in Hood with Dog*, charcoal, *c.* 1906

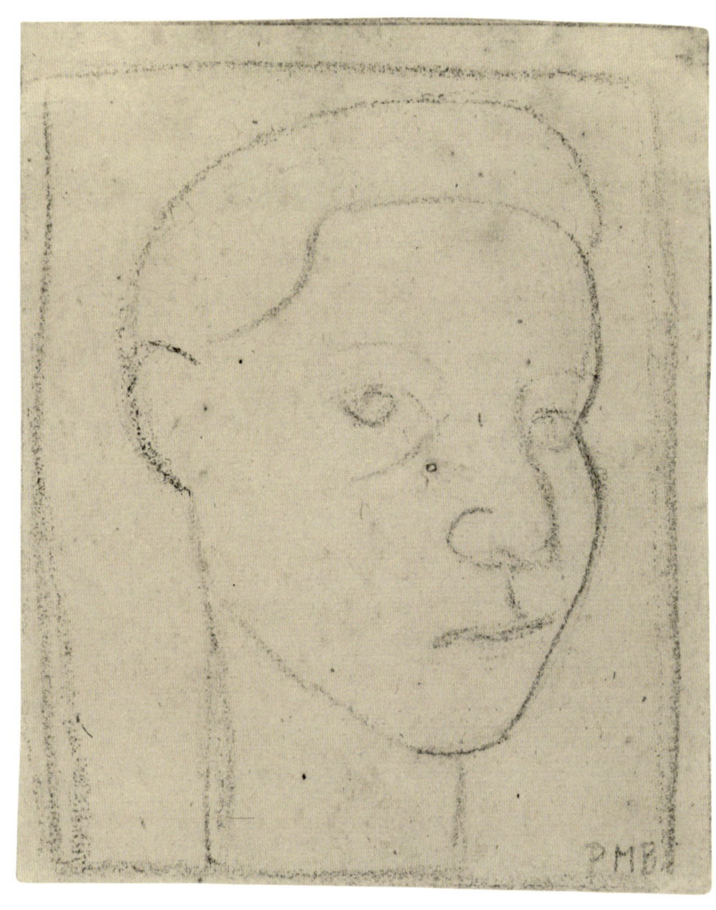

93 Compositional study: *Head of a Woman*, charcoal, 1906

working. She sketched ideas, concepts that referred briefly and in the most basic manner to the reality before her as well as to the more complex picture that was yet to be created. The staged arrangements of 1906–7 already point to a possible way forward.

The question arises as to whether Modersohn-Becker's drawings, if one leaves aside her early academic studies, were always intended as a source of ideas for future paintings. From the drawings we have already discussed – those of 1898 and 1899 (in which she tried out different compositions), 1903 (which she used to explore possible arrangements of figures and identify tried-and-tested pictorial means) and 1905 (which were preparatory works or even substitutes for paintings) – it would certainly appear so. Indeed, Modersohn-Becker later drew on various earlier sketches – for instance, drawings of old people in a seated position – reusing what she had already done and adapting it. Why else would she have taken the Worpswede sketchbooks to Paris with her, since, unlike oil paintings, they could not be reworked or altered?[77] Therefore, it can be assumed that, for Modersohn-Becker, drawing was a means of working up ideas that could be used in further work: to shape the future she so longed for in modern art.

1907: *Intoxicating, Powerful Colour*

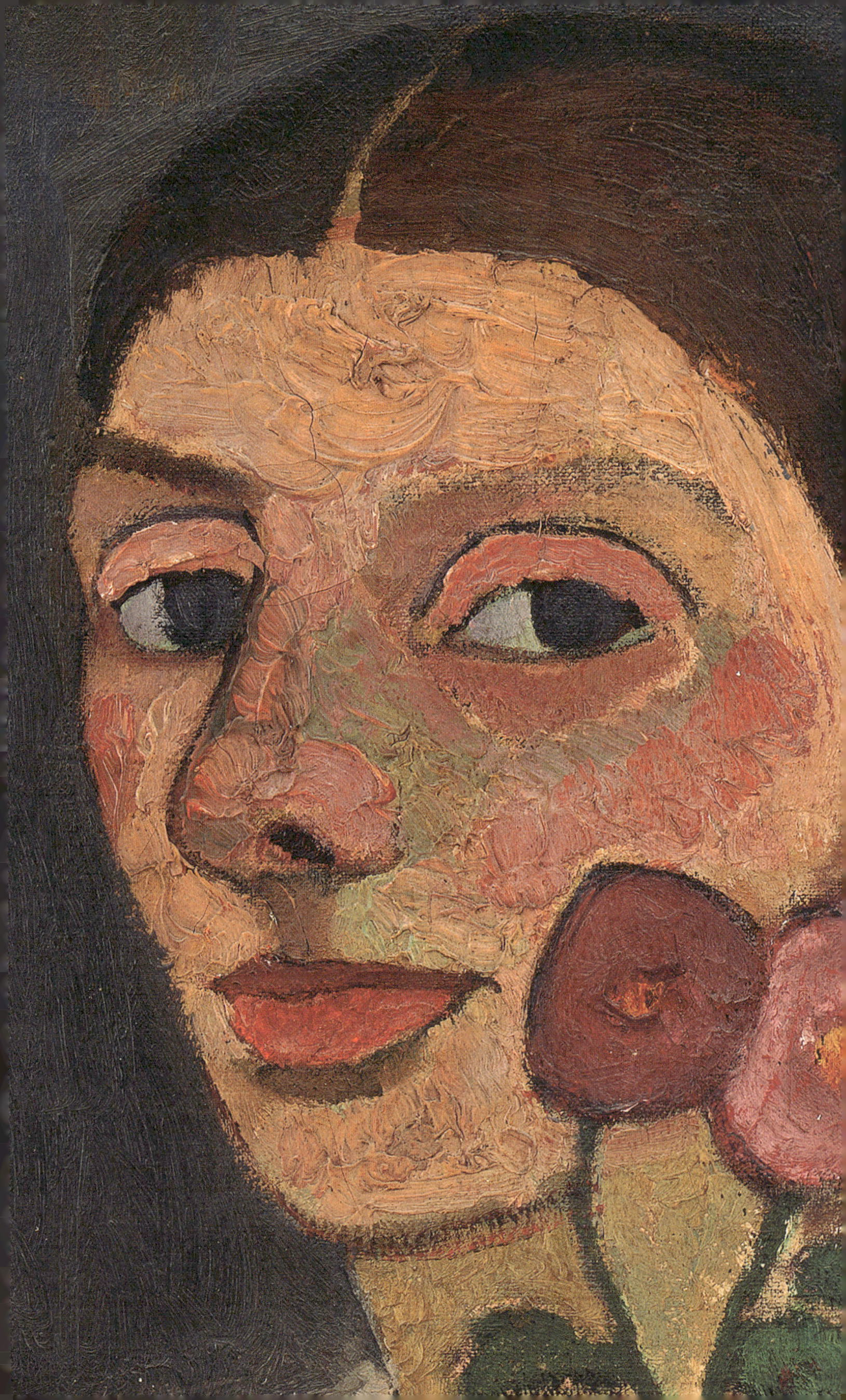

Retreat

At the end of March 1907, Paula Modersohn-Becker, now pregnant, returned to Worpswede with her husband. She was looking for a peaceful environment in which to work, and this, she now thought, she was most likely to find in the long term with Otto Modersohn – with the proviso of a 31-year-old: 'If only you stay healthy and do not die too soon.' Enriched by the stimulus in Paris from classical, culturally diverse and new art, and fortified by the boost to her creativity, she retreated to work on developing her art.

As a peaceful place to work, Worpswede was the obvious choice for practical rather than artistic reasons. However, the place had changed a great deal. The original artists' colony no longer existed. Heinrich Vogeler had worked to keep it together, but he now had quite different ambitions. Fritz Overbeck had moved away. Worpswede was no longer a close-knit artistic community; it was simply a place to live. According to Hoetger, Modersohn-Becker still loved the people there, 'but she lived and acted alone and remained alone'.[78] She herself felt that, as an

Detail of ill. 99

artist, you 'mostly live completely on your own', a sentiment echoed by her sister Herma: 'generally this all happened in incredible isolation'.[79]

Before returning to Worpswede, she had been to see Auguste Pellerin's important Cézanne collection in Neuilly. She was most fascinated by the early works, which at the time were not greatly admired. A few weeks before she was due to give birth, she was reminded of Cézanne – who had died in 1906 – and Paris by a major retrospective of his work at the Salon d'Automne. 'If it was not absolutely necessary for me to be here now, I would have to be in Paris'; 'I really wanted to go to Paris for a week. There are 56 Cézannes on show there!'

In a letter to Clara Rilke-Westhoff from the same period, Modersohn-Becker recalls the time they had both discovered Cézanne – then virtually unknown – at Vollard's in 1900: 'how he is one of the three or four powerful artists who have affected me like a thunderstorm, like a great event'. This first encounter with Cézanne had been a revelation to her, giving her an insight into what art could mean in the modern world, outside the confines of her own country. It is easy to imagine that the decision to make Paris the centre of her life and art could be traced back to that crucial event.

In Worpswede, Modersohn-Becker threw herself into her work. But her words to Otto – with her wish to 'not die too soon' – have a poignancy in light of her own fate. By the end of 1907, she was dead.

94 *Elsbeth between Tiger Lilies*, 1907

                 CHAPTER 7

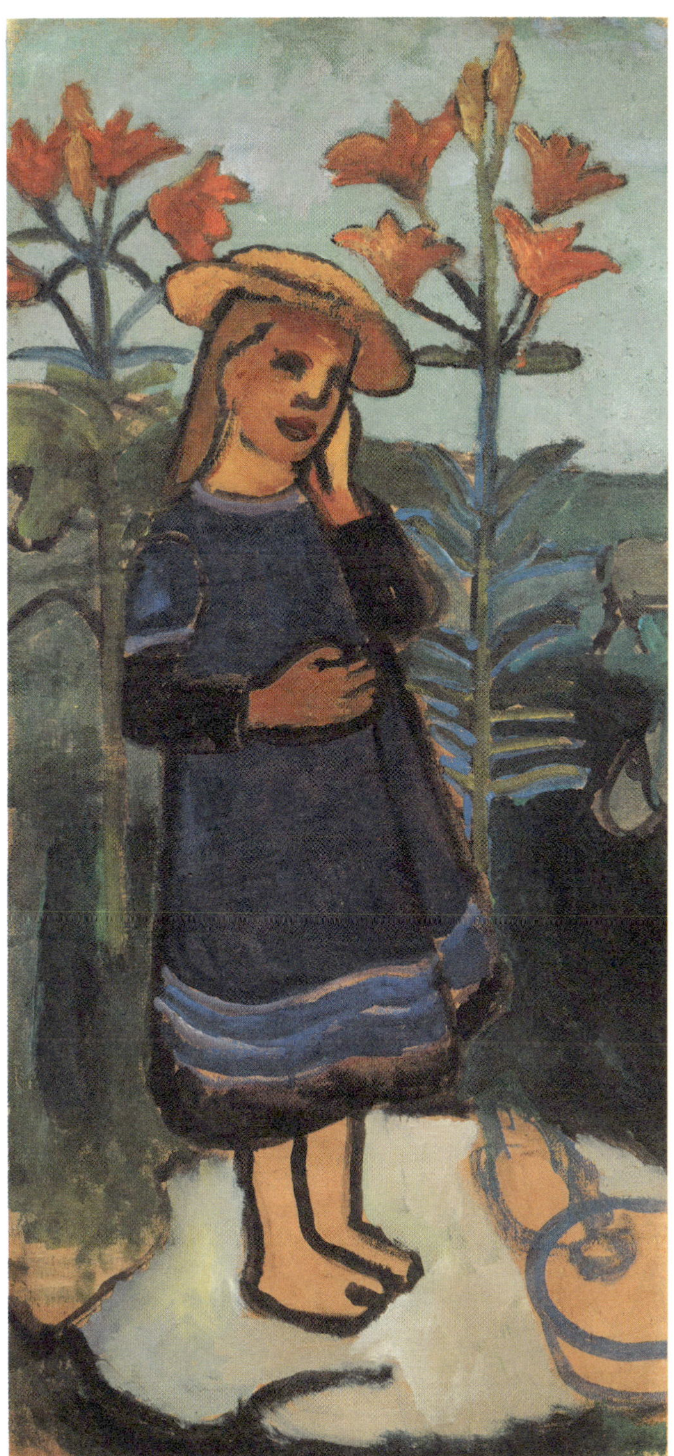

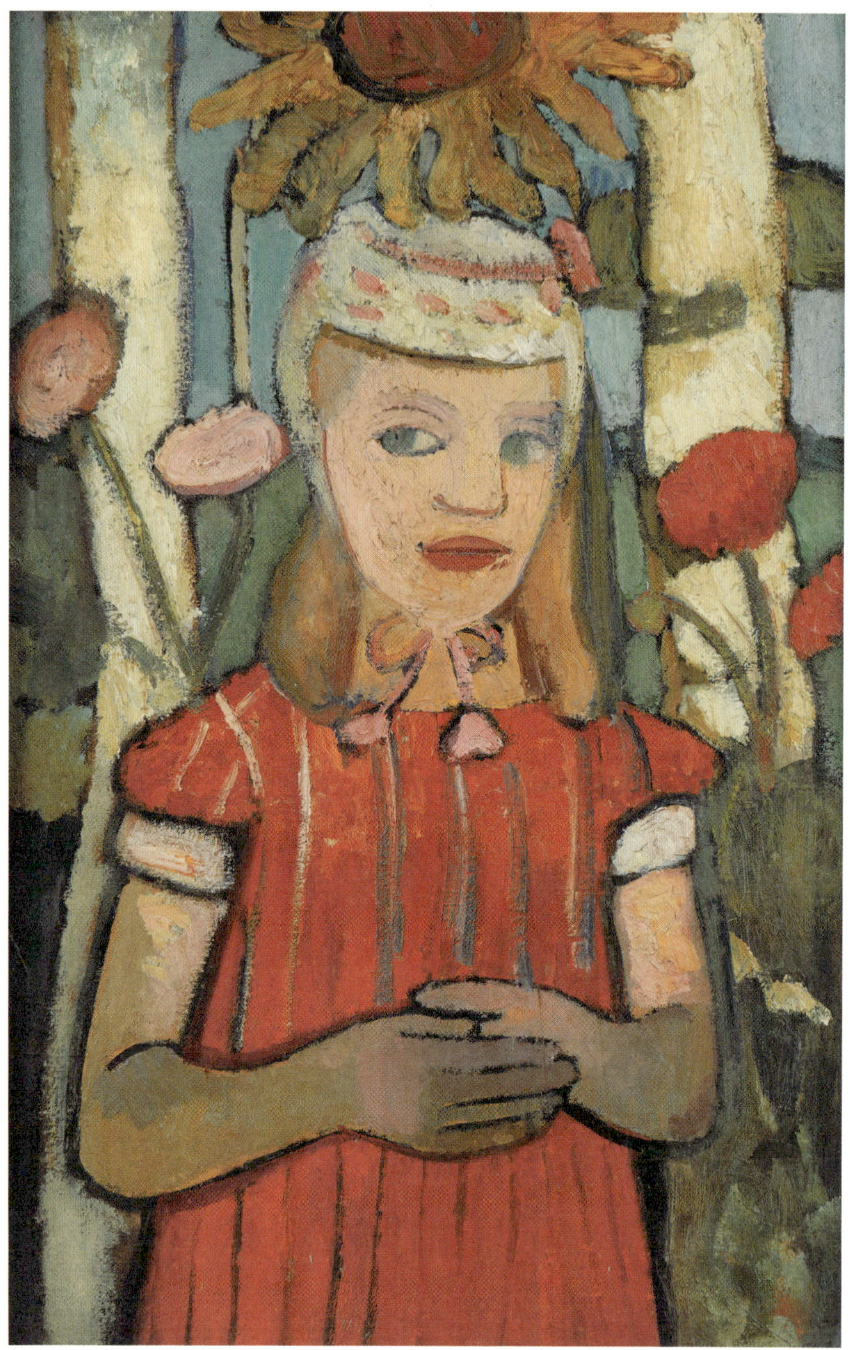

Full of Life

During this period, Modersohn-Becker's work entered a new phase. In March 1906, while she was still in Paris, she had taken a surprising decision: 'My paintings look dark and muddy here. I need to use much purer colours.' In the summer of 1907, a few months before her death, she added that the work she had done in Paris now looked to her 'too cool and too lonely and empty'. She thought that, in order to be complete, the archetypal compositions and the strange mask-like faces obviously needed to be contemporary, natural, filled with life. That was, to use her own words from a journal entry in December 1902, 'the state of being'.

In a letter to Bernhard Hoetger in the summer of 1907, she told him that she was planning fresh experiments and a new departure. She now wanted the colours to be 'intoxicating, full, exciting and powerful'. Picasso's and Modersohn-Becker's paths might have crossed for a little while, but at this point they diverged completely. While Picasso worked on developing the simplification of colour, the crystalline flat shapes and the fragmentation that characterized his Cubist style, Modersohn-Becker relied on bolder colours, the fullness and power of expression, and most crucially of all the qualities that she considered the essence of her figures.

Two pictures, *Elsbeth between Tiger Lilies* (ill. 94) and *Girl in Red Dress with a Sunflower* (ill. 95), were part of this new plan. On a superficial level, the basic composition of a child surrounded by flowers appears to be a continuation of the

95 *Girl in Red Dress with a Sunflower,* 1907

paintings she did in Paris. However, in these later works the formal elements are simplified. The children are no longer in a ritual setting, and the flowers (in the case of ill. 94) or tree trunks and flowers (ill. 95) are much more prominent, defining the scene. In *Elsbeth between Tiger Lilies,* the plants tower above the girl like higher authorities. In *Girl in Red Dress with a Sunflower,* they crowd around the child possessively, encroaching into her space: the leaves of the tall sunflower extend over the girl's cap.

Colour now plays a new role. In *Girl in Red Dress with a Sunflower,* the brightness of the flatly applied red tones dominates the scene. The bold use of colour is further accentuated by the strong black contour lines – a device that was also used by Gauguin and Matisse to intensify colours, but that also recalls Modersohn-Becker's late charcoal drawings. Compared with the Paris pictures, the expressive power of the colours and the stylized plants, which are given equal prominence, infuse the paintings with a new sense of life and an intimacy never seen before. These are no longer rapt figures caught on canvas; they are living, breathing people. Nature is exposed and replaces the ritual features. Again, the harmony between nascent beings and natural forms is evoked, as in the early paintings of children, but here the technique is more advanced. The paintings are reminiscent of medieval depictions of the Garden of Eden, a utopia in which humans peacefully coexist with flora and fauna.

A Different World

If these two paintings are seen as the starting point of this new phase, *Old Poorhouse Woman in the Garden with Glass Bottle and Poppies* (ill. 98) is the culmination. Worpswede once again comes to the fore: 'Dreebeen' is the main figure, now monumental, viewed from a slightly low angle, holding a foxglove stem and surrounded by tall red poppies. Towering above the poppies is a thick, upturned glass bottle on a stick. The scene is painted in dark colours against a light sky. The change of scale but, above all, the conceptual weight of the curious central figure, the plants and the glass bottle turn the scene into a symbolic world. Is the old woman, as Gustav Pauli wrote in 1919, reminiscent of a 'mysterious demonic apparition', an 'otherworldly monster'?[80] Or, as Günter Busch put it less dramatically in 1981, has 'the transposition of the old woman into a fantasy world of dreams of reality found magnificent and grotesque expression' in this picture?[81] At any rate, 'Dreebeen' seems to have been transformed into a mythological figure in this picture.

In Worpswede, Modersohn-Becker immersed herself in another world. The strange stories and 'hallucinations' of the poorhouse residents were an opportunity for the artist to elevate a person like 'Dreebeen', whom she found mysterious, to a fantasy figure in a setting that was deliberately constructed and therefore more intense. Monster or grotesque mythical being – which is she? The way the old woman is holding up the foxglove stem like a 'wand' (Pauli) or a sceptre might be a strong hint.

Comparisons have also been drawn between *Old Poorhouse Woman* and two paintings by Van Gogh: *La Berceuse (Woman Rocking a Cradle)* (1889, ill. 97) and *Portrait of Dr Gachet* (1890, ill. 96). Modersohn-Becker saw two versions of *La Berceuse* and

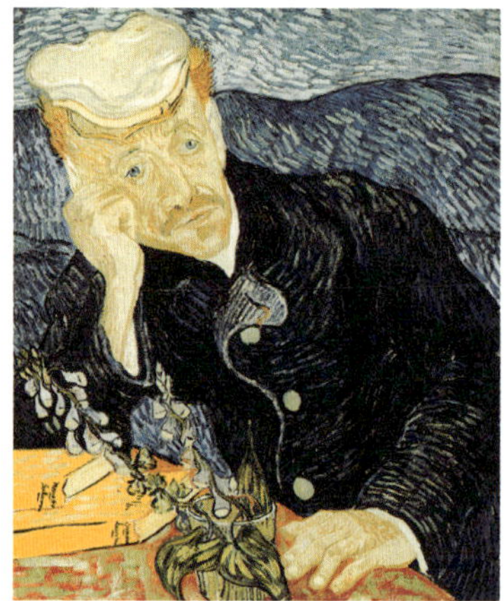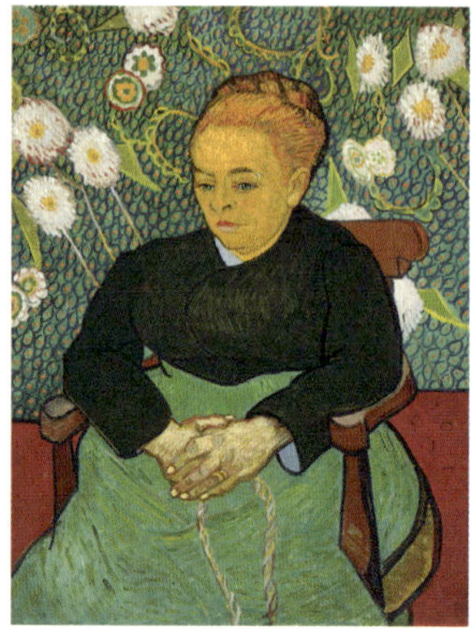

96   Vincent van Gogh, *Portrait of Dr Gachet*, June 1890

97   Vincent van Gogh, *La Berceuse*
(Woman Rocking a Cradle), 1889

OPPOSITE

98   *Old Poorhouse Woman in the Garden with*
Glass Bottle and Poppies, 1907

one of the two versions of *Dr Gachet* in the Van Gogh retrospective at the Salon des Indépendants in 1905, and according to her husband she was particularly impressed by the former.[82] The general arrangement of Modersohn-Becker's painting certainly bears an interesting resemblance to *La Berceuse*, while the foxglove that 'Dreebeen' is holding is a clear reference to the Gachet portrait. In front of Dr Gachet, who is depicted in a melancholy stance, two foxglove stems as drooping and limp as the male figure project into the picture. The foxglove represents the medicine digitalis. As Van Gogh explained to Gauguin in June 1890, he wanted to show 'the deeply sad expression of our time',[83]

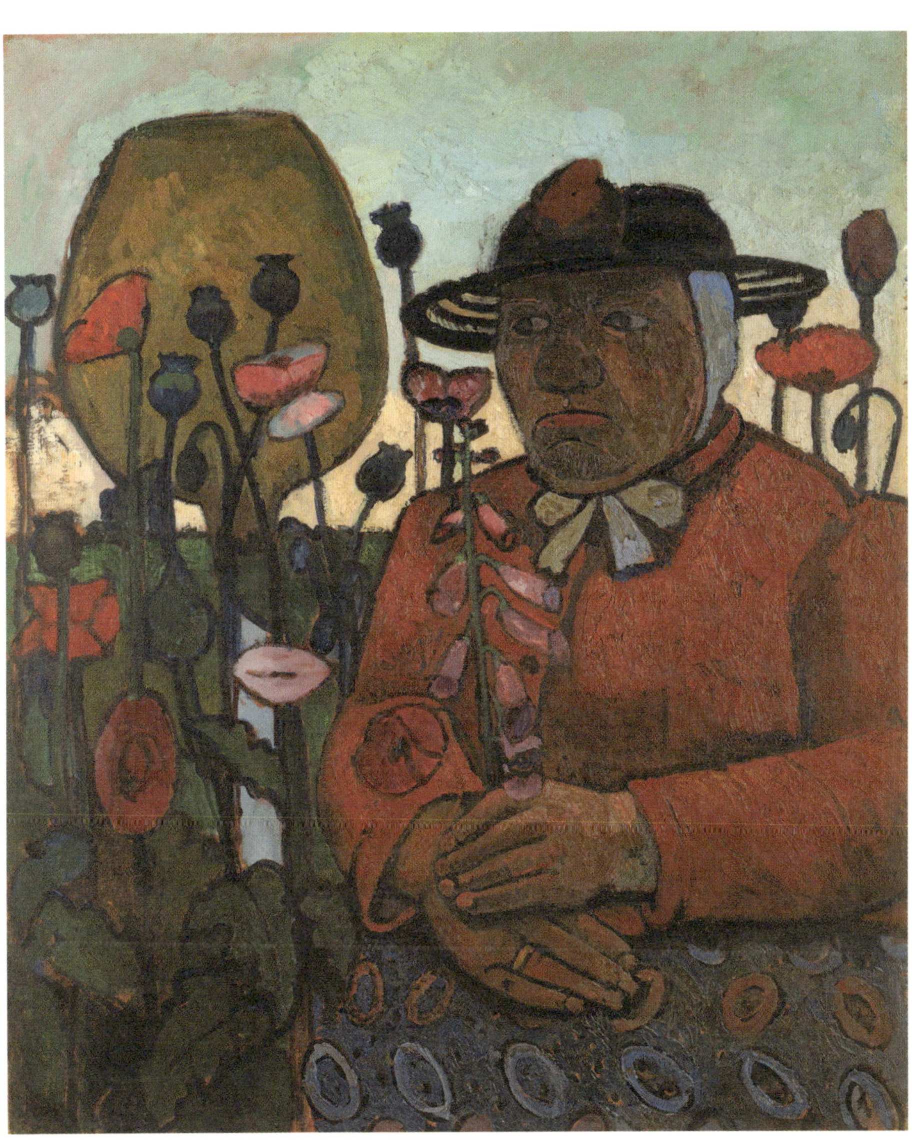

including a symbolic antidote. Modersohn-Becker did not simply adapt the foxglove motif; her painting was a response to Van Gogh's misanthropic view of the times. In complete contrast to the Gachet portrait, her rounded, solid figure looks naturally at peace with herself, holding the medicinal plant high with self-confidence. It is as if 'Dreebeen', here becoming the embodiment of art, has special powers derived from nature. The sturdy stem projects from the surrounding wild vegetation in a deliberate assertion of strength, suggesting an enduring art.

Self-Portrait with Two Flowers in Raised Left Hand (ill. 99), which Modersohn-Becker painted in 1907, shortly before her death, was again part of her plan to lay more emphasis on colour. In the narrow, large-format painting, the figure, her stance, her gaze and the raised flowers in her left hand give the composition an unusually intense unity. The underlying structure is precise. The upper body is shown in three-quarter view; the head is turned slightly and the eyes look directly at the viewer. The curved left hand projects into the picture, holding the flowers at face height, overlapping the lower cheek and at roughly the same level as the lips. The sketchily painted right hand breaks up the composition at the bottom of the picture. The figure is cropped on the right and at the bottom, making the portrait more direct and powerful, and the free, albeit controlled application of the varied, bold tones breathes life into the image.

The subject is neither a type nor an individual; nor is she purely autobiographical or representing her time. The imagery, though given weight by the fact that it is based on a self-portrait, bestows upon the figure an extreme kind of pictorial individuality that has a hieratic quality. There was no other portrait like it in the international art world at the time.

99 *Self-Portrait with Two Flowers in Raised Left Hand,* 1907

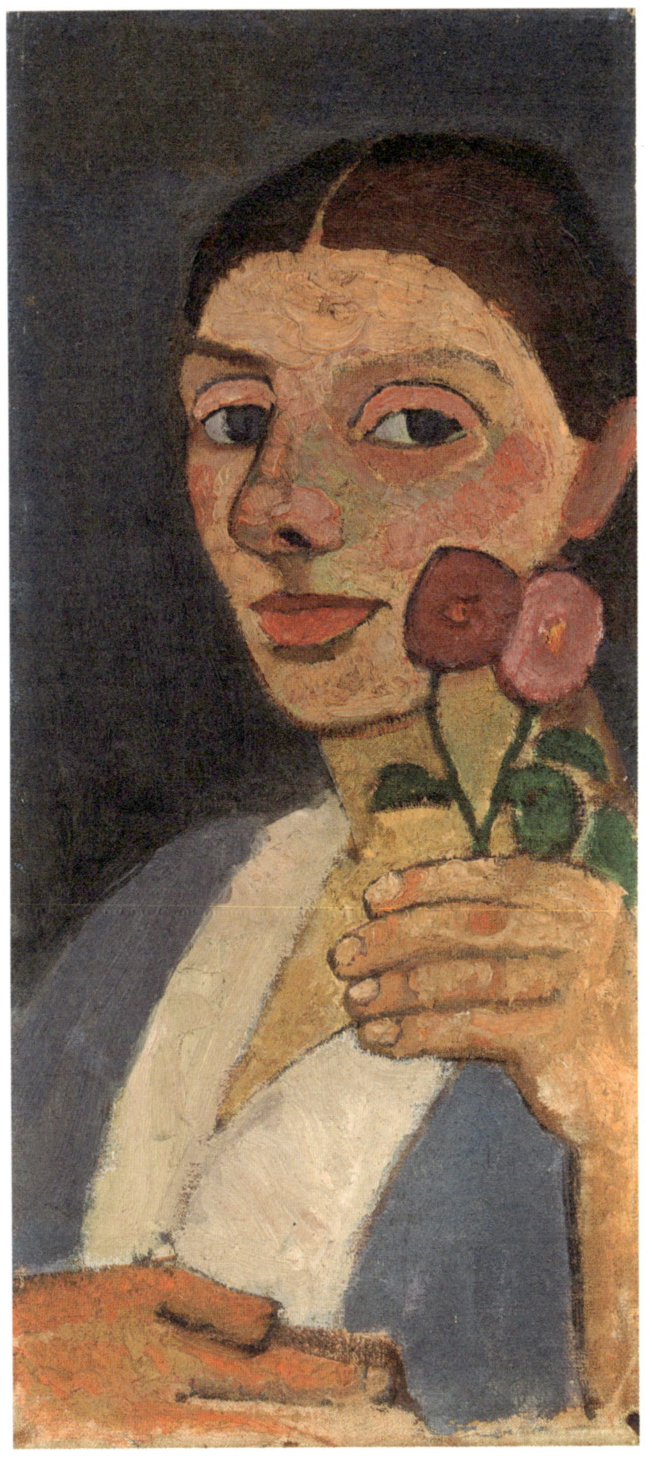

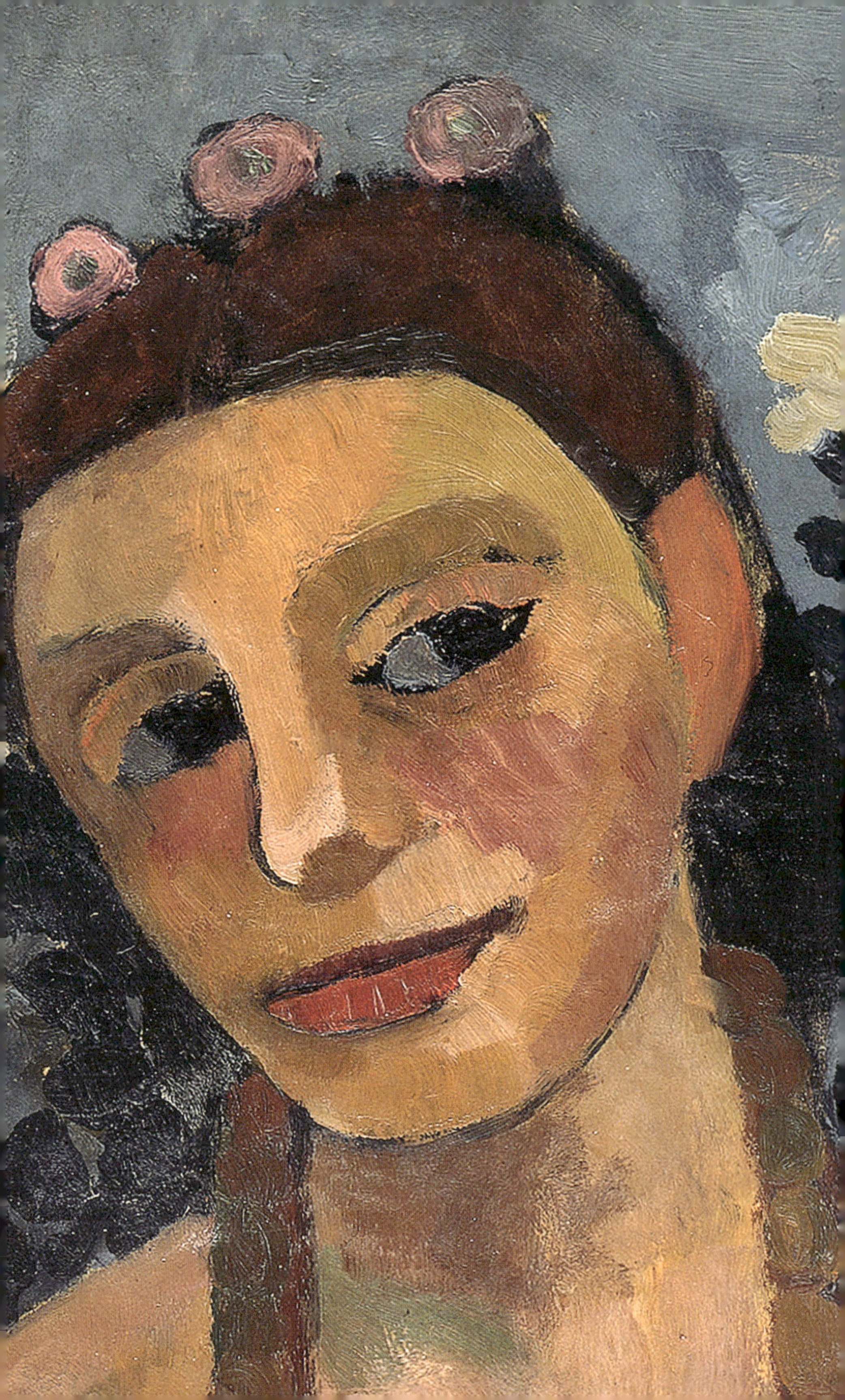

Conclusion

Although something of a loner (drawing a comparison with other artists half a generation older than her, such as Helene Schjerfbeck in Finland, Hilma af Klint in Sweden and Vilhelm Hammershøi in Denmark), Paula Modersohn-Becker made a unique contribution to the emerging modern art scene in Paris. One of the lessons she learnt in the capital of art was not to think about the public reaction. She deliberately chose her own path. At a time when, in studios all over Paris, artists were striving to give their paintings autonomy, she searched for new forms and content. The result was a style of painting that was essentially figurative but had its own rules.

Instead of polishing her own style, she continually experimented with the many stylistic and artistic possibilities of her time, eventually finding a way to exaggerate figures and so develop her own meaningful iconography. Her motifs may have been inspired by the peace of Worpswede, but the thrill of the Paris art world was where she felt at home.

Detail of ill. 76

Modersohn-Becker died of an embolism on 20 November 1907, two and a half weeks after the birth of her daughter Mathilde.

Did she paint differently because she was a woman? Her women look different, as do her children and old people: lost in thought, but self-confidently independent in their ritual strength. The women are not a threat to men, as they are for Edvard Munch; they are not muses, as in the work of Ernst Ludwig Kirchner; nor are they the social constructs of Max Beckmann. Modersohn-Becker's figures have their own, non-sexualized status. They are creatures who embody everything the artist tried to achieve in both form and content. They express her ideas on art and represent a strong, unconventional and progressive art: as she put it in April 1902, 'art that is rich and inventive and only looks to the future'. These people personify the self-image of an artist who made her mark in the modern art world within only a few years.

Chronology

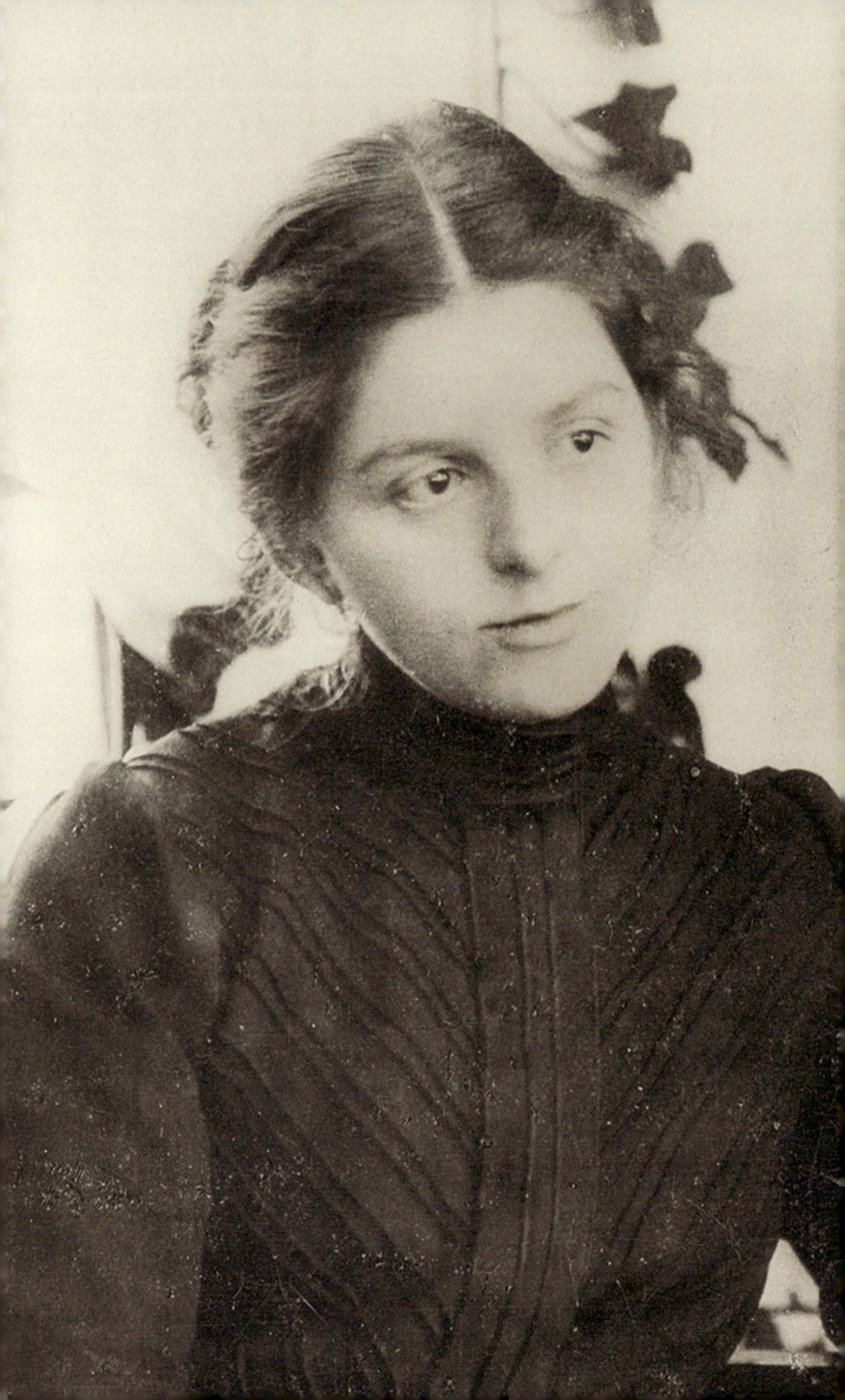

1876–91

Minna Hermine Paula Becker is born in Dresden on
8 February 1876, the third of seven children. Her father,
Carl Woldemar Becker, is building inspector for the Berlin-
Dresden railway. Her mother, Mathilde Becker, is from the
von Bültzingslöwen family, originating in Thuringia.

1888

Moves to Bremen. Her father becomes building surveyor for
Prussian railways.

1892

Stays for seven months with her aunt, Marie Hill, on a country
estate near London. Has drawing lessons at St John's Wood
Art School.

Detail of photograph on p. 215

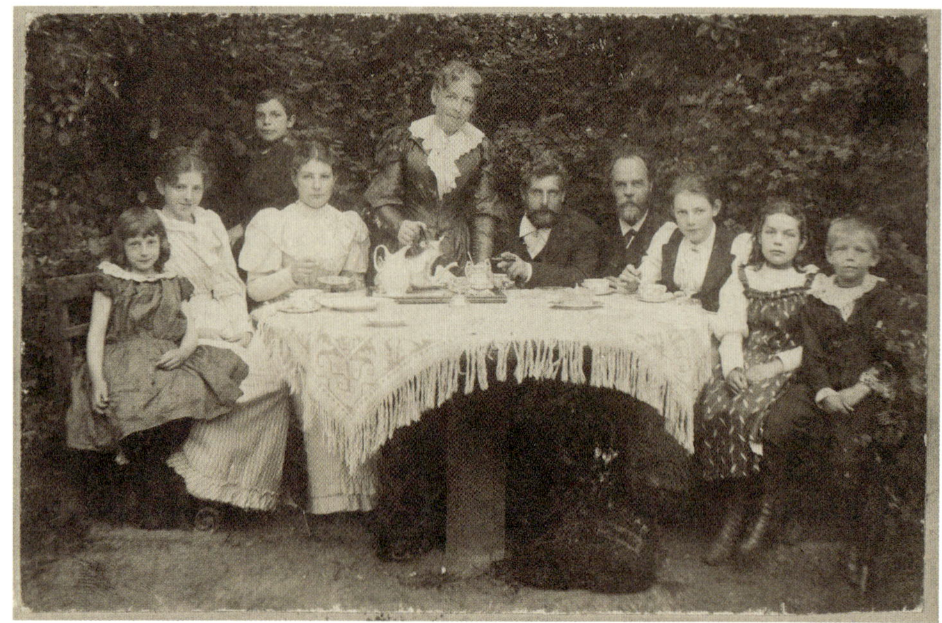

Sunday tea in Bremen, June 1893. From left to right: Herma Becker, Paula
Becker, their cousin Edmund Schaefer, unknown, Paula's mother Mathilde
Becker, Paula's father Woldemar Becker, Uncle Georg Theodor Schaefer,
Milly Becker, unknown, Henner Becker

1893–95

At her father's instigation, she attends teacher training college
in Bremen, graduating in the autumn of 1895. She also
has painting and drawing lessons with the Bremen artist
Bernhard Wiegandt. In April 1895, she sees the first
exhibition by the Worpswede painters at Kunsthalle Bremen.

1896

Starts an 18-month course at the painting and drawing school
of the Berlin Association of Women Artists and Art Patrons,
set up in 1867. Studies at museums in her spare time. Goes to
the Pinakothek and the Schack-Galerie in Munich.

1897

First stay in Worpswede in the summer. Travels to Dresden for
the International Art Exhibition (artists include Degas, Ensor,
Monet, Pissarro, Böcklin, Hodler and Liebermann) and to the
Museum of Art History and the Liechtenstein Museum in Vienna.

First painting.

1898

Further studies in Berlin. Visits a lithograph exhibition at
the Museum of Decorative Arts (artists include Liebermann,
Klinger, Menzel, Puvis de Chavannes, Manet, Redon, Renoir,
Toulouse-Lautrec, Vallotton and Munch). Visits Max Klinger's
studio in Leipzig.

Moves to Worpswede in September. Fritz Mackensen critiques
her drawings. She becomes friends with the budding sculptor
Clara Westhoff.

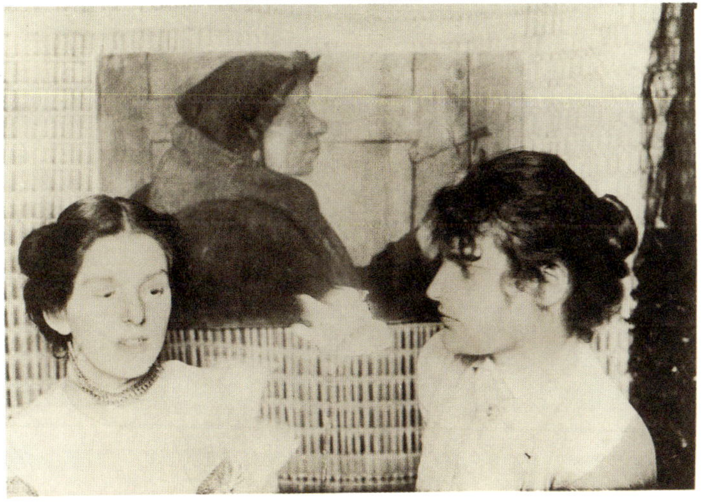

Paula Becker and Clara Westhoff in Paula's studio, *c.* 1899

1899

Travels in Switzerland, visits museums in Munich,
Nuremberg, Leipzig and Dresden. Exhibits her own work at
the Kunsthalle Bremen with Clara Westhoff and Marie Bock,
but withdraws it immediately due to devastating criticism.

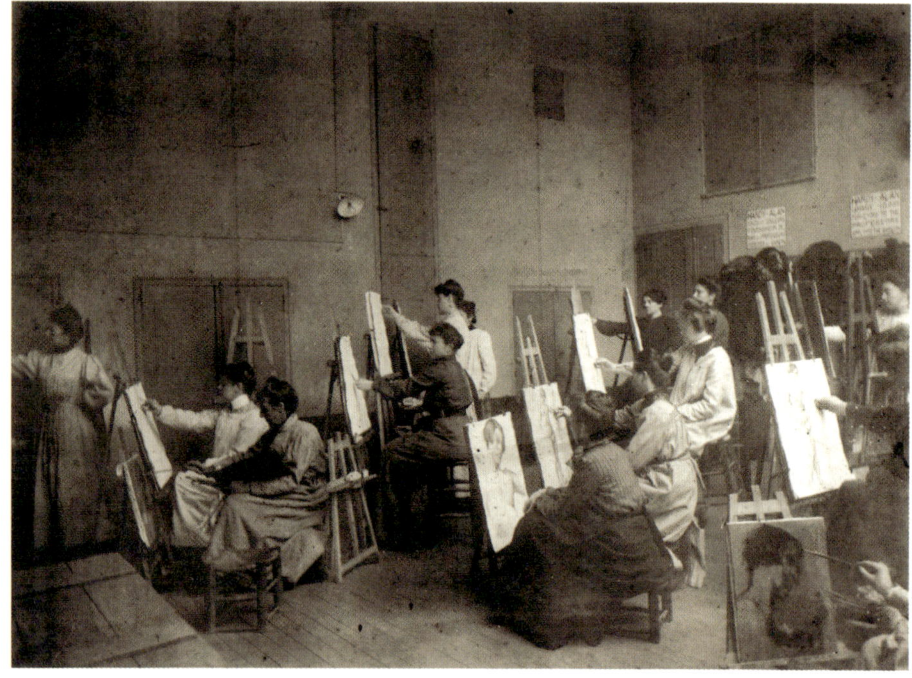

Women's art class at the Académie Colarossi, *c.* 1900

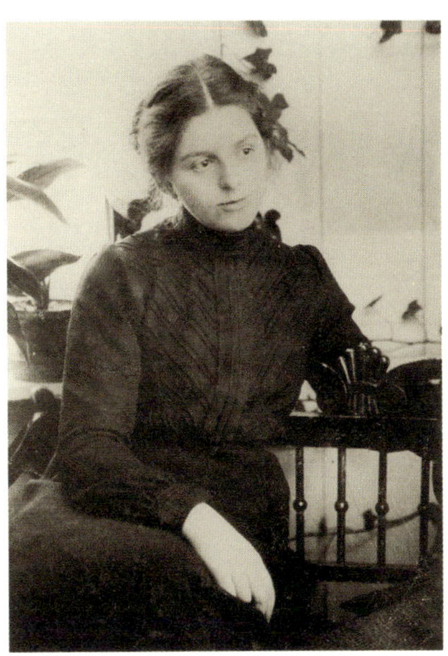

Paula Modersohn-Becker, *c.* 1901

1900

First trip to Paris at New Year 1899. Studio at 9 Rue Campagne
Première. Studies at the private Académie Colarossi and attends
anatomy classes at the Ecole des Beaux-Arts. Visits museums
and art dealers, often with Clara Westhoff. Discovers Cézanne
at the gallery of the art dealer Ambroise Vollard.

Otto Modersohn comes to Paris with Fritz and Hermine
Overbeck and Marie Bock. Joint visits to the Paris Exposition
and the accompanying international art exhibitions at the Grand
Palais and the French centenary exhibition at the Petit Palais.

Returns to Worpswede. Takes lodgings with a farmer,
Hermann Brünjes, in the Ostendorf area, and also works there.
Sunday meetings with the 'family', Clara Westhoff and Marie
Bock, Otto Modersohn, Heinrich Vogeler and Martha Schröder,
at Heinrich Vogeler's home, Barkenhoff. The poets Carl
Hauptmann and Rainer Maria Rilke are occasional guests.

Engagement to Otto Modersohn in September.

1901

At her parents' instigation, undertakes a cookery course in
Berlin. Lives with her aunt, Hermine Parizot, at 61 Eisenacher
Strasse. Visits museums and art dealers. Frequent meetings
with Rilke, who is living in Schmargendorf.

On 25 May she marries Otto Modersohn, who already has
a three-year-old daughter, Elsbeth. Honeymoon in Berlin,
Dresden, Schreiberhau (Szklarska Poreba), Prague, Munich
and Dachau (to see the Hans von Marées collection at the
Schleissheim Palace). Her room at the Brünjes' farm is
converted into a studio.

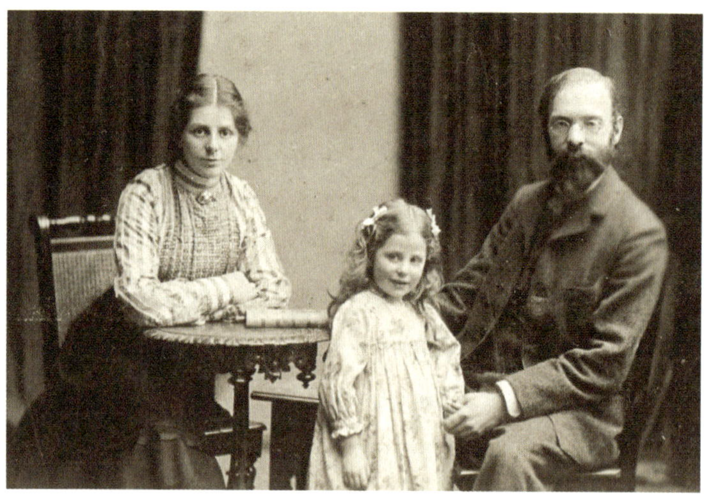

Paula, Elsbeth and Otto Modersohn, *c.* 1902

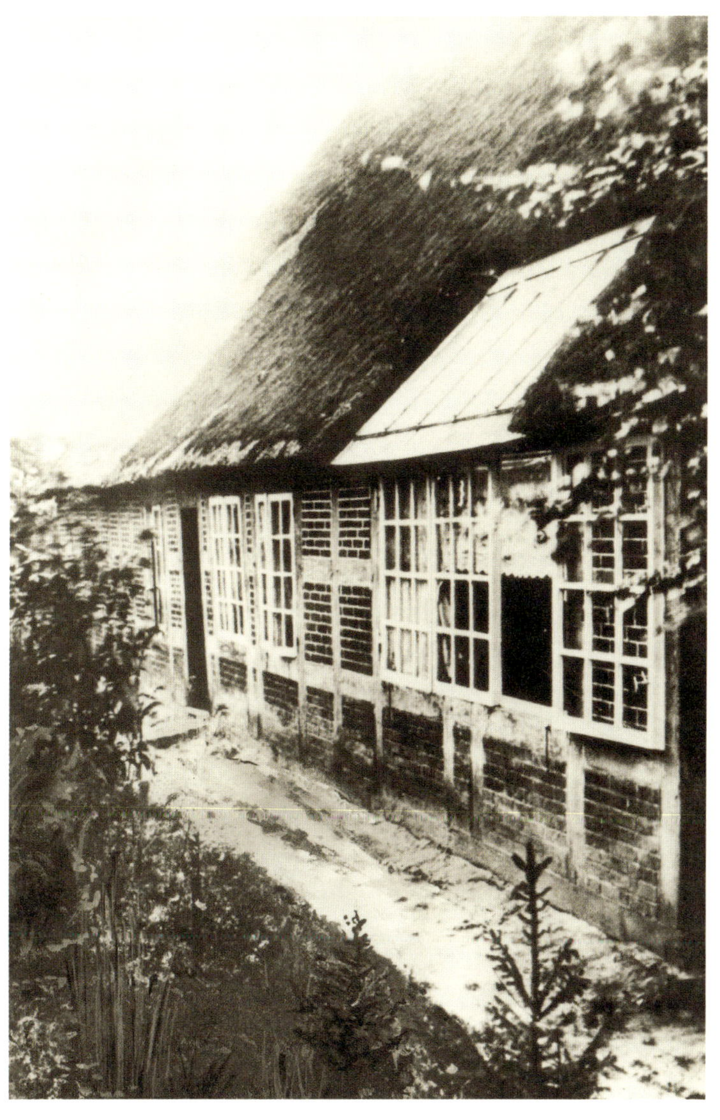

Paula Modersohn-Becker's studio with skylight, at the house
of farmer Hermann Brünjes, *c.* 1902

1903

Second trip to Paris in February. From end of February, her studio is at 29 Rue Cassette. Sketches works in the Louvre, visits exhibitions and art dealers with Rilke and his wife Clara Rilke-Westhoff. Discovers Egyptian mummy portraits from Fayum. Visits Rodin in Paris and Meudon.

Returns to Worpswede in March.

1904

Travels to Dresden, Kassel and Braunschweig with Otto Modersohn. Distanced from fellow Worpswede artists.

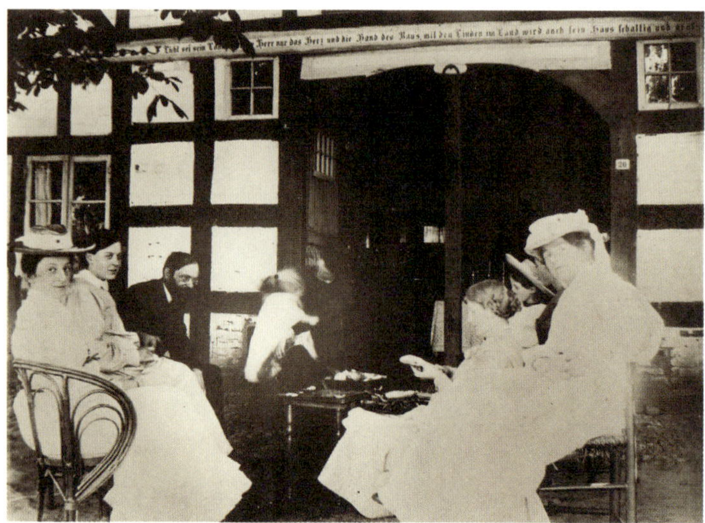

In front of the Vogelers' home, Barkenhoff, *c.* 1904. From left to right: Herma Becker, Philine Vogeler, Otto Modersohn, Heinrich Vogeler, Martha Vogeler, Elsbeth Modersohn, Paula Modersohn-Becker

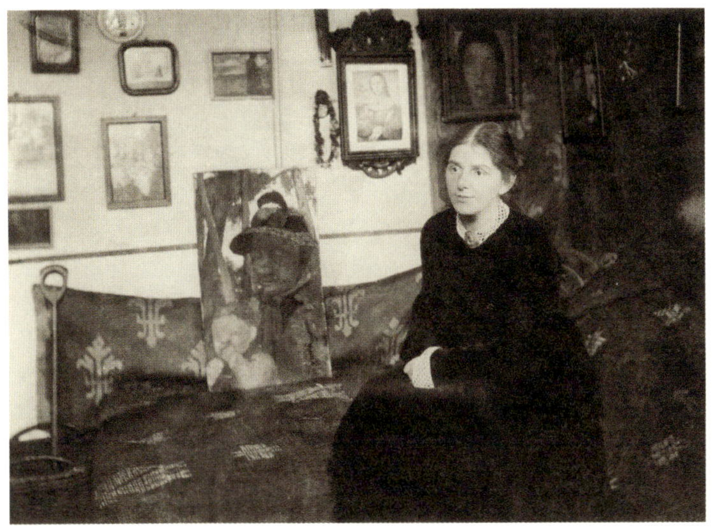

Paula Modersohn-Becker in her studio at Hermann Brünjes's house,
photograph by Karl Brandt, *c.* 1905

1905

In February, she takes her third trip to Paris, where her sister
Herma is doing a language course. Studio at 65 Rue Madame.
Studies nudes at the Académie Julian for a month. Visits
studios of Maurice Denis and Charles Cottet. At the Salon des
Indépendants she sees works by Matisse and the Nabis, as well
as Seurat and Van Gogh retrospectives. At the end of March
Otto Modersohn and other Worpswede artists come to Paris,
and they visit Gustave Fayet's Gauguin collection together.

Returns to Worpswede in April. Visits Karl Ernst Osthaus's
Folkwang Museum in Hagen. At the end of the year she
travels to Schreiberhau with Otto Modersohn, where she
meets the sociologist Werner Sombart.

1906

On her return journey from Schreiberhau, she visits the centenary exhibition at the National Gallery in Berlin.

Moves to Paris in February, leaves Otto Modersohn and Worpswede. Initially in a studio at 14 Avenue du Maine, then, from the end of October, at 49 Boulevard du Montparnasse. Anatomy and life-drawing courses at the Ecole des Beaux-Arts. Excursions with Rilke; they attend the unveiling of Rodin's *Thinker* outside the Panthéon. Aristide Maillol is also present.

The sculptor Bernhard Hoetger encourages her to work intensively on figure paintings, portraits and self-portraits. She creates her most important works. At the end of October Otto Modersohn comes to Paris for the winter.

Four of her paintings are shown in an exhibition by the Worpswede artists at the Kunsthalle Bremen.

1907

Returns to Worpswede at the end of March, partly because she is pregnant. She writes in a letter on 21 October, 'If it was not absolutely necessary for me to be here now, I would have to be in Paris.' Daughter Mathilde is born on 2 November. On 20 November Paula Modersohn-Becker dies of an embolism.

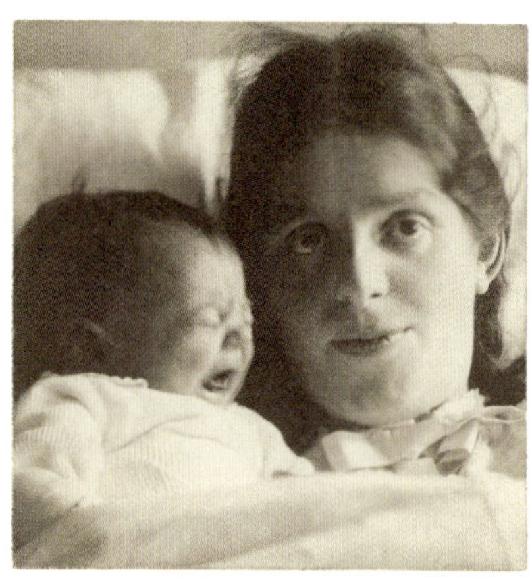

Paula Modersohn-Becker with her daughter Mathilde, November 1907. Photograph by Hugo Erfurth

Notes

1   The quotations from letters and journals are from *Paula Modersohn-Becker in Briefen und Tagebüchern*, Günter Busch and Liselotte von Reinken (eds), revised by Wolfgang Werner, Frankfurt am Main, 2007.

2   Alfred Lichtwark's letters to the administrative board of the Kunsthalle, quoted by Gustav Pauli, in *Kunst und Künstler*, vol. 21, 1922–23, p. 49.

3   Letters from Otto Modersohn quoted from *Paula Modersohn-Becker / Otto Modersohn. Der Briefwechsel*, Antje Modersohn and Wolfgang Werner (eds), Berlin, 2017.

4   Reprinted in *Paula Modersohn-Becker in Briefen und Tagebüchern* (see Note 1), pp. 199–201.

5   Letter of 17 April 1904 from Geneva, in *Max Beckmann. Briefe*, Klaus Gallwitz, Uwe M. Schneede and Stephan von Wiese (eds), vol. 1, Munich, 1993, p. 20.

6   Wilhelm Uhde, *Von Bismarck bis Picasso. Erinnerungen und Bekenntnisse*, Zurich, 1938, p. 119.

7   Ambroise Vollard, *Erinnerungen eines Kunsthändlers*, Zurich, 1980, p. 82.

8   Sketch of Clara Rilke-Westhoff, in *Paula Modersohn-Becker in Briefen und Tagebüchern* (see Note 1), pp. 240–41.

9   Alfred Lichtwark, 'Deutsche Kunst', in *Weltausstellung in Paris 1900. Amtlicher Katalog der Ausstellung des deutschen Reichs*, Berlin, 1900, p. 128.

10   Henriette Mendelsohn, 'Pariser Studientage. Kollegialischer Ratgeber für Malerinnen und solche, die es werden wollen', in *Die Kunst für Alle*, 12th year, 1896–97, p. 151.

11   Anne Buschhoff, 'Bei intimster Betrachtung die größte Einfachheit anstreben – Kinderbilder und frühe Darstellungen von Mutter und Kind', in *Paula Modersohn-Becker und die Kunst in Paris um 1900 – von Cézanne bis Picasso*, Anne Buschhoff and Wulf Herzogenrath (eds), exh. cat., Kunsthalle Bremen, Bremen, 2007, p. 104.

12   Journal, 26 September (1903), in *Paula Modersohn-Becker / Otto Modersohn. Der Briefwechsel* (see Note 3), p. 252.

13   Rainer Stamm, *'Ein kurzes intensives Fest'. Paula Modersohn-Becker. Eine Biographie*, Stuttgart, 2007, p. 136.

14   Clara Rilke-Westhoff, in *Paula Modersohn-Becker. Ein Buch der Freundschaft*, Rolf Hetsch (ed.), Berlin, 1932, p. 43.

15   Herma Weinberg, in *Paula Modersohn-Becker. Ein Buch der Freundschaft* (see Note 14), pp. 16–17.

16   John Richardson, *A Life of Picasso: The Early Years, 1881–1906* (vol. 1), New York, 1991, p. 411.

17 Marc, letter to his mother from Paris, 20 June 1903, in *Franz Marc. Briefe, Schriften und Aufzeichnungen*, Günter Meissner (ed.), Leipzig, 1989, p. 19; Macke, letter to Elisabeth from Paris, 12 June 1907, in *August Macke. Briefe an Elisabeth und die Freunde*, Werner Frese and Ernst-Gerhard Güse (eds), Munich, 1987, p. 127.

18 Lorenz Dittmann, 'Die Farbe bei Marées', in *Hans von Marées*, Christian Lenz (ed.), exh. cat., Bavarian State Painting Collections Munich, Munich, 1987, p. 101.

19 Angelica Hoffmeister-zur Nedden, 'Zur Maltechnik von Paula Modersohn-Becker', in *Paula Modersohn-Becker. Werkverzeichnis der Gemälde*, vol. 1, Munich, 1998, p. 114.

20 Letter to Daniel de Montfreid, 25 February 1901, in *Paul Gauguin. Briefe und Selbstzeugnisse*, Kuno Mittelstädt (ed.), Munich, 1970, p. 164.

21 Letter to Jappe Nilssen, 23 or 24 May 1912, in *Munch und Deutschland*, Uwe M. Schneede and Dorothee Hansen (eds), exh. cat., Kunsthalle der Hypo-Kulturstiftung Munich/Hamburger Kunsthalle/Nationalgalerie Berlin, 1994, p. 73.

22 Letter to Karl von der Heydt, 16 January 1906, in *Rainer Maria Rilke. Briefe aus den Jahren 1902 bis 1906*, Ruth Sieber-Rilke and Carl Sieber (eds), Leipzig, 1939, p. 291.

23 Clara Rilke-Westhoff, in Hetsch (see Note 14), p. 49.

24 Letter to Maria Franck, 13 April 1907, in *Briefe, Schriften und Aufzeichnungen* (see Note 17), p. 25.

25 *Leben und Meinungen des Malers Hans Purrmann*, Barbara and Erhard Göpel (eds), Wiesbaden, 1961, p. 60.

26 Letter to Karl von der Heydt (see Note 22), p. 291.

27 Otto Modersohn, Tagebuch, 15 June 1902, in *Briefwechsel* (see Note 3), p. 175.

28 See Rainer Stamm, 'Parallele Erscheinungen? Modersohn-Becker, Picasso und Matisse', in *Paula Modersohn-Becker. Der Weg in die Moderne*, Uwe M. Schneede and Kathrin Baumstark (eds), exh. cat., Bucerius Kunst Forum Hamburg, Munich, 2017, pp. 36–47.

29 Notebook 23, in Theodore Reff, *The Notebooks of Edgar Degas*, 2 vols, Oxford, 1976, p. 44.

30 Paloma Alarcó, 'Mask of the Primitive', in *The Mirror & the Mask: Portraiture in the Age of Picasso*, exh. cat., Museo Thyssen-Bornemisza, Madrid, 2007, p. 111.

31 Quoted from Daniel-Henry Kahnweiler, *Confessions esthétiques*, Paris, 1963, p. 232.

32 Jack D. Flam, 'Matisse and the Fauves', in *'Primitivism' in 20th Century Art*, exh. cat., Museum of Modern Art, New York, 1984, vol. 1, p. 214.

33 See Jean-Louis Paudrat, 'From Africa', *ibid.*, pp. 139–41.

34 André Malraux, *Picasso's Mask*, New York, 1976, p. 10.

35 See William Rubin, 'Modernist Primitivism. An Introduction', in *'Primitivism'* (see Note 32), pp. 1–73; Jack D. Flam, 'Matisse and the Fauves', *ibid.*, pp. 211–39.

36 Letter to Elisabeth from Paris, 29 June 1907, in *Macke. Briefe* (see Note 17), p. 134.

37 Letter to Kandinsky from Bonn, 5 October 1912, in *Marc. Briefe* (see Note 17), p. 77.

38 Wolfgang Werner, 'Koinzidenzen der Rezeption am Beginn der Moderne', in *Von der Genauigkeit des Sehens. Festschrift für Anne Röver-Kann zum 75. Geburtstag*, Rebecca Duckwitz and Christien Melzer (eds), Bremen, 2018, pp. 166–67.

39 Heinrich Vogeler, *Werden. Erinnerungen*, Fischerhude, 1989, p. 120.

40 *Helene Schjerfbeck. Finland's Modernist Rediscovered*, exh. cat., Finnish National Gallery Ateneum, Helsinki, 1992, p. 70.

41 Lovis Corinth, *Das Erlernen der Malerei*, Hildesheim, 1979, p. 136.

42 Jura Brüschweiler, *Ferdinand Hodler. Selbstbildnisse als Selbstbiographie*, Bern, 1979, p. 7.

43 Letter to Jappe Nilssen, 9 March 1909, in *Edvard Munchs kriseår. Belyst i brever*, Erna Holmeboe Bang (ed.), Oslo, 1963, p. 58.

44 Otto Modersohn, in Hetsch (see Note 14), p. 26.

45 Letter to Emile Bernard, April 1888. See vangoghletters.org.

46 Letter to sister, 9–14 September 1888. See vangoghletters.org.

47 Letter to J. J. Isaäcson, 25 May 1890. See vangoghletters.org.

48 Emil Nolde, *Das eigene Leben* (1931), Cologne, 1994, p. 207.

49 Herma Weinberg, in Hetsch (see Note 14), pp. 12, 15.

50 Letter 17 December 1961, in *Werkverzeichnis der Gemälde*, vol. 1 (see Note 19), p. 32, note 23.

51 Heinrich Vogeler, 'Paula Modersohn-Becker. Zum Gedächtnis einer Frühverstorbenen', in *Das Wort*, no. 11, Moscow, November, 1938, p. 121, quoted from *Paula Modersohn-Becker und die ägyptischen Mumienportraits. Eine Hommage zum 100. Todestag der Künstlerin*, Rainer Stamm (ed.), Kunstsammlungen Böttcherstrasse, Paula Modersohn-Becker Museum Bremen/Museum Ludwig Cologne, 2007, p. 21.

52 Quoted from *Paula Modersohn-Becker in Briefen und Tagebüchern* (see Note 1), p. 727.

53 Karl Scheffler, 'Neue Bücher: Paula Modersohn-Becker von Gustav Pauli; Paula Modersohn-Becker, Briefe und Tagebuchblätter', in *Kunst und Künstler*, 19th year, no. 9, 1921, p. 332.

54 Sebastian Giesen, *Victor Emil Janssen. Selbstbildnis vor der Staffelei*, exh. cat., Hamburger Kunsthalle, 2001, p. 27.

55 Rainer Stamm (see Note 13), pp. 202–3.

56 Wolfgang Werner, 'Selbstbildnis oder Figurenbild?', in *Ich bin Ich. Paula Modersohn-Becker. Die Selbstbildnisse*, exh. cat., Paula Modersohn-Becker Museum Bremen, Munich, 2019, p. 105.

57 Simone Ewald, 'Über die Rolle von Spiegel und Fotografie in Selbstbildnissen', *ibid.*, pp. 18–27.

58 *Werkverzeichnis der Gemälde* (see Note 19), vol. 2, p. 518.

59 Lucian Hölscher, 'Der Aufbruch der Kunst in die Zukunft', in *'Das schönste Museum der Welt'. Museum Folkwang bis 1933. Essays zur Geschichte des Museum Folkwang*, Göttingen, 2010, p. 13; see also Lucian Hölscher, *Die Entdeckung der Zukunft*, Frankfurt am Main, 1999.

60 Letter from Mathilde Becker to Karl Ernst Osthaus, March 1913, quoted from *Ich bin Ich* (see Note 56), pp. 9–10.

61 Quoted from Rainer Stamm (see Note 13), p. 195.

62 Letter to Paula Modersohn-Becker from Vegesack, 17 September 1906, in *Paula Modersohn-Becker in Briefen und Tagebüchern* (see Note 1), p. 559.

63 Karin Schick, 'Das Bild als Kosmos. Zu einigen späten Werken von Paula Modersohn-Becker', in *Paula Modersohn-Becker. Der Weg in die Moderne* (see Note 28), p. 63.

64 Gustav Pauli, *Paula Modersohn-Becker*, Munich 1919, 2nd edition 1922, p. 39.

65 Raphaël Bouvier, 'Le Garçon à la pipe', in *Picasso. Blaue und Rosa Periode*, Raphaël Bouvier (ed.), exh. cat., Fondation Beyeler, Riehen, 2019, p. 205.

66 Karin Schick (see Note 63), p. 67.

67 Letter to Adolf Hildebrand, 20 July 1871, in *Hans von Marées. Briefe*, Anne-S. Domm (ed.), Munich, 1987, p. 73.

68 Letter to sister, first half of June 1890, in *Sämtliche Briefe* (see Note 45), p. 81.

69 Letter to J. J. Isaäcson, 25 May 1890. See vangoghletters.org.

70 Clara Rilke-Westhoff, in Hetsch (see Note 14), p. 43.

71 Werner Spies, 'An einer wilden Grenze. Einzelgänger im Dschungel der Moderne. Das Pariser Grand Palais feiert den Maler Henri Rousseau', in *Frankfurter Allgemeine Zeitung*, 9 May 2006, p. 37.

72 Otto Modersohn, in Hetsch (see Note 14), p. 26; letter to Herma Becker from Otto Modersohn in Paris, 2 March 1907, in *Briefwechsel* (see Note 3), p. 410.

73 Ottilie Reylaender-Böhme, in Hetsch (see Note 14), p. 36.

74 Marion Ackermann, 'Paula Modersohn-Becker und München', in *Paula Modersohn-Becker 1876–1907. Retrospektive*, Helmut Friedel (ed.), Lenbachhaus, Munich, 1997, p. 19.

75 Quoted from *Auguste Rodin. Zeichnungen und Aquarelle*, exh. cat., Westfälisches Landesmuseum für Kunst und Kulturgeschichte, Münster, 1984, p. 30.

76 Emil Heilbutt, 'Aus der achten Ausstellung der Berliner Secession', in *Kunst und Künstler*, 2nd year, 1904, p. 140.

77 Verbal comment by Wolfgang Werner.

78 Bernhard Hoetger, 'Erinnerungen an Paula Modersohn-Becker', in C. E. Uphoff, *Paula Modersohn*, Leipzig, 1919, p. 14.

79 Herma Weinberg, in Hetsch (see Note 14), p. 18.

80 Gustav Pauli (see Note 64), p. 41.

81 Günter Busch, *Paula Modersohn-Becker. Malerin und Zeichnerin*, Frankfurt am Main, 1981, p. 116.

82 Otto Modersohn, letter to Gustav Pauli, 19 July 1919, in Christa Murken-Altrogge, *Paula Modersohn-Becker*, Cologne, 1980, p. 117.

83 Letter to Paul Gauguin, June 1890. See vangoghletters.org.

Selected Bibliography

Paula Modersohn-Becker 1876–1907. Werkverzeichnis der Gemälde, Günter Busch
and Wolfgang Werner (eds), 2 vols, Munich, 1998

Paula Modersohn-Becker 1876–1907. Oeuvreverzeichnis der Graphik, Wolfgang
Werner (ed.), Bremen, 1972

Paula Modersohn-Becker in Briefen und Tagebüchern, Günter Busch and Liselotte
von Reinken (general eds), Wolfgang Werner (ed.), Fischer, Frankfurt am
Main, 1979; published in English as *Paula Modersohn-Becker: The Letters and
Journals*, Günter Busch and Liselotte von Reinken (eds), Arthur S. Wensinger
and Carole Clew Hoey (trans.), New York, 1983

Paula Modersohn-Becker – Otto Modersohn. Der Briefwechsel, Antje Modersohn and
Wolfgang Werner (eds), Berlin, 2017

Paula Modersohn-Becker, The letters and Journals, Günter Busch, Liselotte Reinken
(eds), Northwestern University Press, Evanston, Ill., 1998

Adolf Behne, 'Paula Modersohn und der Übergang zur Bildkonstruktion',
in *Sozialistische Monatshefte*, no. 7, 1923, pp. 294–99

Günter Busch, *Paula Modersohn-Becker. Malerin, Zeichnerin*, Frankfurt am
Main, 1981

Carl Georg Heise, *Paula Modersohn-Becker. Mutter und Kind (Werkmonographien
zur bildenden Kunst 62)*, Stuttgart, 1961

Bernhard Hoetger, 'Paula Modersohn-Becker', in *Genius. Zeitschrift für werdende
und alte Kunst 1*, 1919, pp. 34–37

Gustav Pauli, *Paula Modersohn-Becker. Mit einem Werkverzeichnis*, Leipzig, 1919

Diane Radycki, *Paula Modersohn-Becker: The First Modern Woman Artist*, New
Haven and London, 2013

Rosa Schapire, 'Paula Modersohn-Becker', in *Der Kreis. Zeitschrift für künstlerische
Kultur 3*, 1926, pp. 112–15

Rainer Stamm, *'Ein kurzes intensives Fest'. Paula Modersohn-Becker. Eine Biographie*,
Stuttgart, 2007

Carl Emil Uphoff, *Paula Modersohn-Becker*, Leipzig, 1919

Paula Modersohn-Becker. Ein Buch der Freundschaft, Rolf Hetsch (ed.), Berlin, 1932

Paula Modersohn-Becker. Zeichnungen, Pastelle, Bildentwürfe, Uwe M. Schneede (ed.),
exh. cat., Kunstverein, Hamburg, 1976

Paula Modersohn-Becker. Das Frühwerk, Anne Röver (ed.), exh. cat., Kunsthalle
Bremen, 1985

Paula Modersohn-Becker 1876–1907. Retrospektive, Helmut Friedel (ed.), exh. cat.,
Städtische Galerie im Lenbachhaus, Munich, 1997

Paula Modersohn-Becker. Von Dresden her, Gabriele Werner (ed.), exh. cat.,
Staatliche Kunstsammlungen Dresden, Galerie Neue Meister, Dresden, 2003

'*Rücksichtslos geradeaus malend*'. *Paula Modersohn-Becker, Marie Bock, Clara
Rilke-Westhoff. Die Ausstellung 1899*, Paula Modersohn-Becker Stiftung (ed.),
exh. cat., Paula Modersohn-Becker Museum, Bremen, 2003

*Paula Modersohn-Becker und die ägyptischen Mumienporträts. Eine Hommage
zum 100. Todestag der Künstlerin*, Rainer Stamm (ed.), exh. cat., Paula
Modersohn-Becker Museum (Bremen) and Museum Ludwig (Cologne),
Munich, 2007

*Paula Modersohn-Becker und die Kunst in Paris um 1900 – Von Cézanne
bis Picasso*, Anne Buschhoff and Wulf Herzogenrath (eds), exh. cat.,
Kunsthalle Bremen, 2007

*Paula Modersohn-Becker in Bremen. Aus den Sammlungen Kunsthalle Bremen,
Kunstsammlungen Böttcherstraße/Paula Modersohn-Becker Museum, Paula
Modersohn-Becker Stiftung*, Paula Modersohn-Becker Stiftung (ed.),
Bremen, 1996, rev. ed. 2008

Paula Modersohn-Becker. Pionierin der Moderne, Rainer Stamm and
Hans-Peter Wipplinger (eds), exh. cat., Kunsthalle Krems, 2010

Paula Modersohn-Becker, Michael Juul Holm (ed.), exh. cat., Louisiana
Museum of Modern Art, Humlebaek, 2014

Paula Modersohn-Becker. Berlin – Worpswede – Paris, Mara Folini (ed.),
exh. cat., Museo Comunale d'Arte Moderna Ascona, Turin, 2015

Paula Modersohn-Becker, Julia Garimorth (ed.), exh. cat., Musée d'Art
Moderne de la Ville de Paris, Paris, 2016

Paula Modersohn-Becker. Der Weg in die Moderne, Uwe M. Schneede
and Kathrin Baumstark (eds), exh. cat., Bucerius Kunst Forum,
Hamburg, 2017

Paula Becker & Otto Modersohn. Kunst und Leben, Paula Modersohn-Becker
Stiftung (ed.), Bremen, exh. cat., Paula Modersohn-Becker Museum,
Bremen, 2018

Ich bin Ich. Paula Modersohn-Becker. Die Selbstbildnisse, Frank Schmidt (ed.)
in collaboration with the Paula Modersohn-Becker Stiftung, Bremen,
Simone Ewald, Wolfgang Werner, exh. cat., Paula Modersohn-Becker
Museum Bremen, 2019

List of Illustrations

PMB Stiftung: Collection of the Paula Modersohn-Becker Foundation, Bremen
PMB Museum: Paula Modersohn-Becker Museum, Bremen

Frontispiece: *Self-Portrait*, charcoal, blending stump, 21.5 × 17.7 cm (8 ½ × 7 in.),
    c. 1906. PMB Stiftung
1   *Self-Portrait*, gouache on paper, 24.5 × 26.5 cm (9¾ × 10½ in.), *c.* 1897.
    PMB Stiftung
2   *Peasant Woman Carrying a Forked Branch*, India ink, pastel, pencil,
    44.5 × 74.5 cm (17⅝ × 29⅜ in.), 1898–99. Private collection, Berlin
3   Three studies for etching *Seated Old Woman*, pencil on paper, 41 × 26 cm
    (16¼ × 10¼ in.), 1898–99. PMB Stiftung
4   Sketches for the etching *Seated Old Woman*, pencil on paper, 26 × 40.3 cm
    (10¼ × 15⅞ in.), 1899. PMB Stiftung
5   Compositional studies: *Head in Front of Landscape/ Three Sketches of Woman
    Seated in a Landscape*, pencil on paper, 25.5 × 36.8 cm (10⅛ × 14½ in.),
    1898–99. PMB Stiftung
6   Preparatory drawings for the etchings *Portrait of a Peasant Woman* and
    Seated Old Woman, pencil, 26.1 × 40.3 cm (10⅜ × 15⅞ in.), 1898–99.
    Kunsthalle Bremen/ Der Kunstverein in Bremen
7   Study: *Children with Lanterns*, charcoal, 26.2 × 38.2 cm (10⅜ × 15⅛ in.),
    c. 1901. PMB Stiftung
8   *Children with Lanterns in Front of House*, oil tempera on board, 40.5 × 57.2 cm
    (16 × 22⅝ in.), *c.* 1901. Kunsthandel Wolfgang Werner, Bremen/ Berlin.
    Catalogue raisonné 194
9   *Lady with a Feather Hat*, oil tempera on board, 49.5 × 36 cm (19½ × 14¼ in.),
    1897–98. Private collection. Catalogue raisonné 14
10   *Church in Worpswede*, oil tempera on board, 72.7 × 45 cm (28⅝ × 17¾ in.),
    1900. Kunsthalle Bremen. Catalogue raisonné 48
11   *Interior (Studio in Bremen)*, oil on paper, 34.4 × 31.7 cm (13⅜ × 12 ½ in.), 1897.
    PMB Stiftung
12   *Portrait of a Woman with Poppies*, oil tempera on board, 57.5 × 46 cm
    (22¾ × 18⅛ in.), *c.* 1898. PMB Museum Bremen. Catalogue raisonné 24
13   *Picture Puzzle*, postcard to the artist's mother, Paris, 1 March 1900.
    Private collection
14   *Half-Length Portrait of the Sculptor Clara Rilke-Westhoff*, oil on canvas,
    52 × 36.8 cm (20½ × 14½ in.), 1905. Hamburger Kunsthalle. Catalogue
    raisonné 537
15   Charles Cottet, *Au pays de la mer*, triptych, oil on canvas, 176 × 356 cm
    (69⅜ × 140¼ in.), 1898. Musée d'Orsay, Paris

16 *Self-Portrait in Front of Window with View of Parisian Houses*, oil on paper
on board, 38 × 25.5 cm (15 × 10⅛ in.), 1900. PMB Stiftung, Bremen,
loan from private collection. Catalogue raisonné 49

17 *Birch Trunks in a Landscape*, oil tempera on board, 73.6 × 46.2 cm
(29 × 18¼ in.), *c.* 1901. PMB Stiftung. Catalogue raisonné 250

18 *Birch Trunks in Front of Red House Wall*, oil tempera on board, 53 × 39.8 cm
(20⅞ × 15¾ in.), *c.* 1901. PMB Stiftung. Catalogue raisonné 257

19 Edvard Munch, *The Four Sons of Dr Max Linde*, oil on board,
144 × 199.5 cm (56¾ × 78⅝ in.), 1903. Museen für Kunst und
Kulturgeschichte der Hansestadt Lübeck

20 *Four Children in a Landscape with a Marsh Canal*, oil tempera on board,
55.8 × 41 cm (22 × 16¼ in.), *c.* 1900. Kunstsammlungen Chemnitz–Museum
Gunzenhauser, Eigentum der Stiftung Gunzenhauser. Catalogue raisonné 69

21 *Two Girls by a Birch Trunk*, oil tempera on board, 51 × 54 cm
(20⅛ × 21⅜ in.), *c.* 1902. PMB Museum Bremen, permanent loan
from private collection. Catalogue raisonné 282

22 *Girl Standing in Front of a Goat Shed*, oil tempera on board, 73.3 × 52.3 cm
(28⅞ × 20⅝ in.), 1902. Kunsthalle Emden, Henri and Eske Nannen
Foundation and gift from Otto van de Loo. Catalogue raisonné 327

23 *Dreebeen Seated with Glass Bottle*, oil tempera on board, 52 × 40 cm
(20½ × 15¾ in.), 1903. Private collection, Berlin. Catalogue raisonné 417

24 *Study of Dreebeen Sitting in the Garden*, oil tempera on board, 48.2 × 36.4 cm
(19 × 14⅜ in.), *c.* 1904. Otto Modersohn Museum, Fischerhude, permanent
loan, Ahlers Collection. Catalogue raisonné 481

25 Otto Modersohn, *Anna 'Dreebeen' Schröder in the Garden of the Worpswede
Poorhouse*, oil on board, 41.4 × 58.5 cm (16⅜ × 23⅛ in.), 1902. Private collection

26 Sketch of the Philippe Pot monument in the Louvre, charcoal, 15.6 × 23.8 cm
(6¼ × 9⅜ in.), 1903. PMB Stiftung

27 Sketch of Lucas Cranach's *Venus Standing in a Landscape* in the Louvre,
charcoal, 23.8 × 15.6 cm (9⅜ × 6¼ in.), 1903. PMB Stiftung

28 Sketch of Dominique Ingres's *Mlle Rivière* in the Louvre, charcoal,
23.8 × 15.6 cm (9⅜ × 6¼ in.), 1903. PMB Stiftung

29 Collection of Gertrude and Leo Stein at 27 Rue de Fleurus, photo, *c.* 1906.
Top centre: *Woman with a Hat (Madame Matisse)*, 1905, by Henri Matisse,
Archives and Manuscripts Collection, Baltimore Museum of Art

30 *Paris Street with Child in a Hood, Lamppost and Horse-Drawn Cart*, charcoal
on paper, 29.3 × 21.9 cm (11⅝ × 8⅝ in.), 1905. PMB Stiftung

31 *Horse-Drawn Bus in Paris, Three Men Sitting on Top of the Bus*, charcoal
on paper, 29.8 × 21.8 cm (11¾ × 8⅝ in.), 1905. PMB Stiftung

32 *Group of Women and Children and a Man between Tree Trunks*, charcoal,
21.8 × 29.8 cm (8⅝ × 11¾ in.), 1905. Private collection, Bremen

33 *Portrait of a Girl with Hand Spread across her Chest*, oil tempera on canvas,
41 × 33 cm (16¼ × 13 in.), *c.* 1905. Von der Heydt-Museum, Wuppertal.
Catalogue raisonné 570

34 *Head of a Girl Sitting on a Chair*, oil tempera on canvas, 26 × 21 cm
(10¼ × 8⅜ in.), *c.* 1905. Private collection. Catalogue raisonné 556

35 *Head of Blonde Girl with a Straw Hat*, oil tempera on canvas, 27 × 33.5 cm
(10¾ × 13¼ in.), *c.* 1904. Kunst- und Museumsverein Wuppertal. Catalogue
raisonné 476

36 *Standing and Kneeling Girls Nude in Front of Poppies II*, canvas, 106 × 56 cm
(41¾ × 22⅛ in.), May–June 1906. Museen für Kunst und Kulturgeschichte
der Hansestadt Lübeck. Catalogue raisonné 650

37 *Two Girls in White and Blue Dresses*, oil tempera on board, 54.5 × 36 cm
(21½ × 14¼ in.), May–June 1906. Milwaukee Art Museum, Maurice
and Esther Leah Ritz Collection. Catalogue raisonné 646

38 *Two Girls in White and Blue Dresses with Arms Around Each Other's Shoulders*,
oil tempera on board, 58.5 × 40 cm (23⅛ × 15¾ in.), May–June 1906.
Rauert Collection in the Hamburger Kunsthalle. Catalogue raisonné 647

39 Pablo Picasso, *Green Bowl and Tomatoes*, gouache on wood, 21 × 27 cm
(8⅜ × 10¾ in.), spring to summer 1908. Estate of the artist

40 *Still Life with Asters and Tomatoes*, oil tempera on canvas, 30 × 35 cm
(11⅞ × 13⅞ in.), August 1906. Private collection. Catalogue raisonné 702

41 *Still Life with Goldfish Bowl*, oil tempera on board, 50.5 × 74 cm
(20 × 29¼ in.), May–June 1906. Von der Heydt-Museum, Wuppertal.
Catalogue raisonné 668

42 *Still Life with Terracotta Jug, Peonies and Oranges*, oil tempera on board,
61.5 × 49 cm (24¼ × 19⅜ in.), May–June 1906. Kunsthandel Wolfgang
Werner, Bremen/Berlin. Catalogue raisonné 669

43 *Still Life with Blue Box*, oil tempera on canvas, 27.3 × 35.7 cm
(10 ¾ × 14⅛ in.), 1907. PMB Stiftung. Catalogue raisonné 732

44 *Portrait of Sister Herma with Artichoke Flower in her Raised Hand*, oil tempera
on canvas, 56.5 × 51 cm (22¼ × 20⅛ in.), April–May 1906. Private collection,
Bremen. Catalogue raisonné 640

45 *Portrait of Rainer Maria Rilke*, oil tempera on board, 32.3 × 25.4 cm
(12¾ × 10 in.), May–June 1906. PMB Stiftung, loan from private collection.
Catalogue raisonné 643

46 *Half-Length Portrait of Woman in Black with Handkerchief*, oil tempera on
canvas, 51 × 50.5 cm (20⅛ × 20 in.), spring 1906. Private collection.
Catalogue raisonné 645

47 *Portrait of Werner Sombart*, oil tempera on canvas, 50 × 46 cm
(19 ¾ × 18⅛ in.), spring 1906. Kunsthalle Bremen/Der Kunstverein
in Bremen. Catalogue raisonné 642

48 *Half-Length Portrait of Lee Hoetger with Flower*, oil tempera on canvas,
55.3 × 33.2 cm (21⅞ × 13⅛ in.), August 1906. PMB Museum Bremen.
Catalogue raisonné 687

49 Pablo Picasso, *Portrait of Gertrude Stein*, oil on canvas, 99.6 × 81.3 cm
(39¼ × 32⅛ in.), 1905–6. Metropolitan Museum of Art, New York

50 Page of sketches by Bernhard Hoetger, Paula and Otto Modersohn, with
portraits of Bernhard and Lee Hoetger and of Paula and Otto Modersohn,
on the back of a letter from the Kunsthalle Bremen to Otto Modersohn
in Paris dated 27 November 1906, 22.5 × 29.2 cm (8⅞ × 11½ in.),
29 November 1906. PMB Stiftung

70 *Self-Portrait with Blue, White Striped Dress*, oil tempera on canvas,
49 × 26.5 cm (19⅜ × 10½ in.), summer 1906. Private collection.
Catalogue raisonné 672

71 *Self-Portrait, Right Hand on Chin*, monotype on newspaper, partly
overpainted, 26.3 × 19 cm (10⅜ × 7½ in.), summer 1906. PMB Stiftung.
Catalogue raisonné 673

72 *Self-Portrait, Right Hand on Chin*, monotype on lined paper, 27 × 21.2 cm
(10¾ × 8⅜ in.), summer 1906. PMB Stiftung. Catalogue raisonné 674

73 *Self-Portrait Facing Left, Hand on Chin*, oil tempera on paper on board,
26.8 × 21.4 cm (10⅜ × 8½ in.), summer 1906. Private collection.
Catalogue raisonné 676

74 *Self-Portrait Facing Right, Hand on Chin*, oil tempera on paper on board,
27 × 18.7 cm (10¾ × 7⅜ in.), summer 1906. Private collection.
Catalogue raisonné 677

75 Paula Modersohn-Becker, half-length nude, photo by Herma Becker (?),
May–June 1906. PMB Stiftung

76 *Self-Portrait as a Half-Length Nude with Amber Necklace I*, oil tempera
on board, 62.2 × 48.2 cm (24½ × 19 in.), summer 1906. Private collection.
Catalogue raisonné 678

77 *Self-Portrait with Lemon*, oil tempera on board, 50 × 27.5 cm (19 ¾ × 10⅞ in.),
1906–7. Private collection, Hamburg. Catalogue raisonné 683

78 *Self-Portrait with Camellia Branch*, oil tempera on board on wood,
61.5 × 30.5 cm (24¼ × 12⅛ in.), 1906–7. Museum Folkwang, Essen.
Catalogue raisonné 684

79 Paul Gauguin, *Two Tahitian Women*, oil on canvas, 94 × 72.4 cm
(37⅛ × 28⅜ in.), 1899. Metropolitan Museum of Art, New York

80 *Half-Length Nude Italian Woman with a Plate in her Raised Hand*, oil tempera
on canvas on different base, 55 × 38 cm (21¾ × 15 in.), autumn 1906.
Private collection. Catalogue raisonné 694

81 *Standing Child Nude with Goldfish Bowl*, oil tempera on canvas,
105.5 × 54.5 cm (41⅛ × 21½ in.), 1906–7. Bayerische
Staatsgemäldesammlungen. Catalogue raisonné 696

82 *Two Kneeling Nude Girls*, oil tempera on canvas, 53 × 70.3 cm
(20 ⅞ × 27¾ in.), 1906–7. Private collection. Catalogue raisonné 701

83 *Kneeling Nude Girl with Stork*, oil tempera on canvas on different
medium, 73.5 × 60 cm (29 × 23⅝ in.), 1906–7. Private collection.
Catalogue raisonné 697

84 Pierre Puvis de Chavannes, *Hope*, oil on canvas, 70.5 × 92 cm
(27 ⅞ × 36¼ in.), 1871–72. Musée d'Orsay, Paris

85 Pablo Picasso, *Boy with a Pipe*, oil on canvas, 100 × 81.3 cm (39 ⅜ × 32⅛ in.),
autumn 1905. Private collection

86 *Seated Nude Girl with Flower Vases*, oil tempera on canvas, 89 × 109 cm
(35⅛ × 43 in.), 1906–7. Von der Heydt-Museum, Wuppertal. Catalogue
raisonné 699

87 Pierre Puvis de Chavannes, *Inter artes et naturam*, oil on canvas,
40.3 × 113.7 cm (15⅞ × 44⅞ in.), 1890. Metropolitan Museum of Art

Picture Credits

All drawings and paintings by Paula Modersohn-Becker:
© Paula-Modersohn-Becker-Stiftung, Bremen
All photos: © Paula-Modersohn-Becker-Stiftung, Bremen

INDEX

'Painting is beautiful, but very, very difficult.'

Paula Modersohn-Becker in
a letter from Paris to Otto
Modersohn, 3 August 1906